LMMS: A Complete Guide to Dance Music Production Beginner's Guide

The beginner's guide to exploring, understanding, and rocking the world of dance music using the free LMMS digital audio workstation

David Earl

BIRMINGHAM - MUMBAI

LMMS: A Complete Guide to Dance Music Production Beginner's Guide

Copyright © 2012 Packt Publishing

All rights reserved. No part of this book may be reproduced, stored in a retrieval system, or transmitted in any form or by any means, without the prior written permission of the publisher, except in the case of brief quotations embedded in critical articles or reviews.

Every effort has been made in the preparation of this book to ensure the accuracy of the information presented. However, the information contained in this book is sold without warranty, either express or implied. Neither the author, nor Packt Publishing, and its dealers and distributors will be held liable for any damages caused or alleged to be caused directly or indirectly by this book.

Packt Publishing has endeavored to provide trademark information about all of the companies and products mentioned in this book by the appropriate use of capitals. However, Packt Publishing cannot guarantee the accuracy of this information.

First published: September 2012

Production Reference: 1140912

Published by Packt Publishing Ltd.
Livery Place
35 Livery Street
Birmingham B3 2PB, UK.

ISBN 978-1-84951-704-1

www.packtpub.com

Cover Image by Sandeep Babu (sandyjb@gmail.com)

Credits

Author
David Earl

Reviewers
Tobias Doerffel
Tres Finocchiaro
Paul Giblock

Acquisition Editor
Robin de Jongh

Lead Technical Editor
Susmita Panda

Technical Editors
Vrinda Amberkar
Prasanna Joglekar
Ankita Shashi

Copy Editor
Insiya Morbiwala

Project Coordinator
Vishal Bodwani

Proofreader
Stephen Swaney

Indexer
Monica Ajmera Mehta

Production Coordinator
Arvindkumar Gupta

Cover Work
Arvindkumar Gupta

About the Author

David Earl is a music composer, producer, and performer living in the San Francisco Bay Area. His music has been heard in film, television, audio branding, and video games. David has worked for clients such as Brown Paper Bag, Summit Pictures, Double Fine, Activision, THQ, Lila Rose, Artemis, Sony, Pyramind, Ripesound, and the Juno Company.

David has been balancing a life of intense creativity with a deep desire to teach. For the past 10 years, he has helped to develop various curricula for Pyramind in San Francisco. He is an Apple Certified Logic Instructor, and also teaches Modular Synthesis using Reaktor.

As a purely innocent and altruistic endeavor, David started posting tutorial videos to YouTube as 'sflogicninja' in 2007, as an attempt to help fellow producers. He now has a following of over 25,000 subscribers worldwide. He has since started creating tutorials for MacProVideo, and creates additional video material for Pyramind Online—the online counterpart to their brick and mortar training center.

David has collaborated with other writers in his field, but *LMMS: A Complete Guide to Dance Music Production* is his first official effort.

> I would like to thank my wife for putting up with my late night writing sessions. I also give deep thanks and gratitude to Artemis Robison, without whose efforts this book, quite possibly, would not have happened.
>
> I would also like to thank all of the mentors that I've had over the years. Mentors such as David Occhino, Mike Dana of Fresno City College, Andy Newell of Ripesound, Steve Schick at Fresno State, Jordan Rudess of Dream Theater, Mark Bacciarini, Lance Freeman, and Fresno State's entire music department. Without learning from these teachers, there is not a chance I could have been doing what I do today, and it is because of them and others, who I may not have listed here, that I feel compelled to pass my knowledge on to those willing to learn.

About the Reviewers

Tobias Doerffel is the founder and lead developer of LMMS (and is living in Germany). He has been working on LMMS since 2004 and also runs and supports other Open Source projects, such as iTALC. He has been studying Applied Computer Science with a focus on Computer Engineering and is currently working as a Software Engineer.

> I'd like to thank all the supporters and active members of the LMMS community. It's great to see the creative results from people all over the world using LMMS.

Tres Finocchiaro was born in 1981 in upstate, New York and had an early interest in computing and technical writing. He got his first computer in 1993, an IBM PCjr, on which he learned the BASIC programming language. In 1999, Tres was exposed to the Linux computer operating system when visiting his brother in Buffalo, NY. Soon after, Tres began refining his skills and interests in computing and other Linux-related projects, such as the public domain, free software, and the Open Source community.

Tres began by working with the Oneida Indian Nation's Turning Stone Casino in Upstate NY, where he was employed as a Cashier. Two years later, Tres was hired as a Computer Operator and was nearing the completion of his Associates Degree in Computer Networking Systems. Eight years later, Tres is a key component to the IT operations at Turning Stone as an Application Development Analyst, which includes computer programming and support as well as technical writing. For years, Turning Stone has played a key role in providing Tres with the structure to succeed while allowing for creativity to expand his knowledge in both computing and technical writing.

After writing and creating several computer programs for the work place, Tres started the community-based printing program jZebra as a side-project from home. The jZebra, a small, web plugin, has had great success and is used by businesses in countries all over the world, including Britain, Indonesia, and Germany (to name a few). The jZebra is free software that prints barcodes, receipts, and ID badges, and the source code is offered for others to learn and collaborate from.

In addition to the jZebra project, Tres is also an active member of the Ubuntu Desktop Linux community and LMMS music community, and he is a blogger, husband, and father as well.

> I would like to thank Tobias Doerffel for his contribution to music production, Packt Publishing for giving me this opportunity, and my wife for her unsurpassed patience.

Paul Giblock is a Researcher at The Joint Institute of Computational Sciences in Oak Ridge, Tennessee. He holds a bachelor's degree in Computer Science, and is currently working toward his master's degree at the University of Tennessee in Knoxville. Paul started contributing to LMMS in 2006 when he added the LB302 synthesizer. Since then, he has assisted in porting LMMS from Qt3 to Qt4, creating the Controller framework, enhancing MIDI support, updating plugins, and improving various aspects of the graphical user interface. He also added the Soundfont Player, LFO Controller, Peak Controller, and Stereophonic Matrix plugins. Paul is currently interested in high performance computing, human interface design, and digital signal processing.

www.PacktPub.com

Support files, eBooks, discount offers and more

You might want to visit www.PacktPub.com for support files and downloads related to your book.

Did you know that Packt offers eBook versions of every book published, with PDF and ePub files available? You can upgrade to the eBook version at www.PacktPub.com and as a print book customer, you are entitled to a discount on the eBook copy. Get in touch with us at service@packtpub.com for more details.

At www.PacktPub.com, you can also read a collection of free technical articles, sign up for a range of free newsletters and receive exclusive discounts and offers on Packt books and eBooks.

http://PacktLib.PacktPub.com

Do you need instant solutions to your IT questions? PacktLib is Packt's online digital book library. Here, you can access, read and search across Packt's entire library of books.

Why Subscribe?

- Fully searchable across every book published by Packt
- Copy and paste, print and bookmark content
- On demand and accessible via web browser

Free Access for Packt account holders

If you have an account with Packt at www.PacktPub.com, you can use this to access PacktLib today and view nine entirely free books. Simply use your login credentials for immediate access.

Table of Contents

Preface	**1**
Chapter 1: Gearing Up: A Preflight Checklist	**7**
Getting a studio ready to thump	8
System requirements	8
Installing LMMS	9
Installing LMMS on Windows	9
Installing LMMS on Linux	10
Installing LMMS on Mac OS X 10.6 and above	10
LMMS resources or where's my stuff?	11
File management – keeping it together	12
Managing project versions	13
Time for action – saving our first project	13
Playing sessions at other studios	15
Setting up MIDI for LMMS	16
MIDI keyboards	16
Control surfaces	17
Setting up MIDI in Windows	18
Time for action – setting up MIDI in Windows	19
Setting up MIDI in Linux	19
Time for action – setting up MIDI in Linux using ALSA	20
Installing MIDI in Mac OS X	20
Getting sound out of LMMS	21
Getting on the mic	21
Dynamic microphone	22
The condenser microphone	22
A brief introduction to sound cards and audio interfaces	24
Great resources for inspiring sounds	25
Radiohead	25

Indaba music	26
Remix comps	26
CCmixter	27
Making custom samples	**28**
Avoiding painful microphone feedback	29
Time for action – recording with a microphone	**29**
The art of listening – controlling your listening environment	**33**
Composing on the fly – laptop configurations	33
Cutting out the world – choosing earbuds	34
Composing in a room with studio monitors	35
Computer noise, room noise, and hum	35
Corners are bad	36
Hardwood floors need a rug	36
Parallel walls aren't great	36
Absorption versus diffusion	36
Speaker choice and placement is important	37
Get a good chair	38
Summary	**38**
Chapter 2: Getting Our Feet Wet: Exploring LMMS	**41**
What kind of electronic musician are you?	**41**
Opening the LMMS default song and making noise!	**42**
Time for action – opening a new song template	**42**
The Main Menu bar	43
The Project menu	44
The Edit menu	44
The Tools menu	45
The Help menu	45
Clicking through the toolbar	45
The top row of buttons on the left-hand side	45
The bottom row of buttons on the left-hand side	47
Other features of the toolbar	52
Exploring the goodies in the side bar	54
Using the Beats+Bassline Editor	**55**
Time for action – setting the stage to build a beat	**55**
Time for action – adding drums to the Beats+Bassline Editor	**56**
Time for action – creating a beat pattern	**57**
Our first tweaking of samples	58
Time for action – editing samples with the Audiofile processor	**58**
Time for action – adding elements and variation to our beat pattern	**60**
Adding instruments to the Beats+Bassline Editor—Bass	61
Time for action – adding bass to the Beats+Bassline Editor	**61**
Our first tweaking of a synth	62

Time for action – editing note length and root pitch in the	62
Beats+Bassline Editor	62
Exploring the Piano Roll editor	64
Time for action – opening a pattern in the Piano Roll editor	64
Time for action – changing the pitch of the bassline	65
Using the Piano Roll in the Song Editor	66
Time for action – muting instruments in the	66
Beats+Bassline Editor	66
Time for action – enabling a Piano Roll in the Song Editor	67
Time for action – enabling a MIDI keyboard controller	67
in the Song Editor	67
Getting the Mixer to work in our project	68
Time for action – routing an instrument to a channel on the FX Mixer	69
What plugins are and where we can put 'em?	70
Time for action – exploring FX	70
Summary	73

Chapter 3: Getting Our Hands Dirty: Creating in LMMS — 75

Starting our beat with the basics	75
Time for action – making the most basic of beats	76
Time for action – fitting the bass in	80
Other styles in dance music	83
Chicago style house music	83
Time for action – creating Chicago style house music	83
New York House	86
Acid House	87
Breakbeat	88
Jungle, Drum and Bass, and Braindance	88
Tasting the ingredients of dance music	89
Drums	89
The bass drum	90
The hi-hat	90
The snare drum	92
The tom-tom	92
Basses	93
The upright bass	94
The electric bass	94
The synth bass	95
Drum machines	97
Samplers	100
Other notables	101
Summary	**102**

Table of Contents

Chapter 4: Expanding the Beat: Digging Deeper into the Art of Beatmaking — 103
- Starting fresh — 103
- Time for action – setting up long form patterns — 104
- Time for action – adding harmonies to beats — 106
  - Placing the bass — 109
- Time for action – making the bass pitch friends with our harmony — 109
  - Giving the beat a turnaround — 111
  - The importance of knowing just a little music theory — 112
    - The major scale — 112
    - How to figure out a major scale — 113
    - The minor scale — 114
    - Putting a number to a note — 115
- Time for action – using the key of the song — 115
  - Simple guidelines for the bass — 118
  - Twiddling knobs to set the beat — 119
    - Tweaking the bass tone — 119
- Time for action – sweeping a filter using automation — 119
- Time for action – panning and volume automation — 124
  - Using automation on instrument effects — 129
- Time for action – putting reverb on the clap and twiddling it — 129
- Summary — 134

Chapter 5: Making Spaces: Creating the Emotional Landscape — 135
- Using the Song Editor — 135
  - Getting the Beats+Bassline Editor's pattern into the Song Editor — 136
- Time for action – moving a pattern into the Song Editor — 136
  - Different elements for the Song Editor — 138
    - Adding new parts to the Song Editor from the side bar — 139
- Time for action – bringing in instruments — 139
  - Inputting notes into the Piano Roll in real time — 141
- Time for action – playing the notes in the Piano Roll editor — 141
- Time for action – using panning to spread the song out — 145
  - Blending the old with the new — 148
- Time for action – delaying those stabs! — 149
  - Delay versus reverb — 152
  - Using FX channels to reduce CPU usage — 156
- Time for action – setting up reverb on an FX bus — 156
  - Listening to the masters of space — 159
- Summary — 163

Chapter 6: Finding and Creating New Noises — 165
- Sampling audio — 166
  - Early sampling — 166
  - The grey area — 167

Table of Contents

Getting into LMMS samples	168
Time for action – creating a pattern completely from samples, with a drum loop	**168**
The art of sampling	174
Digital recording	175
Recording on the main computer	175
Software for grabbing audio goodies	175
Unbalanced versus balanced cables	176
Using handheld recorders	180
Finding sounds on the Internet that won't get you sued	182
Time for action – sound sculpting in Audacity	**184**
A note about bits and samples	192
Summary	**196**
Chapter 7: Getting It All Stacked Up	**197**
Get your loop set	**198**
Time for action – setting up the loops	**198**
Adding instruments	203
Time for action – making our basses	**203**
Making that break dirty	206
Time for action – dirty bass	**206**
Send that sound out to get effected	209
Time for action – sending clones through effects	**209**
Adding in the smooth	212
Time for action – adding the ambient elements	**212**
Using samples in the Song Editor	**215**
Time for action – adding a sample track	**215**
Summary	**220**
Chapter 8: Spreading Out the Arrangement	**221**
The art of arranging	**222**
Analyzing Imagine by John Lennon	223
Time for action – breaking down Imagine by John Lennon	**223**
The purpose of the bridge	224
The art of the break	225
Time for action – analyzing One	**225**
Laying it out for our project	227
Time for action – spreading out the loop	**228**
Summary	**236**
Chapter 9: Gluing the Arrangement Together	**237**
The art of the transition	**237**
Using dropouts	238
Time for action – creating a dropout with the accompanying pitch fall	**239**
Creating filter sweeps	244

Time for action – creating a filter sweep	245
Time for action – adding in effects over time	250
Summary	253

Chapter 10: Getting the Mix Together — 255
What is mixing? — 255
- Audio energy — 256
- Digital clipping and you — 256

Time for action – separating audio streams — 259
ABCs of mixing — 263
- Volume balancing — 263
- Panning and stereo separation — 264
  - Low frequency sound — 264
  - Drums — 265
  - Keyboards, leads, and pads — 266
  - Vocal samples — 266
  - Other panning considerations — 267
- Dynamics — 268
  - Compressors and limiters — 269

Time for action – using compression in LMMS — 270
- Filtering — 274

Time for action – using EQ — 275
- Types of equalizations — 276
- Delay-based plugins — 280

Time for action – exploring echo and simple delays — 280
- The Haas effect — 282

Time for action – exploring Freeverb — 283
- Plates, springs, and convolution — 284

Time for action – exploring vintage reverb — 286
- Automation — 287
- Exporting the mix — 287
- Mastering — 290

Summary — 292

Chapter 11: Getting into Instruments — 293
The instruments of LMMS — 293
The language of synthesis — 294
- The main parts of an instrument — 294
  - The Oscillator section — 295
  - Parameters of the Oscillator section — 298

Time for action – exploring oscillators — 299
- Types of synthesis — 302
  - Mix — 302
  - Phase modulation synthesis — 303

Frequency modulation synthesis	304
Sync	305
Amplitude modulation	305
Time for action – exploring different synthesis methods	**305**
Experimenting with subtractive synthesis	308
Time for action – activating instrument filters	**308**
Using modulation	310
Using envelopes	310
Using LFOs	312
Time for action – assigning modulators in LMMS	**312**
Using the Function tab	317
Chords	318
Arpeggio	319
Arpeggio modes – Sort and Sync	321
The different instruments of LMMS	322
Bit Invader	322
Kicker	323
LB-302	324
Mallets	325
Organic	328
FreeBoy	330
PatMan	332
SF2	333
Vestige	334
Vibed	335
ZynAddSubFx	337
Summary	**338**
Chapter 12: Where to Go from Here	**339**
Guilds, societies, and such	339
ASCAP	340
BMI	340
SESAC	341
Where to sell my stuff	343
Beatport	343
iTunes	343
CD Baby	344
Tunecore	344
Music labels	344
Community	345
User groups	345
Soundcloud	346
Summary	**347**

Appendix: Pop Quiz Answers	**349**
Chapter 3: Getting Our Hands Dirty: Creating in LMMS	349
Chapter 4: Expanding the Beat: Digging Deeper into the Art of Beatmaking	349
Chapter 5: Making Spaces: Creating the Emotional Landscape	350
Chapter 6: Finding and Creating New Noises	350
Chapter 7: Getting it All Stacked Up	350
Chapter 8: Spreading Out the Arrangement	350
Chapter 9: Gluing the Arrangement Together	350
Chapter 10: Getting the Mix Together	351
Index	**353**

Preface

Welcome to *LMMS: The Complete Guide to Dance Music Production*! This book has everything you need to get started making electronic music. Not only does this book help you understand the inner workings of LMMS—a great music production program—it also guides the reader down the path of creating a song from the beginning to the end. Some history of dance music is explored along the way, as well as making your own noises and becoming a part of the music community at large.

What this book covers

Chapter 1, *Gearing Up: A Preflight Checklist,* explores settings, parameters, and preferences we need to get LMMS off the ground. We'll also explore creating sound libraries of samples without fear of getting sued. Before we make music, we need to get our studio in order!

Chapter 2, *Getting Our Feet Wet: Exploring LMMS,* explores the LMMS layout. LMMS has six main editors, and we'll explore the function of each, and how they will contribute to our process. We will also explore the way these editors work with each other.

Chapter 3, *Getting Our Hands Dirty: Creating in LMMS,* starts making music! Dance music is based on patterns, and in this chapter we will explore pattern-based music. We will take a close look at the different instruments used in electronic music production and their use in popular dance music patterns. We'll also make some basic patterns that are representative of some of the most popular dance music styles.

Chapter 4, *Expanding the Beat: Digging Deeper into the Art of Beatmaking*, starts exploring basic sound creation techniques using some of the instruments built into LMMS. In this chapter, we'll also start making sense of our music by creating a good, basic arrangement of our music. We'll also explore changing parameters of LMMS over time with automation.

Chapter 5, *Making Spaces: Creating the Emotional Landscape*, explores creating atmosphere and texture in our arrangement using ambience, reverb, and other techniques. In this chapter, we'll get familiar with artists that used ambience effectively in dance music. We will also explore controlling effects so that they change over time, creating dynamic movement in our music.

Chapter 6, *Finding and Creating New Noises*, explores some basic recording techniques, and where to put noises once we have them. Sampling is a technique of recording sounds in the real world and incorporating them in an instrument that can play them back musically. We will also explore playing samples in the Song Editor as well as the AudioFile Processor.

Chapter 7, *Getting It All Stacked Up*, explores the technique of loop stacking. In dance music, there is a process known as "subtractive arranging". We are going to take the first step in making our dance music arrangement by creating a very dense loop of music, and explore how the different elements of the loop fit together.

Chapter 8, *Spreading Out the Arrangement*, extends the loop that we created in *Chapter 7, Getting it All Stacked Up*, to create an arrangement. We will add additional content to our already dense loop, and explore the art of subtractive mixing.

Chapter 9, *Gluing the Arrangement Together*, explores the art of transitions and automation. Our arrangement works well at this point, but we need to still add life and movement to our music. Altering parameters over time to create builds and transitions is key to a dynamic piece of electronic music.

Chapter 10, *Getting the Mix Together,* explores mixing, which has to do with balancing the volume of all of our parts so that they all have a place in our sonic space. Now that everything has been put in place, we need to balance all of the elements of our song.

Chapter 11, *Getting into Instruments,* explores making awesome sounds and how to apply these sounds to a song. Now that we have been through all of the stages of production, it's time to explore the details of the instruments built into LMMS. LMMS has some powerful instruments under the hood. In this chapter we'll become musical mechanics.

Chapter 12, *Where to Go from Here*, explores the various guilds, unions, and such we need to know about to participate in the music industry at large. Making music is one thing. Getting it into the world is something else! We will also explore some of the newer methods of distribution of music that have come about recently and even how to share music with social networks.

Appendix, *Pop Quiz Answers*, contains the answers to all the pop quiz questions for all the chapters.

What you need for this book

To follow this book, you will need a copy of LMMS for Linux, Windows, or Mac OS X, running on a PC or Mac. A knowledge of music theory is not necessary!

Who this book is for

This book is for anyone who has ever aspired to create music in the dance music vein. Whether a beginner or an intermediate, this book does not simply explore how LMMS works. It also guides the reader through a production workflow that goes from making beats to mixing a finished arrangement that can be shared with the world at large!

Conventions

In this book, you will find several headings appearing frequently.

To give clear instructions of how to complete a procedure or task, we use:

Time for action – heading

1. Action 1.
2. Action 2.
3. Action 3.

Instructions often need some extra explanation so that they make sense, so they are followed with:

What just happened?

This heading explains the working of tasks or instructions that you have just completed.

You will also find some other learning aids in the book, including:

Pop quiz – heading

These are short multiple-choice questions intended to help you test your own understanding.

Have a go hero – heading

These practical challenges and give you ideas for experimenting with what you have learned.

You will also find a number of styles of text that distinguish between different kinds of information. Here are some examples of these styles, and an explanation of their meaning.

Code words in text are shown as follows: The downloaded installer from `lmms.sourceforge.net` will simply install the application and it will be located in your `Programs` folder."

New terms and **important words** are shown in bold. Words that you see on the screen, in menus or dialog boxes for example, appear in the text like this: "To find out which you are running, click on the **Start** button in the lower-left side of the screen".

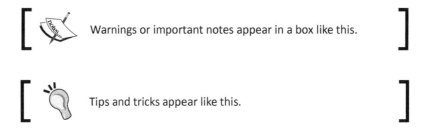

Warnings or important notes appear in a box like this.

Tips and tricks appear like this.

Reader feedback

Feedback from our readers is always welcome. Let us know what you think about this book—what you liked or may have disliked. Reader feedback is important for us to develop titles that you really get the most out of.

To send us general feedback, simply send an e-mail to `feedback@packtpub.com`, and mention the book title in the subject of your message.

If there is a topic that you have expertise in and you are interested in either writing or contributing to a book, see our author guide on `www.packtpub.com/authors`.

Customer support

Now that you are the proud owner of a Packt book, we have a number of things to help you to get the most from your purchase.

Errata

Although we have taken every care to ensure the accuracy of our content, mistakes do happen. If you find a mistake in one of our books—maybe a mistake in the text or the code—we would be grateful if you would report this to us. By doing so, you can save other readers from frustration and help us improve subsequent versions of this book. If you find any errata, please report them by visiting http://www.packtpub.com/support, selecting your book, clicking on the **errata submission form** link, and entering the details of your errata. Once your errata are verified, your submission will be accepted and the errata will be uploaded to our website, or added to any list of existing errata, under the Errata section of that title.

Piracy

Piracy of copyright material on the Internet is an ongoing problem across all media. At Packt, we take the protection of our copyright and licenses very seriously. If you come across any illegal copies of our works, in any form, on the Internet, please provide us with the location address or website name immediately so that we can pursue a remedy.

Please contact us at copyright@packtpub.com with a link to the suspected pirated material.

We appreciate your help in protecting our authors, and our ability to bring you valuable content.

Questions

You can contact us at questions@packtpub.com if you are having a problem with any aspect of the book, and we will do our best to address it.

1
Gearing Up: A Preflight Checklist

When creating electronic music, it's a good idea to take some extra time to choose your gear carefully for the task at hand. You should also be mindful of the environment you are working in. A studio can theoretically be just about anywhere these days, from a hotel room to a well-tuned control room. It's important to choose the right tools for the right circumstances.

Here is what we're going to explore in this chapter:

- Check our system requirements
- Show how to install LMMS on various operating systems
- Get familiar with the location of LMMS resources
- Control our project assets
- Configuring MIDI devices for use with LMMS
- Configuring audio devices for use with LMMS
- Setting up your sample library – how not to get sued
- The art of listening: how to help a room sound better
- Ergonomics: make music! Continue to have feeling in your hands!

Getting a studio ready to thump

Your studio should be like a good restaurant. A chef will have a favorite knife, good stoves, and a clean, orderly kitchen. A music studio should have a well-configured computer, decent monitors, and good ergonomics (seriously, we'll be sitting here for hours, so let's at least be comfortable, right?) These priorities are important, whether creating 5-star cuisine under the wrathful eye of Gordon Ramsey (Gosh I'm hungry right now), or creating electronic music.

In this chapter, we'll be talking about setting up our music studio so that we get the most out of LMMS from the computer and operating system to our desks and headphones. So let's get started, already!

System requirements

Your computer is the control center of your studio. A computer will impact not only how music is made but also how it is performed. This means major decisions like desktop or laptop, to minor decisions such as deciding which audio effects will save your computer's processor from working too hard.

If you are using a desktop or laptop, you need a Windows or Linux compatible PC. An Apple Mac will also work for LMMS. LMMS is efficient and can run on all kinds of computers. The basic specifications are: 1 GHz processor with at least 512 megabyte of RAM

LMMS plays nicely with older CPUs and is very efficient. But it's still ambitious to think that you are going to rock the house with a single core processor and roughly half a gigabyte of RAM. You'll hit the wall pretty quickly when using software instruments and effects.

A better bet would be a multi-core computer with at least 2 gigabytes of RAM. Multiple processors means more plugins and tracks. You also need enough RAM for the operating system as well as the application you are running. In the electronic music world, more CPU power and RAM means more tracks, more instruments, and speedier handling inside LMMS, as well as your other applications.

The operating system you choose will be determined by your own personal preference, and what other applications you wish to run on your computer. LMMS works on the following:

- Windows
- Linux-based operating systems (GNU Linux, Ubuntu, Fedora, SuSE, Mint, and so on)
- OS X (with some limitations)

Stability is key when making electronic music. The more stable your system is, the more work you'll get done. If you don't plan to perform with LMMS, get yourself a desktop. If you need portability for performance or creating music on the go, a laptop would be the better fit. Windows and Linux seem to be the most stable operating systems to run LMMS on as far as operating systems are concerned. The OS X version is a port of 4.1.0, at the time of writing this book and is slightly less stable.

Now this could be considered 'optional', but as a general rule, you should always have an external drive for music projects. Hard drives are inexpensive these days and will ensure that your internal hard drive, whose responsibility is to run your operating system, remains less cluttered and fragmented from electronic music production.

Your external hard drive should meet these optimal specifications:

- 7200 rpm
- The drive should have Firewire 800, USB 2.0, eSATA, or other high-speed bus
- Approximately 250 GB to 1 TB

Your external hard drive needs to spin fast so that it can play many samples and audio files concurrently. Having an external drive also means easier transport if you'd like to take your sessions to other studios.

LMMS works with any active audio output that your computer has. It can use a headphone output or a more expensive external audio peripheral that hooks up to speakers.

If you would like to use a piano keyboard controller to enter notes into LMMS, there are many manufacturers that have products on the market. Simply install the appropriate driver that comes with the MIDI controller and LMMS will be able to see the device.

Installing LMMS

LMMS installers can be downloaded from the following link:

`http://lmms.sourceforge.net/download.php`

Installing LMMS on Windows

The Windows operating system comes in several flavors. The versions of Windows operating system that LMMS is compatible with are the following:

- Windows 2000
- Windows XP
- Windows 7
- Windows Vista (32-bit and 64-bit)

Windows is installed from a factory CD. Windows versions come in both 32 and 64 bit. 64-bit applications have a lot more power than 32-bit applications. This is essentially because the application can access more RAM more efficiently. 64-bit operating systems give applications the ability to access more than 4 GB of RAM. If your operating system has 64-bit capability, I highly recommend it. LMMS runs beautifully in 32-bit as well, so if you are currently working in 32-bit, you'll still have a lot of power.

Windows 7 can be installed as either a 64 or 32 bit platform. To find out which you are running, click the **Start** button in the lower-left of the screen. Then go to **Control Panel | System Maintenance**, and click **System**. You can view the system type here.

Installing LMMS is very easy. Make sure to choose either 32-bit or 64-bit from the `lmms.sourceforge.net` site.

The downloaded installer from `lmms.sourceforge.net` will simply install the application and it will be located in your `Programs` folder.

Installing LMMS on Linux

LMMS was born on Linux! Linux is a free operating system that is very popular as an alternative to Apple and Windows platforms. Linux also comes in many flavors. I would suggest checking out Ubuntu. The download for Ubuntu can be found here:

`http://www.ubuntu.com/download`

You will need to burn this installer to CD, run it from a memory stick, or you can even run Linux inside Windows. Nothing like having your cake and eating it too!

Installing LMMS on the Linux platform is detailed here:

`http://www.linuxmusicmaker.com/2011/07/easy-install-lmms-0412-using-ppa-on.html`

Installing LMMS on Mac OS X 10.6 and above

For those of us who would like to try LMMS on OS X:

- `http://www.mediafire.com/?5nv6r7yb2ac72gp`
- `http://www.zshare.net/download/91015791d82670a9/`

The OS X version is currently 4.1.0 and is fairly stable. It is a port, however, and is not available directly from the folks at `lmms.sourceforge.net`. Use at your own risk!

To install LMMS, simply drag the downloaded application to your applications folder.

LMMS resources or where's my stuff?

The LMMS application is fairly self-contained, but there are many pre-defined areas that LMMS looks to for its resources.

When we open up LMMS for the first time, we can see where LMMS is looking for its resources by opening the **Edit** menu and selecting **Settings**, followed by clicking on the folder icon on the left-hand side of the menu:

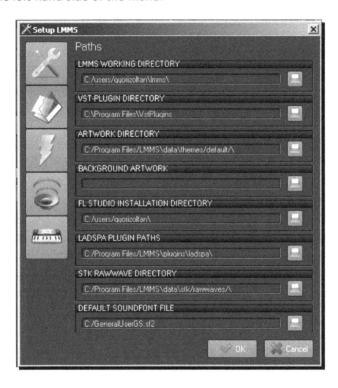

This will show us where LMMS is currently pointing to for its resources.

Here's where all those paths are looking:

- The **WORKING** directory is where our projects and presets for software instruments are stored.
- The **VST PLUGIN** directory is where our installed third-party VST plugins are stored.
- The **ARTWORK** and **BACKGROUND ARTWORK** directories are where we can put custom artwork for changing LMMS' appearance. There are several users on the Internet who have developed custom skins to make LMMS more attractive to the eye.

- The **FL STUDIO INSTALLATION** directory is only for Windows users who already have the **Fruity Loops** application installed on their computer. If it's on the computer, LMMS can access its FLP files for importing into an LMMS session.
- The **LADSPA PLUGIN PATHS** directory is where LADSPA plugins are located. **LADSPA** stands for **Linux Audio Developers Simple Plugin API**. Yeah, it's a mouthful, but there are a lot of LADSPA plugins that we can get from the Internet and incorporate them into our studio. They're made by a loving community of developers.
- The **STK RAWWAVE** directory contains raw wave files and samples.
- The **SOUNDFONT** directory can use soundfont files for sampled instruments. Soundfont files are single documents that are a container of sound files used in simple sampler architectures.

With the exception of the **WORKING** directory, we can use all of the other directories in their current locations to get up and running.

As for that **WORKING** directory, we should point that to our shiny new external drive we have. This is the best place to have all of our projects running. Again, please get an external drive!

File management – keeping it together

We need to be diligent, almost religious, about file management. File management is what allows us to work on projects over time and not have them suddenly stop playing back right. We aren't all going to be able to write the hit dance song of the century in one night, so we need to be sure that files are named properly and are headed in the right direction when we save. The **WORKING** directory is a nice start, but we need to start thinking about projects that might have several revisions.

It's a good idea, when starting a song, to immediately go to the file menu and choose **Save As**. Here's what will happen if we don't: we work on the best song we've ever created and suddenly, inexplicably the program crashes and our work will be destroyed never to be recovered. It's happened to the best of us. If you do not save immediately, your song is only an 'I-forgot-to-plug-the-power-supply-into-my-laptop' away from oblivion.

When saving your project, there are three directories that should pop up when we save, as you can see here:

These are three very important folders. When we have instruments or effects that have been custom-tweaked, their settings are saved in the **presets** directory. These settings will then be available to you in all future projects. This is how to build a palate of sounds that give our songs a specific and unique signature.

The path shown in the previous image shows the default directory on the internal drive. To use a folder on an external drive, simply create the folder on the external drive and drag the folder into the left panel of the **File Save** dialog box.

When we collect samples, we will toss them in the **samples** folder. They will also be available in our future projects in an easily accessible side bar.

Managing project versions

The **projects** directory is where our projects will live. LMMS projects contain a lot of information. They reference presets, samples, MIDI sequences, and all kinds of other important assets. As we create new projects, though, this folder is going to get really messy. The way to handle file management is to create subdirectories within the **projects** directory and concentrate on version management.

When working on a project, we get inspired. We try new things. We can sometimes destroy old work when we're in that mode, so it's important when working on electronic music to save versions of your project along the way, so that the perfectly good work we did yesterday does not get ruined by the inspired work we do today.

Time for action – saving our first project

Working with versions is simple. It's mostly about naming your files correctly and using subfolders. Let's save a project as **First_Time_Out_v1**:

1. When we do this, we should be presented with a menu that looks something like the following:

2. Now we need to add a new directory by hitting the following button:

3. This creates our new directory, which I'll name **First_Time_Out**:

It's important to note that we're using underscores. This is a method of substituting spaces so that there's no issue with the way the computer sees this file. It's a holdover from the days when having a space in the name of your file could mean bad news.

4. We're now going to save into this folder. Use the name **First_Time_Out_v1**:

What just happened?

Now we have our first version of the song. So let's say we work for a night on this project and put it away. The next night we create a new project with a new subdirectory and go to town. When we revisit **First_Time_Out_v1**, we should save **First_Time_Out_v2** and continue working. If we decide to change direction on the piece, we can save a new version mid-stream. When we do this, we should indicate what the new version has that is different from the first. We should be descriptive. Something like **First_Time_Out_v3_DubstepAttempt**. If our new direction doesn't work, no problem! Just revert back to the previous version and save it as **First_Time_Out_v4**. Always be working on the latest version. Even if you backtrack, create a new version. This way you'll be able to take a trip, come back, and know exactly where you have been with your current song.

Many people wonder why version management is so important. It's really just about making sure that at every step of the way we are giving ourselves a chance to see the progress that we've made on a project. Some people will not follow these rules and end up saying things like, 'LMMS lost my file!' or 'My Computer put my file somewhere!!'

No. No, it didn't.

Playing sessions at other studios

When sharing a project with others, we need to keep a few things in mind:

- The other studio may not have our samples
- The other studio may not have our presets
- The other studio may not have our VST instruments and effects

LMMS projects will save preset data in them for a specific project, but our samples that we usually have access to will not necessarily be there. There are a couple of easy fixes for the samples and presets, but the VST plugins may be a bit more difficult.

Remember that external drive we got? The one that is so easily portable?

If this is where our **WORKING** directory is, we can simply take our drive to the other studio and re-point the settings window of the other studio's LMMS application to our drive while we are there.

Now we have access to all of our presets and samples again. Nice, huh?

Make sure that when leaving, the old settings are restored. It can freak a studio owner out if all of a sudden their computer is trying to find another drive for their resources. Jot a note down or take a screenshot of where their **WORKING** directory is located before pointing to another drive. Change the settings back before leaving. Unless playing a practical joke, in which case you are on your own.

VSTi and VST plugins are usually third-party plugins that aren't necessarily free. We may not be able to copy the VST plugins to the other studio's drive and use them. If they are freeware, we're ok. If not, the plugins may not open at all and cause havoc at the other studio. Be sure to check and see which plugins are freeware and which ones aren't. We can always write the effect to the audio of the tracks that have VST plugins on them. This way the audio will play back with the effect on someone else's LMMS application. To accomplish this, hit the red button on the track you need to export, as you can see in the following image:

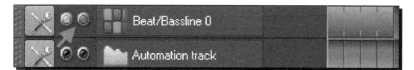

Then go to the **File** menu, and choose **Export....**

Now that the track alone will be saved as an audio file, we can bring this file back into our project and play it on a sample track. That should solve any compatibility issues between studios (we should also save a version of this called **First_Time_Out_v5_StudioVisit** to keep our versions straight).

Gearing Up: A Preflight Checklist

Setting up MIDI for LMMS

MIDI controllers come in all kinds of shapes and sizes. Most virtual studio applications are based around the MIDI keyboard as a primary source of MIDI input. In LMMS we don't necessarily need a keyboard to write electronic music. We can write MIDI data in one of LMMS' many editors. Sometimes entering MIDI data from a keyboard is faster, though. Here are some examples of MIDI controllers:

MIDI keyboards

Some MIDI keyboards are built solely for the purpose of entering MIDI notes into your music program, but others have a bit more going on than that. Here are some MIDI keyboard controllers that pack in some additional hardware such as knobs and sliders to allow us to control LMMS' parameters:

- M-Audio Axiom Pro:

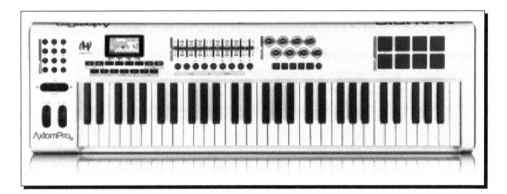

- Novation SLmkII:

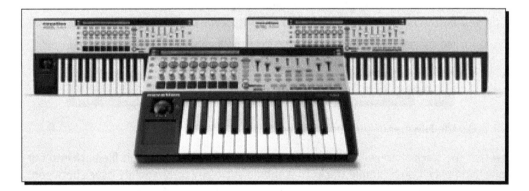

- Akai MPK49:

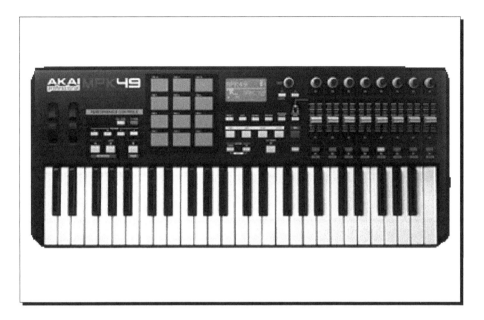

Control surfaces

MIDI control language allows us to automate knobs and sliders in LMMS using real physical knobs and sliders out here in the real world. Some control surfaces these days don't even have a keyboard, since many of us want just the knobs and sliders. A lot of electronic music artists prefer to write note information rather than play the notes from a keyboard. Here are some controllers without piano keys. We call them control surfaces:

- KORG nanoKONTROL 2:

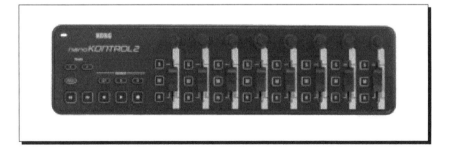

Gearing Up: A Preflight Checklist

- Novation Zero SLmkII:

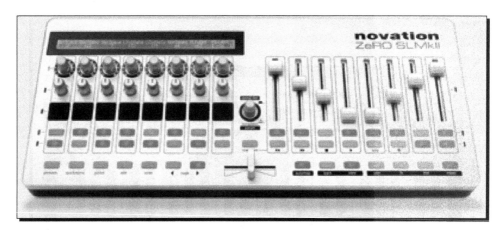

- Akai MPD32:

Setting up MIDI in Windows

Setting MIDI up in Windows requires us to do a little bit of work. Here is how we get it done:

Time for action – setting up MIDI in Windows

If you are using Windows, you will likely need to download a driver for the controller:

1. Go to the manufacturer's website and look under their downloads section to get the current driver. Be sure to download the 32-bit or 64-bit driver depending on which OS is running. After downloading the driver, we need to install it. If you are running Windows 2000 or XP, you should go to **Start | Control Panel | Add Hardware and Devices**.

2. When adding a new hardware device, Windows will ask for the new driver. Simply point to the directory that contains the new driver and we're good.

What just happened?

In Windows 7, there may be issues with drivers that are slightly older. Some drivers made for Vista need to be set to **Compatability Mode** to get them to work in Windows 7. To get to **Compatability Mode**, simply right-click the driver and select **Properties**. The **Properties** tab will have a checkbox for **Compatability Mode**. Try this out. If it doesn't work, you'll need to ask the manufacturer if they'd please get Windows 7 drivers up, as soon as possible. Most manufacturers have made the move to Windows 7 drivers, but it's good to have this technique if something goes awry.

Setting up MIDI in Linux

Setting up MIDI in Linux can be a little tricky, but LMMS has done its level best to include the ability to use MIDI controllers without much hassle.

MIDI and audio in Linux have come a long way, but have been notoriously difficult to set up properly. Some of the issues of latency and compatibility have been addressed by the development of ALSA.

> **ALSA** stands for **Advanced Linux Sound Architecture**. It's the link between your computer's Linux operating system and your MIDI and audio devices. You can find the currently developed drivers here:
>
> http://www.alsa-project.org/main/index.php/Main_Page

Most Linux hosts will automatically install ALSA and all of the appropriate drivers, so usually your audio interface or MIDI interface is automatically detected.

Time for action – setting up MIDI in Linux using ALSA

Linux uses an open source MIDI driver system. Let's look at the process of setting up Linux for MIDI:

1. In your **Settings** menu in LMMS, select the area that looks like the following:

2. Once you are in this menu, you should see the ALSA setup and all MIDI devices available to LMMS:

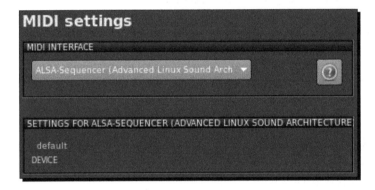

What just happened?

Just choose ALSA and hopefully your devices will be shown in the dropdown menu underneath 'MIDI INTERFACE'. Most soundcards, casual or professional should be detected by the operating system making the setup in ALSA a breeze.

Installing MIDI in Mac OS X

LMMS should automatically see any OS X ready MIDI devices that you have connected to LMMS. The current build of LMMS is **CoreMIDI** compliant, so you should be able to use a controller immediately. Most modern MIDI devices use CoreMIDI, so set up should be painless and simple.

Getting sound out of LMMS

In the **Settings** window, audio settings are here:

In the Windows version, you can choose SDL and PortAudio. **SDL** is the traditional backend audio interface, and works quite well. **PortAudio** is more modern and allows for many different backend audio systems, and offers more latency control:

The light grey area is where we select how the system is accessing the audio card(s) and the area below that is where we select the specific card we wish to use. This window is similar on OS X and Linux as well.

To test an audio driver, open one of the sample projects and play it. If we hear something, we're good!

Getting on the mic

Microphones come in all shapes and sizes as well as price points. A microphone is essentially the opposite of a speaker. A speaker pushes and pulls on air, making waves that tickle our ears. A microphone receives sound and converts it to an electrical wave that can be amplified and can be sent into a computer, audio mixer, or public address system.

Microphones come in two major categories, with a couple of odd exceptions here and there.

Dynamic microphone

The Shure SM58 – the most popular dynamic mic in the world is as follows:

Dynamic microphones are the tough guys of microphones. They aren't usually delicate, due to the fact that they have very simple electronics. Dynamic microphones use a membrane to vibrate along with sound waves, moving a coil that is between two magnets. The vibration of the coil creates an electrical current that flows down a cable to be amplified. The amplifier used to boost the signal before sending that signal along to be used in recording is called a **microphone pre-amp**. The volume knob at the pre-amp is called a **trim knob**. This is what a dynamic mic looks like from inside:

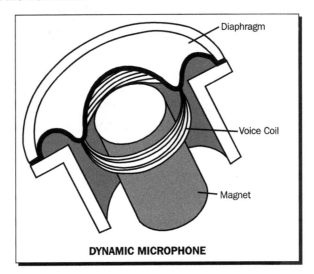

The condenser microphone

The AKG Perception condenser microphone is shown as follows:

Chapter 1

Condenser microphones are the sensitive type. The main difference between a condenser mic and a dynamic mic is that a condenser needs a little electricity to get the job done. It's less rugged than the dynamic mic and way more sensitive, so it usually lives in the studio instead of going out on stage.

Condenser microphones have a very thin, flat conductive sheet called a **diaphram** that is suspended in front of an electrified backplate. Any movement of the diaphragm disturbs the electrical field between them, making a signal. Condensers then take this information and have a bunch of circuitry that convert the signal into something our audio interface would like. It still needs a pre-amp. The signal is usually very detailed compared to the dynamic mic. If you plan on screaming a bunch, the dynamic may be a better choice. If you are a crooner, you should think about getting a condenser mic (although they tend to be more expensive). Here's what the inside of a condenser mic looks like:

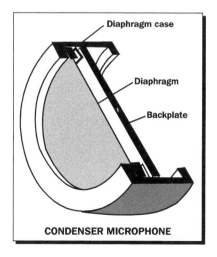

If you are just starting to record things, I would suggest investing in a dynamic mic from a company like Shure, AKG, or Electro-Voice. They are well established and you can find them online for pretty reasonable prices.

A brief introduction to sound cards and audio interfaces

When you need to get an audio signal out of your computer to some speakers, or get some sound from the outside world into your computer, you need an audio interface.

All computers these days have audio interfaces built into them. They are usually enough to get the job done for most music-making endeavors. To reduce noise, get a clearer sound, and get recorded music to sound nice and open and clear, an external audio interface is usually a good idea. Audio interfaces connect to a computer via USB, Firewire, or have a card in the computer with a cable that hooks into an external box. Here's an example of an external USB/Firewire interface:

On this particular interface, we have input-level trim knobs on the left, speaker volume, and headphone volume.

On the right, there are indicator lights that show us the audio's volume coming in and out of the device. This interface has a pretty nice meter. It has a green area lit up where the audio is at a comfy volume. The yellow area tells us the volume is getting close to peaking and the red area is the audio peak. We don't want audio to peak on input because it will distort. We also don't want it to peak the output, because it will distort as well.

An external audio interface like this gives us a lot of information. If you are using an internal soundcard that came with your computer, you are going to have to rely on the meters in the software you are using and your ears to tell you whether your volume is too loud or not.

Great resources for inspiring sounds

When setting up our system, we'll want to start populating our hard drive with samples, loops, and other audio files to use in songs. Many electronic artists still get caught using samples that haven't been cleared. By cleared, I mean that when you sample a CD, record, mp3, or any other audio file from an artist, you need to ask permission to use it.

Heck, just the act of asking may get you noticed by the artists you are pulling from, right? It's worth a try, I guess. Most of the time you get a cold shoulder, though, so I generally advise against it.

There are many, many artists out there that are trying to get their music remixed. I suggest using Google to look up current remixing competitions on the web. I've seen remix contests of everyone from Depeche Mode, Nine Inch Nails, and Sasha, to Peter Gabriel, Ok GO, and Radiohead. Here are some links to get you started:

Radiohead

Radiohead is one of the most well-known bands in the world, and they just love having their music remixed. Check out their site (http://www.radioheadremix.com/) regularly for tweaky strange sounds and lilting English voices:

Indaba music

Indaba music (http://www.indabamusic.com/home) is relatively new on the scene, but has a regularly awesome set of artists who are willing to let other artists take a crack at their work. They also provide a networking solution for artists who are looking for producers, remixers, and so on. Their roster of talent is impressive and they also have sample packs available for download:

Remix comps

Remix comps (http://www.remixcomps.com/) is a site that is always on the lookout for who is putting a remix contest out in the world. It's certainly more of an aggregate site, but one that has found remix contests for everyone from Alicia Keys to Kaskade:

CCmixter

CCmixter (http://ccmixter.org/) is another great site that actually has public domain sample packs for downloading and using. They are using a different type of copyright, creative commons that allows for other artists to use the sampled works free of litigiousness. They also have a community of remixers and artists, so it can be a great place to find other like minds in the electronic music field:

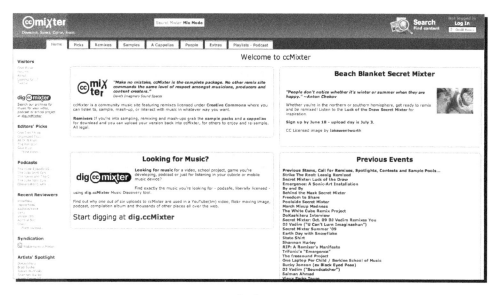

Remixing is a fantastic way to hear the sub mixes of elements from great artists. After digesting them, remixing is a way to get started by pushing the envelope of what can be done in LMMS. We'll be exploring techniques in remixing in Chapters 6 through 9, that will show how to integrate samples from other artists into our own remix. If a remix is good enough, it may even be chosen to be featured on the artists' next album, which is a cool way to get exposure.

Making custom samples

We'll be creating our own audio samples in *Chapter 6, Finding and Creating New Noises*. We'll need to acquire another piece of open source software to get the recording done.

To start out, I would suggest **Audacity**: `http://audacity.sourceforge.net/`

An example of an audio sample is shown as follows:

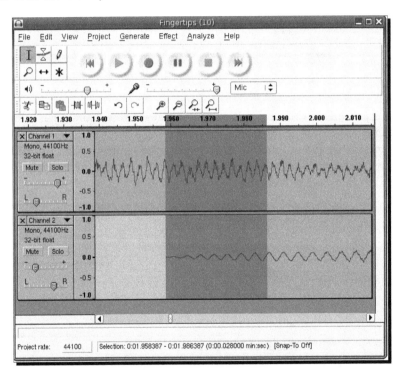

Audacity is an excellent multi-track open source audio recording and editing platform for Windows, Linux, and OS X. It's easy to use and ridiculously powerful. Here are the best links for the manual, Wiki, and other goodies related to Audacity:

- `http://audacity.sourceforge.net/`

Chapter 1

- `http://audacity.sourceforge.net/help/documentation`
- `http://wiki.audacityteam.org/wiki/Audacity_Wiki_Home_Page`

After downloading, Audacity can access the audio input and output of the computer from its **Preferences** page, which is under the **Audacity Menu**. Windows and OS X will use their own system based drivers and you can choose your device in the **Preferences** menu. If using Linux, ALSA will be available through your Preferences menu, and Audacity should have access to the current sound device.

Avoiding painful microphone feedback

When a microphone is hearing itself play through speakers, a feedback loop occurs that can severely hurt yourself and your neighbors. Ear-splitting feedback is never fun, so follow this simple rule first:

> When sampling using Audacity, use headphones, turn the output of the audio interface down, or turn speakers off.

Time for action – recording with a microphone

Ok, now that we're safe from feedback, we have a couple of options. Let's start with recording with a microphone:

1. Under **Preferences**, choose **Devices**, and make sure the device is set to record only one channel or Mono.

2. Get something to sample. Maybe a cat, dog, or loud sibling.

3. Grab a mic.

4. The microphone will need to be plugged into an audio interface that has the ability to boost the microphone's audio signal properly. Also, check to see if the microphone requires **Phantom Power**. Phantom Power is not some strange mutation. It's a 48-volt power signal that a condenser mic requires to power its capsule properly.

5. Once the microphone is plugged in, turn up the trim (audio input volume) on the audio interface. Most audio interfaces have a bright red light that flashes when the audio interface is getting too much signal. Don't let the signal get so loud that red lights begin to flash. We want plenty of room to be able to scream or whisper. If we don't have that room, we get clicks, pops, and distortion.

6. There is a transport bar in Audacity that looks like the following:

7. This is where you can pause, loop, stop, rewind, fast-forward, and record in Audacity.

8. Grab the thing you are about to record (be careful if it is) and hit the red 'record' button in the Audacity transport bar.

9. Audacity will automatically create a new track according to your preferences and start recording. Once the recording is done, you can either mouse over the stop button and hit stop or you can use your space bar to stop. The audio file will then appear in the editing window of Audacity as follows:

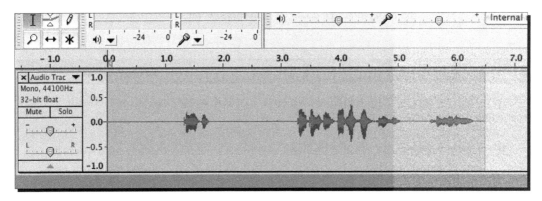

10. Samples should never have a lot of space at the top (beginning) of the file. If we want to trigger this sample in a song, then we need to crop the file. Audacity makes this kind of editing very simple.

11. To zoom in a bit, we need the zoom tool. It looks like a magnifying glass in the upper-left corner of the screen, where our toolbox is located. The toolbox looks like the following:

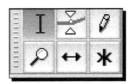

12. The zoom tool is just underneath the selector tool, which is what we are using right now. Click the zoom tool and select all that dead space before the audio starts. You will get a screen that looks like this:

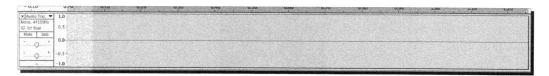

13. Now use your selector tool to select that area of dead space. You can adjust either side of the selection by holding down the *Shift* key.

14. Now hit *Delete*! We now have a sample that starts right at the first sign of audio:

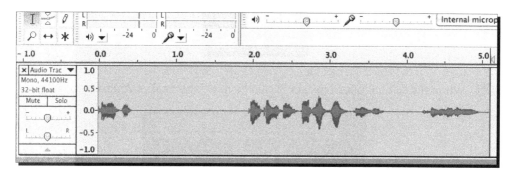

15. You can also delete dead space from the middle of the file with the same technique.

16. Ok, we can let go of that poor creature we just sampled and start using this recording. Samples need to be saved to the **samples** folder in our **WORKING** directory.

17. In Audacity, go to **File** | **Export....**. We'll choose the 16-bit PCM for the audio file settings to give us a standard wave file. Make sure to save to the **WORKING** directory on that nice, spacious external drive.

18. It's recommended to create subdirectories in the **samples** folder to keep yourself organized. Let's call this sample **poor_creature.wav** and put it in a subdirectory called **Animals**.

19. When that's done, open LMMS, and we will see the sample show up in our handy sidebar!

20. In LMMS, this is where you'll find your samples:

21. When the sidebar opens up, you'll see the new folder called **Animals**:

22. And here's our poor creature!

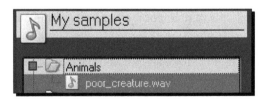

What just happened?

We've just made a sound and added it to our LMMS **My Samples** library!

This is how we can start building our library of custom sounds for LMMS. We can also simply drag audio files into Audacity's edit window or record multiple tracks at once. Audacity also has the ability to write effects to audio files, create volume envelopes, and mix several files together. Layering samples can be a lot of fun and Audacity is one of the easiest multi-track recorder/editors out there.

The art of listening – controlling your listening environment

A studio can be anywhere these days. Some people produce great albums from their bedroom. Some folks write dance music on planes. We've heard this a lot lately, due to the simple fact that studios are so affordable, compact, and powerful, people are making all kinds of claims.

Experience tells me that humans are infinitely adaptable. Someone who flies a lot will discover the pros and cons of creating in that environment. People who record in their bedroom will become accustomed to the limitations of their space as well.

Let's explore some of the different solutions to making dance music in different scenarios. I'd like to start with the light-on-their feet laptop composer.

Composing on the fly – laptop configurations

When you are composing on a laptop and you aren't at home, it's a good idea to have some options in the headphones department. It's also not a bad idea to find a bus-powered audio interface that gives you nice, clear sound. A portable interface means that you can also potentially have a microphone on you to record the occasional vocal or street lunatic.

Bus-powered devices are powered from the computer's bus which are usually USB and Firewire. New bus systems such as Thunderbolt are on the way. Using a bus-powered device means you aren't carrying power supplies.

We've already discussed the CPU and RAM specifications of the laptop we need. We have also agreed that a little external drive is a very good idea.

When choosing a drive for a laptop, I suggest going for a pocket drive that is bus-powered. The trick with being mobile is to travel light, and 'bus powered' means that the drive doesn't have to be plugged into a wall to make it work. When you plug the drive into a USB or Firewire-type port, it gets its power from that port as well!

Even though the drive is bus-powered, it can still be 7200rpm. It needs to be fast and have a fast bus speed. I personally am a fan of the G-drive, and the FreeAgent drives from Glyph have been nice to me.

So we have our project drive, how about the interface?

The audio interface can also be bus-powered. The PreSonus AudioBox is quite inexpensive and gives you nice, clean headphone output and mic preamps for recording in the outside world. I find this device to be the best bang for the buck, but would highly recommend checking some of the other contenders out there. It's a great template for everything you need in a mobile device, though. That is, small, light, bus-powered, and nice preamps.

Cutting out the world – choosing earbuds

Now for listening. Laptop music makers are headphone people. When out in the world, we want to shut the world out so we can work. When we're in a quiet environment, clarity and accuracy is key.

I am a huge fan of in-ear buds for when I am out in the world. I would suggest anything by **Ultimate Ears** or **M-Audio**. If you think you're getting good quality from Skullcandy or Apple earbuds, you are gravely mistaken. Be picky about your earbuds and try to research where they come from. Most earbuds come from the same manufacturer and are simply renamed and repackaged. Avoid these at all costs.

When looking for earbuds, I suggest you look first for isolation. How well do they cut the background noise down? When on a plane, train, or automobile, you'll want earbuds that attenuate the outside world at least 30 db. You don't want to be turning your earbuds up to compensate for outside noise. Doing this could damage your hearing.

Once you've found earbuds that are good at isolating, listen to the mixes you are familiar with. The better the earbuds are, the more extended the low end and high frequencies will be.

If you are in a more controlled environment, I would suggest a set of open-ear headphones for referencing your mixes. My favorite low-cost high-performance headphones are the **Grado SR80** headphones. These were suggested to me by audiophiles and mastering engineers. They are under $100 and sound wonderful. I've actually mixed on them and been happy with the result. The other thing about these headphones is that you can actually talk to people in the room while you have them on. They are an open-ear design, which means that you can be aware of your surroundings if you have someone over that's asking you how the mix is coming along. I don't know how many times I've been mixing on closed-ear headphones and hit the ceiling when someone tapped my shoulder to get my attention.

It should be said that you need to be very, very mindful of your headphone volumes. Don't blow your ears out listening to mixes. Try to find a comfortable listening volume and stick with it so you get some consistency to your mix. Listening loud means that you could be distorting the mix or getting an inaccurate read on what's happening.

So that's about it for the laptop! You don't need much to get by in that configuration. It's somewhat important that when you are writing on a laptop, try to sit with good posture in a comfortable chair if you can. Sitting in a cafe is cool, so long as you aren't hunched over the laptop with your arms cramped up. This is how you get bad tendonitis of several kinds. I had bicep tendonitis, and I have to say that it really sucks.

Composing in a room with studio monitors

So let's say that we're composing in a room with speakers and a desktop computer. What kind of configuration is going to give us the best sound?

Well, rooms come in all shapes and sizes. If the room is bigger, it can be good to have your speakers away from the wall a bit with some kind of dense materials behind them. If we are in a small space, it's good to have our speakers closer to the wall so that the waves coming from the speakers can develop properly, and we aren't sitting in the middle of the room.

A couple of good general rules are the following:

Computer noise, room noise, and hum

Keep in mind that computers are noisy and sometimes even the power in your room can cause noisy recordings. In a perfect world, your computer should live in a climate-controlled box, or if you have a large, airy closet it can live there. As for hum and buzz, try separating your audio cables from your power cables. Many times hum is introduced into audio because the electricity flowing through a power cable will jump into an audio cable.

Many of these noise issues can be taken care of with filters and audio programs that are commonly available, but I highly suggest that you get good, clean recordings in the first place.

Corners are bad

Try to minimize corners in your room. Put something dense in them to take the corner out. A popular material for taking out corners is **Owens Corning 703 Insulation**. It's very sturdy, doesn't shed much, and if you cover it with cloth like burlap (usually used to make potato sacks), or other simple heavy-duty fabric, it makes a great bass trap. We don't need to be fancy. Just put the 48x24" panel in the corner and see what happens. The results are pretty great. If you can't find any Owens Corning 703 nearby or on the Internet, there are alternatives out there that are still very good. Most insulation will work fairly well as long as it is dense and is well covered, so that you aren't breathing fiberglass. If you find it hard to find fiberglass or it's cost-prohibitive, try packing old clothing into the corners tightly. If you can get it to stay in place, you will still get the advantages of bass absorption.

You see, corners in your room amplify bass frequencies. This means that when we listen to mixes, we hear more bass than what's actually there. This may sound cool when we're listening, but when mixing, accuracy is key. We want our mixes to be accurate so that when we go play our mix in the car it translates.

Hardwood floors need a rug

If we are living in an older building, we might have hardwood floors. Hardwood floors look really nice, but they are very reflective. This can cause sound waves to bounce between the floor and ceiling. Putting a rug down makes a world of difference on hardwood floors.

Parallel walls aren't great

Like our floors and ceilings, we need to try and minimize parallel surfaces whenever possible. Sound waves will bounce from these walls and sum together in the center of the room, giving us a boost in certain frequencies. Creating uneven surfaces will minimize this effect. Even having a curved piece of wood on the wall will help keep the negatives of this effect down.

Absorption versus diffusion

Many folks talk about sound-proofing a room. They usually mean making a room silent to the outside world and vice versa. In our studio, we're going to focus less on sound-proofing and think more about treatment.

Taking out the corners of the room and laying a rug down will help control the over-hyping of certain frequencies in a room. What we don't want to do is cover every surface of our room with sound absorption material. This can actually affect the way we hear a mix and will make the room sound lifeless. A good rule of thumb is to use absorption in the corners, floor, and ceiling, and on the back wall to use diffusion.

Diffusion is a way of scattering sound waves so that they lose their energy. The larger waves get broken into smaller ones that don't sum together very well. **Absorption** takes that same audio energy and simply converts it into heat and absorbs most of the heat energy. Absorption is generally used to control low frequency sound, and diffusion scatters the high frequency reflections in the room.

Using diffusion on reflective surfaces means we get to keep a bit of life to the room and our mixes will sound more open and clear. Diffusion panels are kind of pricey, but they are out there. It's good to do research on diffuser panels rather than try to make some of your own. Homemade diffusers can often do more harm than good. Good diffusion requires good math.

That said, let's say we need to save up for some diffusion. In the meantime, put a lot of stuff in your room on the walls. Books can be good because they have both mass and uneven surfaces. Load up the walls so that you have very uneven surfaces all over the place. As long as you aren't listening at insane volumes, you should notice a difference.

A good way to see how well our room is doing is to play a mix and stop it quickly. We may hear a bit of a tail. Did it sound low frequency? High frequency? Did it last long? If we hear a low tone after stopping, more absorption would be a good idea. If we hear fluttering echoes, diffusion is the answer.

Speaker choice and placement is important

The speakers we use in our studio are extremely important. When choosing your first pair of studio monitors, you should never pick a set of monitors simply because they sound 'good'. Sometimes speakers that sound good have less in the midrange, where our ears are very sensitive, or some other bias. We want monitors that are accurate. Accuracy is the king when we are creating music for the masses. Whether our audience is on a laptop or a high-fidelity system, we want our mix to sound good on just about anything, and our monitors are the key to giving us the truth about what's going on.

Monitor choice is very personal, but it can be expensive. In my studio I use Mackie HR824 powered monitors for my speakers. Since I do this stuff for a living, I spent a pretty large amount on them, because they are ruthlessly accurate. Speakers can be very expensive, but there are some manufacturers such as **M-Audio**, **Logitech**, and **Bose** that are trying to create smaller speaker systems for computers that still sound very good. I've been known to write music for advertisements from a tent using headphones, but if you can afford it, try to get the best speakers you can.

Speaker placement should be roughly an equilateral triangle with our head as one point and the speakers' cones as the other two points. This setup will give us the most accurate stereo image and center. Don't put a bunch of stuff over or between the speakers if you can get away with it. Also, we need to try not to have our speakers sitting on our desk or any large surface. Buy some inexpensive monitor stands to de-couple them. Anything a speaker touches will vibrate. The smaller and more isolated the surface, the better!

Get a good chair

You laugh! No, no. I'm serious.

We are about to embark upon a long journey that is absorbing and intense. Time tends to fly by in the studio and before you know it, the sun is coming up and we're looking happy but bleary-eyed at the clock. It's ok to do this and it's invigorating to have one of those all-night sessions making music. The trick is to be able to do it again after a short recovery period.

If you don't make your studio ergonomic, you will suffer the same fate as those who get carpal-tunnel syndrome from writing too much code or crunching too many numbers. If you work in an office during the day or have a job that requires you to use the computer for more than just music making, you MUST make this a priority. Nothing sucks more than not being able to make music because your arm hurts too much. I've been through this kind of thing and it kept me from working for a couple of weeks.

If you have a good chair, don't hunch over and have your screen at least 3 feet away from your face, you can work longer and healthier. If you have a good chair, you can save your back as well. Hey, isn't that what Craigslist was made for? Get a good chair for cheap. We found mine hardly used on Craigslist for about $200 and it's an $800 chair. My health is worth it.

Summary

In this chapter we:

- Installed LMMS
- Found out where LMMS put all of its contents
- Explored how to get audio into LMMS
- Talked about the function of microphones and audio interfaces
- Talked about how to get our listening environment tuned up
- Explored the differences between using a laptop and a desktop computer

What we've done in this chapter is lay the foundation for our journey making music in LMMS. Making electronic music is a blast, and we tend to let the basic disciplines of organization, preparation, and health – go out the window when we want to get started RIGHT NOW.

The thing is, when we have the right gear for the job, LMMS is more stable. When we understand where our resources are, we are never more than a couple of clicks from our presets and sample libraries. When we make bad choices in a project, we can go back to an earlier version. If we understand how sound and MIDI are used by our operating system, we can troubleshoot problems. If we want to remix or sample other artists, there are many places to do so legally. When we have a room and headphones we can trust to tell us what's going on in our mix, our music sounds better.

This chapter was installing more than just applications, hard drives, and samples. We're installing confidence in our studio. That confidence helps creativity flow from us, knowing that we can trust our system, our ethics, our ears, and our personal style of production, be it on the run or rooted in the lab at home.

Now that the prep work has been done, let's get our feet wet!

2
Getting Our Feet Wet: Exploring LMMS

Now that we've discussed studio practices and put our studio together, it's time to explore LMMS.

In this chapter, we'll be doing the following:

- Open the LMMS sample session
- Explore the Song Editor
- Make sense of the Mixer
- Investigate Editor Windows
    - Piano Roll
    - Beats and Bass
    - Automation
    - FX Plugins
    - Controller Rack
    - LADSPA Effects
- Get the Song Editor and the Mixer to work together

What kind of electronic musician are you?

So here we are, ready to finally boot up LMMS and get crackin'. When we first open LMMS, we are presented with a blank template song. This is like a blank canvas ready for us to start making music with. After we have set up all of the preferences and settings from *Chapter 1, Gearing Up: A Pre-flight Checklist* we should be ready to just jump in with both feet and get some work done.

Before we get going, we need to understand what our best workflow is. Maybe you are a piano player. You may want to use a keyboard controller to record notes into LMMS. Maybe you are an obsessive-compulsive tweaker and want to have meticulous control over every iota of data being written into LMMS and prefer to use your mouse. Your workflow is a way of creating the path of least resistance between you and your music.

To understand which workflow is going to work best for a given individual, we need to explore our tools. In electronic music, there are some tools and techniques that have been developed over the past thirty years that make getting your music out of your head and into the world easier.

Computer programs that are used to create and manipulate digital audio are called **Digital Audio Workstations**, or **DAW**s. A DAW is your music making environment. In this case, we are using LMMS.

When you first open a new document in any DAW, it usually has two main windows; an **EditorWindow**, and a **Mixer**. The **Editor** is where you create and arrange your sounds and the **Mixer** is where you balance the volume of the sounds and adjust their sonic characters. DAWs also employ other additional editors that allow you to manipulate sounds in compelling ways. This is something that distinguishes one DAW from another. Different DAWs will use different, specific sets of editors, depending on what kind of content they are creating.

LMMS is all about making electronic music, so its tools are focused on creating, editing, and mixing electronic music. It still employs a lot of the standard tools that one may find in any other DAW, but its specialized tools are a lot of fun.

Opening the LMMS default song and making noise!

Let's open up LMMS and see how it is laid out. No better way to do that than to open up a blank template and get our feet wet.

Time for action – opening a new song template

Let's open a new song template. If you are using Windows or Linux, the application will show in the **Program Menu**. If you are using the Mac version, double-click on the LMMS application to open it and then do the following:

1. Go to the LMMS **Project** menu and choose **New**.

2. Go to the **Project** menu and choose **Save As**.

3. Choose a name for this project and save.

Chapter 2

What just happened?

So we have a song template open now and it looks similar to the following screenshot:

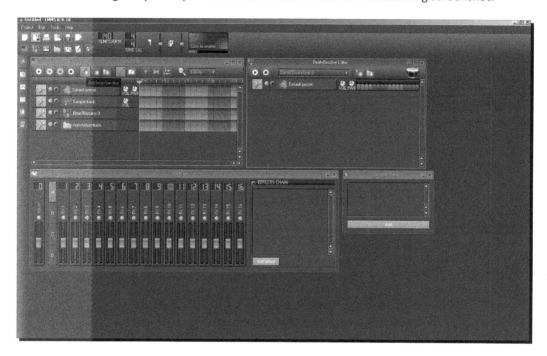

Remember how I said that most DAWs will usually open two main windows? Well, as we can see here, LMMS actually starts us with a bit more than that. To make it easier for us to get around, let's have a look at this song template and get familiar with its layout.

The Main Menu bar

The **Main Menu** bar is where we can choose to **Open**, **Save**, and adjust the preferences of our project. We can also use the **Tools** menu to undo and redo actions that we've performed in any editor within LMMS:

Here's a quick rundown of what these menus are for:

The Project menu

Here is what the **Project** menu looks like when opened:

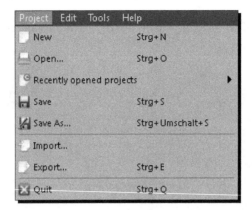

The **Project** menu is where we:

- Open projects
- Save projects
- Import elements of the current project to another project
- Export elements of the current project to another project
- Create a new project
- Open a recent project
- Quit LMMS

The Edit menu

Let's explore the **Edit** menu:

The **Edit** menu lets us:

- Undo an action
- Redo an action
- Adjust the settings of your session

The Tools menu

The **Tools** menu allows you to look through a list of audio effects available to LMMS:

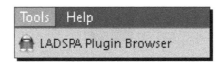

The Help menu

This menu will give useful info to us if we get lost. Your cursor will transform into a question mark and anywhere you click, you'll get info on what that area is for.

Clicking through the toolbar

The toolbar is where we are able to quickly access many of the same actions as our **Project** menu mentioned earlier. It also allows us to select the different editors we will be using in LMMS to edit our music. The toolbar is a great navigation tool that also defines some of the base parameters of our project as well:

The top row of buttons on the left-hand side

Here's a heads-up on each of their functions:

- This button opens a new blank project. This functions just as the **Open New Blank Project** menu from the **Project** pull-down menu:

- This button opens a project from the template. When we use this button, LMMS will ask us for a template to start a new project from:

Getting Our Feet Wet: Exploring LMMS

- This button opens an existing project (a project you created before). This button will open our LMMS projects location and we can open a saved project from there:

- This button opens a recently opened project. This is essentially a drop-down menu that will list the last projects you have worked on. This can be a quicker way to get to a more recent song, since it doesn't open a browser window:

- This button saves the current project:

When we first open LMMS, if we are starting a new endeavor, we should always hit this button first. We will save this project to the LMMS `project` folder designated in our preferences. Be sure to give the project a name that's memorable!

A word to the wise

Don't save songs as dates. We will never remember what they were. Try naming them descriptively, so that when we are looking into our `project` folder a year from now, we'll remember that `Duck Quack` was that silly ditty we wrote while giddy on Red Bull.

- This button exports the current project. This button will actually save your project as a `.wav` or `.ogg` file that you can listen to in the car, on the iPod, or any other music listening apparatus of your choice:

The bottom row of buttons on the left-hand side

These buttons are called the **Window Controls** and this is where we are able to select the different editor windows in LMMS that we are going to use. Here's a quick list of both the buttons' functions and our available editors:

- This button shows us the **Song Editor**:

    The **Song Editor** is where we will be arranging the various parts of our song. This editor is where we decide what instruments we use, what parts we listen to, and which parts we are choosing to edit. It is an overview of our song. This is what the **Song Editor** looks like in our session:

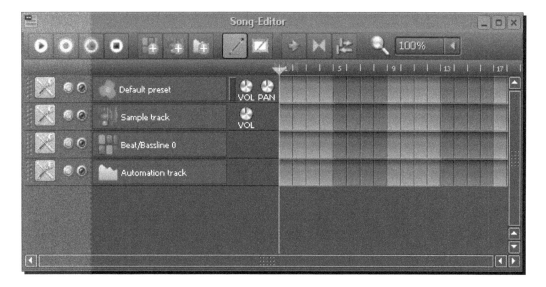

- This button shows us the **Piano Roll** editor:

    The **Piano Roll** editor is where we can look inside of a pattern and create notes for our song.

Think of the **Song Editor** as our overview and the **Piano Roll** editor provides us a *micro* level view. The **Song Editor** will have the sections of our song. The **Piano Roll** lets us look inside of that section and create note data and move that data around.

> The **Piano Roll** editor is named after the piano rolls of old player pianos. Player pianos were automated pianos from the early 20th century that played songs by themselves. They read a printout of a song that was nothing more than a series of holes in a page of paper. The holes were arranged so that if you were looking at the roll sideways, the holes' vertical position determined pitch, and the length of the holes would determine how long the piano held a note for before releasing. This simple visual premise has been used to edit notes in computer music for over 40 years. Rather surprising what technology holds out over the centuries.

If we double-click on a pattern, the **Piano Roll** opens. Here's what the **Piano Roll** editor looks like in our session:

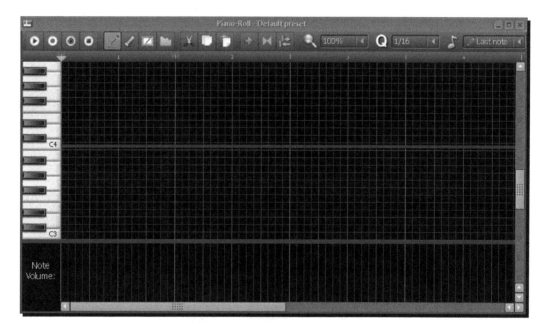

- This shows us the **Beats+Bassline Editor**:

The **Beats+Bassline Editor** is the backbone for LMMS generated dance music. In this editor, you stack various instruments and samples to create a beat and bassline using an old technique that was originally developed for drum machines from the 70's and 80's. This method is a grid-based technique that is very easy to use. All we do is drag an audio file or instrument into the **Beats+Bassline Editor** and the editor will create a 16-segment sequencer. **The Beats+Bassline Editor** also allows for easy organization of **Song Editor** elements by allowing us to add and remove them.

The **Beats+Bassline Editor** looks similar to the following screenshot:

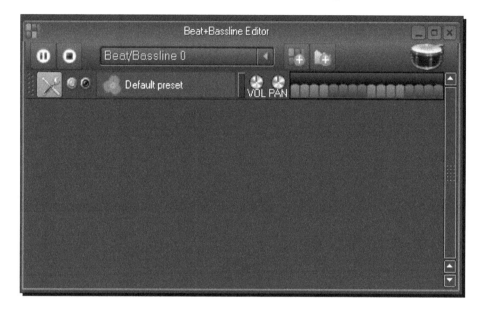

- This button shows the **Automation Track Data**:

Automation Track Data is shown in regions on the **Song Editor**, as well as the **Beats+Bassline Editor**. It allows us to change parameters in LMMS over time. Automation is a great way to add life to any composition. Gradually fading the volume of an element in and out of a track is the most obvious way to use automation. More esoteric uses will add extra variety to the sounds of your samples and synthesizers over the course of a song. Electronic music can be very repetitive if you don't add something that changes gradually over time. The last thing we want music to be is static.

Here's what the automation data of an **Automation Track** looks like:

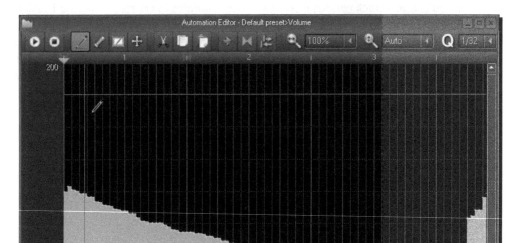

- This Button hides and shows the **FX Mixer**:

The **FX-Mixer** is where audio from all of our samples and instruments are summed together. In LMMS, you have the ability to send any instrument or sample to any channel strip of the audio mixer. Ultimately, these audio channels sum together at the master output. The master output is what we are going to hear when our project is done. All of the audio energy from all of the elements we are using will add up here and we want to be sure that all of that audio energy doesn't overload the mixer. This can lead to **clipping**, a term used for when an audio signal has more amplitude than the mixer allows and starts sounding, well, really bad. Clipping creates a kind of harsh distortion that you probably don't want to include in your music.

The audio mixer has 64 stereo channels available to use. In all, that gives us 128 audio channels.

In the mixer, we'll be balancing volumes from our instruments and samples and adding audio effects. The **FX-Mixer** looks similar to the following screenshot:

- This button shows our **Project Notes**:

Project Notes are used to help us keep track of changes that we are making in a song and allows us a written memory of what we did last night at 4 AM. Sometimes when in the creative flow, it's a really good idea to keep track of what you've done so that when you revisit the project, it'll be easy to slip back into the flow of things.

- This button shows us the **Controller Rack**:

The **Controller Rack** is a list of controllers that we can assign to almost any parameter in LMMS. When we create a controller in the **Controller Rack**, then any knob that we are using in LMMS can access that controller and allow itself to be controlled.

An example of a way this would be used is **panning**. Let's say that we want a sound to pan slowly from ear to ear as we listen to it. We could use the **Automation Track** that we talked about earlier to do this. The **Controller Rack** will automate the panner over time, but slightly differently. To create a reoccurring pan from left to right over time, we would need to write automation by hand. The controller rack's **LFO effect** will control the pan knob of an instrument over time and does not require an automation lane to do so. An added bonus is that an LFO in the controller rack can be assigned to multiple locations.

> **Some new terminologies:**
>
> Panning: The movement from left to right (or vice versa) in the stereo field.
>
>
> LFO: It stands for **Low Frequency Oscillation**. LFO is an electronic signal that creates a rhythmic pulse or sweep and is used to modulate a synthesizer or other sound source, to give the sound more complexity and variation over time. Some examples of LFO effects are tremolo, vibrato, and phasing but the possibilities are endless!

The **Controller Rack** looks similar to the following screenshot:

Other features of the toolbar

- This indicator is the **TEMPO** and time signature indicator. Our song defaults to a tempo of **140**. While working on this chapter, you may choose to slow the song down. Simply double-click on the tempo and change the value to speed the song up or slow it down.

    To the right of the **TEMPO** is our time signature. The numerator and denominator of this fraction lets us know some handy musical stuff. The top number is how many beats there are in a bar. The lower number tells us the value of those beats (that is quarter note, eighth note, and so on.). Most dance music is in **4/4** time, but artists have been known to bend the rules. I actually highly recommend it:

- This is our main output volume. Your main output volume will control the output of LMMS to your speakers:

- This is our **Master Pitch Control**. LMMS actually gives us the ability to change the pitch of the entire project on the fly! This is pretty cool. Imagine we have a friend over that wants to record a sample of their operatic singing voice. We can change the pitch of our song to match their vocal range. Brilliant!

- This is our **CPU Usage Display**. This wacky display actually tells us how our computer's brain is working with all of the data that we are throwing at it. There's a cute oscilloscope pounding away and a little bar below it that's giving us our processor load. The animated oscilloscope is cool looking, but the little bar at the bottom is the important part. When we start reaching 80 percent of our CPU's available load, we might want to try making our project more efficient, so our session doesn't start having anomalies because the computer is overtaxed:

[Oscilloscopes are electronic instruments used to visualize the wave shape of an electrical signal, such as your CPU usage.]

Exploring the goodies in the side bar

The **Side Bar** is the vault of goodies that we can integrate into our session. The **Side Bar** contains **Instruments**, a **Project Browser**, a **Sample Browser**, a **Presets Folder**, a **Home Folder Browser**, and a **Hard Disk Browser**:

To access the **Instruments**, **Samples**, and **Presets**, LMMS is a drag-and-drop affair. If we find an appropriate kick to use in the **Beats+Bassline Editor**, we simply drag the sample into the **Beats+Bassline Editor** and a 16-step sequencer will automatically appear. **Presets** work the same way. Simply drag a **Preset** from the **Side Bar** into the **Song Editor** or **Beats+Bassline Editor** and you're golden! This process of dragging-and-dropping assets from the **Side Bar** makes it a breeze to get a song started.

Speaking of which, I think it's time we started using these windows. Let's get acquainted with the basic functions of our editors, starting with **Beats+Bassline**!

Using the Beats+Bassline Editor

This is the fun part of using LMMS. When LMMS first opens, we are given a **Beats+Bassline Editor** on the right-side of the screen. If you don't see that editor, go to the handy-dandy toolbar to select the button that opens it up! It looks similar to the following:

The **Beats+Bassline Editor** that we are given may have a default instrument loaded. I love synths, (this instrument is a synthesizer instrument), but I think we should start using the **Beats+Bassline Editor** with samples and build a beat. Building a beat with drums is the heart of electronic dance music and we need to lay a solid foundation.

Time for action – setting the stage to build a beat

It is time now to get our **Beats+Bassline Editor** ready for action:

1. Open the **Beats+Bassline Editor** by clicking on its icon. This is what we will see:

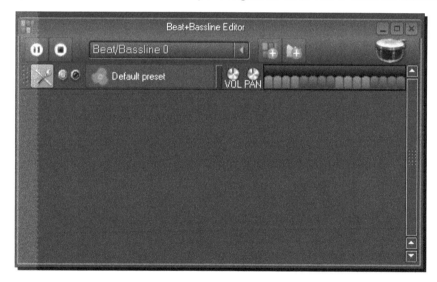

2. To get rid of the synth that is currently being used in here, click on the icon that looks the following:

Getting Our Feet Wet: Exploring LMMS

3. This icon will bring up the following menu, where we can choose to remove this track. Let's go ahead and remove it:

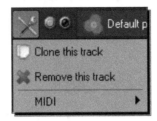

What just happened?

We just created an empty editor, now let's get down to business!

Time for action – adding drums to the Beats+Bassline Editor

Now that we have an empty editor, let's go grab ourselves a bass drum. Head over to the **Side Bar** and choose the **Samples** tab, giving us a list that looks similar to the following screenshot:

1. Open up the `drums` directory by double-clicking on it.

2. Inside this folder are some juicy samples that come packaged with LMMS. To get our bass drum, (`bassdrum02` looks like a good bet...) into our **Beats+Bassline Editor**, simply drag it from the **Side Bar** to the **Beats+Bassline Editor**, in the blank workspace. A new 16-step sequencer will appear. Groovy:

Chapter 2

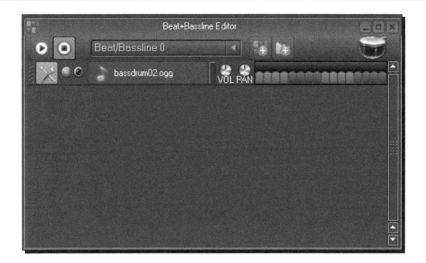

 A sequencer is an instrument that plays a sample or sound in whatever pattern or sequence we choose.

What just happened?

Now that our sample is loaded into the **Beats+Bassline Editor** and we've got a sequencer to play that sample, we can start creating a pattern.

Time for action – creating a beat pattern

Let's make a beat, using the steps of the **Beats+Bassline Editor**:

1. When a sample is loaded into the **Beats+Bassline Editor**, an instrument is created to play the sample and next to that instrument we have a **Volume** knob, a **Pan** knob, and 16 little segments. Let's click on the first segment and then every fourth segment following:

2. This is going to give us the standard, no-frills, dance kick drum. In the dance community, this is usually called *four on the floor*. Hit your *Space bar*, or click on the **Play Icon** to have a listen.

Getting Our Feet Wet: Exploring LMMS

3. Let's get another element in there. A clap would be a good bet for our next instrument. Let's go back to the **Side Bar** and grab ourselves a clap from the same menu we ordered the bass drum from. Just drag-and-drop like before. Have you noticed that clicking on the sample in the **Side Bar** lets you know what it's going to sound like? Handy, huh?

4. When the clap is imported into the editor, we'll get another 16-step sequencer to work with. Click on the fifth and thirteenth segment. Now we have something that looks similar to the following screenshot:

5. To audition our little rhythm, hit the *Space bar* while the editor is selected. We will hear a bass drum and clap playing that sounds very much like the foundation of a dance project.

What just happened?

Congratulations! You've just created your first basic beat! We created a four on the floor kick pattern to set up our dance beat. When we added the clap, it created emphasis in the rhythm on step *5* and *13* of our 16 step sequencer. Now that we have our meat and potatoes beat together, let's start adding the spices.

Our first tweaking of samples

One issue we might hear is that our bass drum is doing some weird pitch stuff. `Bassdrum02` from our sample library has a little *strangeness* happening to its pitch. It sounds like the sound gets higher as it plays. Let's open the **Audiofile Processor** and see if maybe we can tweak it slightly to get the sample to not sweep up in pitch so much.

Time for action – editing samples with the Audiofile processor

The **Audiofile Processor** is an excellent way to incorporate sound files into a project. Let's explore it:

1. Double-click on this area:

2. We will now see the **Instrument Editor** which will look similar to the following:

3. The **Audiofile Processor** has our bass drum sample loaded in it and we're going to try and clip the tail off of our sample a little bit.

4. See the knob that says **END**? Click-and-hold on that knob until you get a value of about **60**.

 To get a precise setting for a value in LMMS, double-click the knob you wish to use. A parameter can be entered from your computer's keyboard.

What just happened?

You'll see that the sample's endpoint has pulled forward a bit (that is towards the right). This means our sample is not playing all the way through and that strange, pitched tail of the sample is now sounding more normal.

After we've done this, our bass drum sounds a bit better, but now it clicks a little at the end. The **Audiofile Processor** has a lot of modulation parameters that we can play with to carve the sound to smooth the kick out even more, but for now, let's get some more sounds into our editor.

Time for action – adding elements and variation to our beat pattern

Let's add additional content to our pattern. Adding variation will help keep things from getting repetitive or gasp boring:

1. Hit your *Space bar* to temporarily suspend playback of the editor.

2. Go to the **Side Bar** and drag over `hihat_closed01`.

3. In the new step sequencer, let's put that hi-hat on these beats:

4. Now hit the *Space bar* again.

5. This pattern works well, but maybe we want a little more variation in the hi-hat. We can add steps to our step sequencer by right-clicking in the step area and choosing to add more steps. The more variation and the longer the sequence, the less repetitive our project will sound.

6. When we right-click on the pattern, we get the following menu:

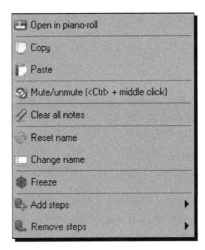

7. In this menu, let's head down to **Add steps**. Choose **Add 16 steps**. Do this for all of the patterns.

Chapter 2

8. Now our sequencer should change to reflect the new extended hi-hat pattern! Drag the window out to make the steps easier to see.

9. Let's add some new steps into the mix. Try this:

10. Now let's add the 16 steps to our kick and clap. We will simply repeat the patterns they have and maybe create a slight change on the kick at the end of the pattern to indicate the pattern's turnaround. Here's an example of a newly tweaked pattern that is 32 beats long:

What just happened?

We now have rhythmic foundation for a rudimentary dance song. Congrats! Now, let's get bass in there.

Adding instruments to the Beats+Bassline Editor—Bass

How can you have a good dance project without bass? Well, some purists may argue that you can get away with only drums, but not me. We need bass to give our song a musical foundation.

Time for action – adding bass to the Beats+Bassline Editor

We need to assign a bass to our pattern. We will be using the **Triple Oscillator Synth** to get the job done:

1. Go to your **Side Bar** and click on your **Instrument Plugins Tab**. It looks similar to the following screenshot:

[61]

2. There are plenty of cool instruments there, but we're looking for the **Triple-Oscillator**. The icon looks similar to the following screenshot:

   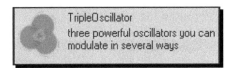

3. This **Synth** should do well for our bass synth. Let's drag it over to the **Beats+Bassline Editor**. This will, once again, add a step sequencer to the editor. Be sure that once it is in the **Beats+Bassline Editor** that you add 16 steps to it.

4. Now we have three drums and a bass. Let's do something simple to start with as far as the bass is concerned. Have it play on the off-beats. So we'll be clicking on the off-beats. The pattern should look similar to the following screenshot:

5. Press your *Space bar* and let's check it out!

6. Whoa! Didn't that sound great?

What just happened?

What's happening is that our instrument is holding the notes too long when it plays. Let's edit this instrument.

Our first tweaking of a synth

Do not be afraid! For complete control of our sounds, we need to start exploring the basics of tweaking a sound in LMMS.

Time for action – editing note length and root pitch in the Beats+Bassline Editor

Almost all instruments in the electronic music world give us the opportunity to shape the pitch and duration of sound using simple parameters. Let's have a look at some of the ways we can use the basic synth parameters to bend the sound to our will:

1. Click on the synth in the editor and then look for this area:

2. Let's click on the area called **ENV/LFO**. This should open a screen that looks similar to the following screenshot:

 An **envelope** is a way of altering the knobs controlling an instrument over time.

3. This area of the instrument is where we are going to alter the length of the triggered sound. There are seven knobs related to how this particular envelope is affecting volume on this instrument. We're going to deal with the **HOLD** knob.

4. Turn the **HOLD** knob to **0**.

5. Now our sound has the proper length. It's pitched a bit high, though.

6. Look to the keyboard at the bottom of the instrument. Do you see the green area?

7. This green area denotes the **root pitch** of the instrument. One way that we can change the pitch of this bass is to raise the root pitch up to **C5**. Just grab the green area and drag it up there. You can also type the value in directly as we have done before with other parameters. Do you hear the pitch change? That's because the key that is being played is now an octave down from the root pitch of the instrument. This is a really quick way to drop our bass into a more bass-like range. This bass line isn't really saying a whole lot, musically. Maybe it's time that we varied the pitch using another editor.

Exploring the Piano Roll editor

Now that we have the rhythm cruising along in our **Beats+Bassline Editor**, we should add some variation to the pitch of the bass instrument. For this, we are going to use the **Piano Roll** editor to change the pitch on specific steps of the sequence.

Time for action – opening a pattern in the Piano Roll editor

1. To open the pattern in the **Piano Roll**, right-click on the bass pattern and choose **Open in piano roll**. It is the first choice in our menu:

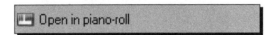

What just happened?

What we will see now is a representation of our stepped pattern in **Piano Roll** form. The note grid of the **Piano Roll** shows pitch vertically and time position of the note horizontally. The width of each green vertical line on the grid is the length on that note:

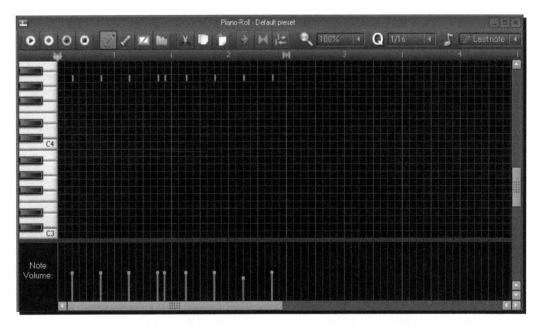

Below the grid, we can see the velocity of the note.

 Velocity is the term for how hard the note is being played.

Technically, if we were playing a piano, velocity would be how fast our finger was speeding towards the key when the note was played. On a piano, if our finger is playing a key at breakneck speed, we would get two effects. The note would be really loud and the timbre of the note would change as well, sounding more bright and harsh. In LMMS, velocity is assigned to note volume. If we want to adjust the volume of each individual note, we would go to the bottom of the **Piano Roll** and adjust the vertical length of each green line to give volume variation in the pattern. The shorter the line, the lower the volume and vice versa.

Clicking where it says **Note Volume** on the left side of the lower grid will give us **Note Panning**:

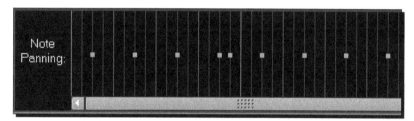

Now the lower grid is being used to pan each individual note. When the dots are vertically centered, then the sound is being distributed evenly between the left and right channel of your project. When moving the dot up, the note is panned right. When moving the dot down, we get more in the left channel.

Time for action – changing the pitch of the bassline

1. So let's simply grab a couple of notes and move them to create some variation of our bass line. Try grabbing and moving these notes vertically to give us the pattern similar to the following screenshot:

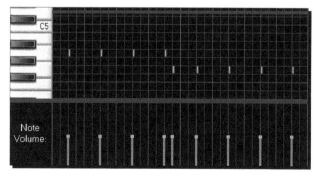

What just happened?

Now we have a bass line that changes. When we have the **Piano Roll** open, we will only hear the instrument we are editing. If we hit the *Space bar*, the **Piano Roll** will play back our bass line to us alone. To hear it in context, we need to return to the **Beats+Bassline Editor**. You can select the **Beats+Bassline Editor** at any time and have a listen to the bass line during this tweaking session.

The default tool in the **Piano Roll** editor is the **Pencil** tool. The **Pencil** will create events wherever appropriate. If you are in the *note grid*, then the pencil makes new notes and can be use to shift notes in pitch and time. In the *volume/pan grid* below, it adjusts volume and panning per note.

If you right-click, you'll have an **Eraser**. As long as you hold the right mouse button down, you will be erasing note data in the note grid.

Using the Piano Roll in the Song Editor

When using a bass in the beats+bassline pattern, shifting pitch, volume, and panning is fine. If you plan on creating more drastic changes or want to have a bass line with multiple note length values, I suggest creating an instrument in the **Song Editor** and using the **Piano Roll** editor there.

Time for action – muting instruments in the Beats+Bassline Editor

The **Beats+Bassline Editor** is very basic and is very good for creating patterns. When we need to be more melodic or use chords, we should use the **Piano Roll** in the **Song Editor**:

1. Let's go mute the bass line in our **Beats+Bassline Editor**. We are going to create a bass line in the **Song Editor**. To mute the bass line, simply click on the green button to the left of the instrument's name:

What just happened?

Now we've muted our original bass line and can start in on the **Song Editor** window.

Chapter 2

Time for action – enabling a Piano Roll in the Song Editor

1. To enable a **Piano Roll** in the **Song Editor**, simply double-click next to the first instrument we see; the **Default preset** triple oscillator synth. A black region will appear next to the synth, showing us where we are going to write our note information:

What just happened?

In LMMS terminology, that black area is called a **block**. Think of blocks as blank paper that you are about to write your masterpiece on. Blocks can be moved around in the **Song Editor** to create an **arrangement**.

Remember how we got instruments into the **Beats+Bassline Editor**? Well, the **Song Editor** works the same way. Simply grab a sample, preset, or instrument from the **Side Bar** and drop it on the **Song Editor**'s **track list**. The track list is the area we currently see the **Default preset** synth that we create a block for a second ago.

Unlike the **Beats+Bassline Editor**, the **Song Editor** does not perform step sequencing. Its primary editor will be the **Piano Roll** editor.

When using the **Beats+Bassline Editor**, you can have several instruments open at the same time and have them play notes at specific times. In the **Song Editor**, you can create blocks next to a **Beats+Bassline Editor** and that will determine how many bars and beats of the sequence in the editor will play.

Time for action – enabling a MIDI keyboard controller in the Song Editor

In the **Song Editor**, if we want to use a MIDI keyboard controller, it's pretty simple:

1. On the instrument you wish to allow input for, click on its **Track Tools** icon:

2. In this list, we see three options: **Clone this Track**, **Remove this Track**, and **MIDI**.

[67]

3. If we choose **MIDI**, we can designate which of the MIDI controllers hooked up to our system we want to use:

What just happened?

Now we have the ability to record MIDI notes directly into the **Piano Roll editor** if we get bored with inputting all of the notes by hand. We'll do some of that in *Chapter 5, Making Spaces: Creating the Emotional Landscape*.

Getting the Mixer to work in our project

We've already defined what a **Mixer** does, but how do we decide what instrument goes to a specific **FX Channel**?

LMMS has a very different approach from other DAWs as to how it allows routing to the mixer.

When you create an instrument, no matter whether in the **Song Editor** or the **Beats+Bassline Editor**, you have the option to route it to whatever FX channel you decide is appropriate. If you do not choose an FX channel, it will automatically be routed to the **masteroutput**, which goes directly out to your headphones or monitors. If you choose not to define an FX channel, you can still adjust the volume of the instrument at the instrument itself, right on the front panel. Here's the area of the instrument where we can choose our FX Channel. I'm showing our bass from the **Beats+Bassline Editor** we created:

Time for action – routing an instrument to a channel on the FX Mixer

It is important to be able to separate out audio streams from different instruments in LMMS. Let's assign the instrument now:

1. If you grab the illuminated number above where it says **FX CHNL**, you can drag up and down to change the assignment of this instrument to the **Mixer**. These channels can have effects placed on them, pass the audio through the plugins, and then send the audio on its way to the master channel.

2. Let's try assigning the bass line to **FX Channel 1**. We should see the audio playing through the **FX-Mixer** now. Oh wait... we don't!

What just happened?

Oh, that's right. We muted the bass line in the **Beats+Bassline Editor**. Go and unmute that instrument and we should now see the audio playing through the **FX-Mixer**:

Those of you coming from a traditional DAW background may find this a bit confusing. Each instrument having its own set of plugins, panning, and volume—as well as having a routing through the **FX-Mixer** seems a bit strange. LMMS approaches digital audio and electronic music in a unique way that is different from the goliath DAWs. I know I found myself scratching my chin a couple of times, but once you get the hang of it, it makes sense.

What plugins are and where we can put 'em?

Plugins are audio effects that we can apply to instruments and **FX** channels in the **Mixer**. If you want your sound to be reverberating and huge, there are effects for that. If you want your instrument or sample to sound dirty and raw, there are plugins for that as well. Plugins are used to help shape the timbre of the sound and give us something more interesting.

Plugins are usually applied to a project when the project is getting ready to mix down. There are exceptions, though. Sometimes, we need to use plugins to take a sound that's vanilla and make it more of a spiced curry. This way when we use that sound in our song, we are more inclined to use it in a more emotionally appropriate way.

When we are using plugins to create a sound we want to play with while we are composing, we usually put it directly on the instrument of choice. Remember this menu?

There's an area called **FX** that we want to check out.

Time for action – exploring FX

Using effects chains, we can send a sound into new spaces and created interesting timbres. We will be essentially creating a sequence of processes that will alter the sound at each step:

1. Go to the bassline instrument we are using in our **Beats+Basslines Editor** and click on **FX**. You will see the following screenshot:

2. There is a button next to the area that says **EFFECTS CHAIN**. Click on this button to enable your plugins.

3. After clicking the **Enable** button, click the **Add effect** button. You'll be presented with an impressive list of plugins that are included with LMMS. These plugins have an interesting descriptor: **LADSPA**.

> LADSPA stands for **Linux Audio Developer Simple Plugin API**. These plugins are all free and are constantly being created in the Linux community. This is why, when you open the **Add effect** list, there are so many choices.

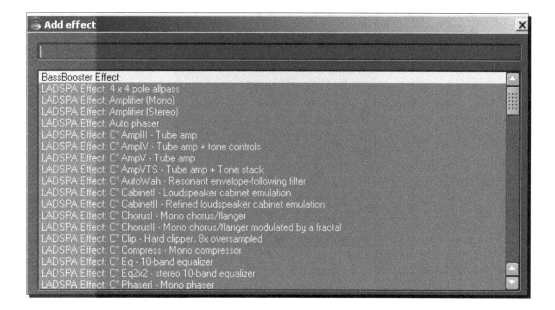

4. When you click on an effect, it will give you a description of the effect below. All you have to do next is click **OK**. Let's select **LADSPA Effect C* AmpIII – Tube Amp**.

What just happened?

This places the effect in the effect chain of the instrument. In this case, we don't have any other effect. In the future, we might add a reverb. If we did, then the distorted signal would flow into the reverb before leaving the instrument on its way to the **Mixer**. This is why it's called an effects chain.

When the effect is in the chain, we have some basic controls and more advanced controls. First, we have control over the wet versus dry signal, **Decay**, and **Gate** for this specific plugin:

If we choose the **Controls** button, we get the more fine controls for the effect. In this case, that would be **gain**, **temperature**, and **drive**:

We can also apply effects at the **FX Mixer**. To do this, we simply select an FX channel by selecting its name with our pointer. The effects chain will be to the right of the **Mixer**. In our case, we are going to select FX channel **1**:

This effect chain works exactly like the other in the instrument. The difference here is that we can have more than one instrument going through this effect at a time. Take for instance the **Kick**, **Hi-hat**, and **Clap**. Those could all be sent to FX channel **1** and that FX channel could have an effect that could affect them all at once. This might be good, for example, if we wanted our drums to sound like they were in the same room together. We could apply a small reverb on the FX channel and send all of the drums through that.

Once you have adjusted the volumes at the instrument and panned them to the left and right speaker using the panning knob, the **FX-Mixer** would be the final place to adjust your volumes before the audio was to be recorded to disk to play on a personal audio device like a phone, iPod, or other device of your liking. Getting the levels correct is very important and the plugins you use will help adjust the overall color of your mix so that it sounds good on any system you play it on.

We will be exploring mixing later in *Chapter 10*, *Getting the Mix Together* and *Chapter 11*, *Getting into Instruments* in which we explore the techniques of mixing in LMMS.

Summary

Well my, my, my. That was a lot of information.

Believe it or not, this is just scratching the surface of how LMMS works and as far as music-making environments are concerned, LMMS is simpler to understand than other DAWs out there. In this chapter, we covered the following:

- Getting a grip on the default template that opens with LMMS
- Exploring workflow in LMMS
- Using the toolbar
- Using the **Side Bar**
- Defining the **Beats+Bassline Editor** and how it's used
- Defining the **Piano Roll editor** and how it's used
- Using the **Song Editor**
- How sound gets from the editors to the **FX Mixer**
- How to use effect chains

Now that we've had an overview of LMMS, we're going to start getting to work on getting creative. Using the LMMS environment, we'll be exploring how to make really interesting house, techno, and trance music. We'll be analyzing patterns, creating sounds, and using advanced techniques to get the foundations laid so that we can do what we like in LMMS. These foundations are not specifically being laid so that you create music in LMMS for the rest of your life. The point is to help you take this program as far as you can and have applicable skills that will allow you to create good music in any program you use. Many of the concepts in LMMS will port over to any program that you may use in collaboration. LMMS will be another tool in your arsenal that you'll reach for when you need something that LMMS does really well. In the following chapters, I'm going to be applying skills that I have learned in other studios and other programs to give you a leg up in LMMS.

Onward!

3
Getting Our Hands Dirty: Creating in LMMS

We've explored LMMS and its various editors and menus, so it's time to get this party started. In this chapter, we are going to explore what patterns are good foundations for dance music.

Specifically, we'll cover:

- Exploring pattern-based electronic production
- Introducing the elements of a good rhythm pattern
- Exploring different dance music genres
- Exploring dance music arrangements
- Exploring the Beat+Bassline editor
- Using the Piano Roll to perfect patterns

Starting our beat with the basics

Most of the essential ingredients can be created in the **Beat+Bassline Editor**. Dance music has a fairly long lineage and there are many cousins in this family. We're going to start with some basic patterns and move our way up through different genres and styles to give ourselves a basic education in different dance music languages.

Let's get started by making our first beat:

Time for action – making the most basic of beats

The foundation of all modern dance music comes from the simple four on the floor dance beat. We're going to use the **Beats+Bassline Editor** to get us there:

1. Open LMMS and save this project as **Basic Dance Beat**.
2. Open the **Beat+Bassline Editor**.
3. Open the **Instrument plugins** tab on the sidebar menu as follows:

4. Drag the instrument called **Kicker** to the **Beats+Bassline Editor**, as shown in the following image:

5. Now we have a **Kicker** and a **Triple Oscillator Synth** ready to go in the **Beats+Bassline Editor**. Now all we need to do is create our pattern. Create your kick pattern on the first, fifth, ninth, and thirteenth beat:

Chapter 3

6. This ridiculously simple pattern is going to be the basis of a whole lot of dance music styles. This type of kick pattern is called **four on the floor**.

7. Now go back to the sidebar and open up the **My samples** tab. Click on **hihat_closed_01.ogg**. The hihat tone should be short and crisp:

8. Now drag that hihat sample into the **Beats+Bassline Editor**. It'll show up under the **Kicker** as follows:

9. The hihat is going to be on the 'off' beats of the pattern. In other words, it's going to play when the kick is not playing. Insert a hihat every third beat:

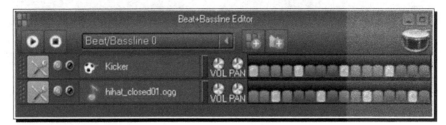

10. Let's hear how this sounds so far. Hit your spacebar while the **Beats+Bassline Editor** is open, and you'll hear the kick and hihat.

11. This pattern is the basis of most dance music, but at a tempo of 140 we are limiting ourselves to the techno genre. Notice how fast the kick and hihat appear to be playing? Let's get our tempo down to something a little less frantic.

12. Go to the toolbar and change the tempo from 140 to 125:

13. Tempos are a big deal in dance music. Tempo can make the difference between a trance style and house style. Time signature will remain 4 beats to a bar, though.

14. From now on, when talking about patterns, we will be referring to the beats within the bar. Our pattern has one bar with sixteen beats per bar. These are called, aptly, sixteenth notes. Every two sixteenth notes equals an eighth note and every 4 sixteenth notes equals a quarter note, which is what our song is based on.

15. Hit your spacebar. Sounds a little less frantic, right?

16. Now we should adjust the volume of the kick and hihat. They're kind of loud. Drag the **VOL** knobs to put the Kicker's volume at around 50% and the hihat around 25%:

17. Now we can add our clap. Go to the sidebar and choose **clap02.ogg**:

18. Drag the sample over to our **Beats+Bassline Editor** and place the clap on beats five and thirteen:

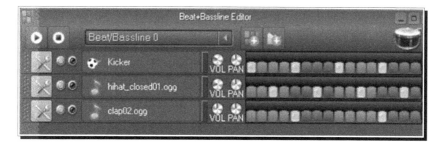

19. The kick and the clap. It's like Yin and Yang. Okay maybe not, but it is what gets people dancing. We'd better adjust the volume of that clap to around 25% so it doesn't take our heads off:

20. Now hit your spacebar and have a listen. Sounds familiar? It should. This basic rhythm is the building block of popular music from disco to modern pop.

What just happened?

We used the **Beat+Bassline Editor** to create the rhythm for our dance music project. This pattern has been popular for dance music since the seventies, when disco was around. Later on, when disco was considered a scourge on pop music, there were these giant discos that needed people in them. DJs in urban centers like Detroit and Chicago started taking drum machine synths and made a new kind of dance music to fill the clubs. This is where it all began!

Now we should add a bass line to our pattern.

Time for action – fitting the bass in

The bass in dance music provides a lot of information to the listener. Although closely related to the kick, it gives us the musical foundation for the song. Where it fits in time also declares what kind of style we are going for. We're going to start with a four on the floor bass:

1. Go to your sidebar and open the **My samples** pane.

2. In this pane, you'll see other folders besides the drums we used earlier. This time, select **basses**:

3. We're going to use **synth_acid02.ogg**. Drag it over to the **Beats+Bassline Editor**.

4. Once there, match the timing of the bass with the kick drum:

5. Make sure to adjust the volume of the bass so that you can still hear the kick.

6. Now let's move the last bass note to the fourteenth beat. That little change at the end of the pattern should do a lot to keep the pattern from sounding too repetitive.

7. Let's vary the pitch on the bass note. Right-click on the last bass note. This opens a **Piano Roll** editor. Alternatively, pressing *F7* or clicking the **Piano Roll** icon will do this too:

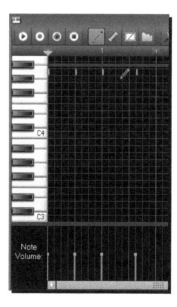

8. Grab the last note and raise it two steps higher.

9. Close the **Piano Roll** and listen to the bass along with the rest of your beat.

10. Go to the second note of the bass, and if you have a mouse-wheel, turn the mouse-wheel up and down. You'll see the shade of green go from brighter to darker. This is the volume of that note. The darker the shade, the lower the volume, as shown in the following image:

11. Having the bass to be on the beat is fine for some house music styles, but when things began evolving in the dance scene, Trance DJs were putting the bass on the off beat like so. Give it a try:

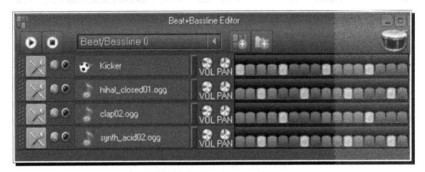

12. This is considered a **Techno** or **Trance** bassline. The rhythm of the drums is essentially the same, but the bass placement gives a very different feeling. This provides heavier kicks, which slammed harder in the club. To check out a PsyTrance bass rhythm, add a note behind each bass note. The effect is a bit more frenetic:

13. To hear Trance rhythms at their proper tempos, set your tempo to 140-145 beats per minute. You'll hear that Techno and Trance are fast and furious, requiring programming that leaves enough space to let each voice be heard.

What just happened?

Using the **Piano Roll** editor in concert with the **Beat+Bassline Editor**, we were able to add a simple bassline to our pattern.

Pattern-based music creation is a quick and easy way to start building elements for our song. The **Piano Roll** allows us to alter pitch, note length and timing. We will be constructing melodies and atmospheric sounds using the **Piano Roll**. At this point, press the spacebar or click the stop button in the **Beat+Bassline Editor** to stop the song before moving on.

Other styles in dance music

Now we'll start a new pattern and explore other dance music styles. To do this, we'll need to create another beat and bassline, which we'll do right inside the **Beat+Bassline Editor** itself. These patterns will need to be a bit longer than the previous patterns we've created.

Chicago style house music

For this section, we are going to explore some of the first styles of house music created for the dance floor. Chicago style house music is considered one of the first house music ever made, and was pioneered by the likes of Larry Heard and Marshall Jefferson.

Let's explore this style.

Time for action – creating Chicago style house music

First, let's create a bassline in the **Beat+Bassline Editor**. We'll need a new editor with an extended length. Let's do it!

1. Create a new pattern in the **Beat+Bassline Editor** by clicking on the add beat and bassline button. The button looks like the following:

2. Now that we have a new pattern, the pattern will be called **Beat/Bassline 1**, as shown in the following image:

This also adds a Beat+Bassline track to our Song editor. We can toggle back to our previous pattern by clicking on the drop-down menu triangle to the left of the add beat+bassline button. What's really cool is that all of our settings for the instruments are still there!

3. Go to your sidebar, click the "star" icon to open the **My Presets** pane and look for a new bass sound. We're going to use the LB302, so locate its folder, and drag the **Oh Synth** preset to your **Beats+Bassline Editor**.

4. Now we need to extend the pattern we have here. To add beats, right-click in the steps area and choose **Add steps** from the drop-down menu. Let's add **16 steps**, as shown in the following screenshot:

5. Repeat this step for every instrument in the **Beat+Bassline Editor**.

6. Now we should stretch the screen out to make things easier to see. Grab the lower right-hand corner of the **Beat+Bassline Editor** to give yourself room:

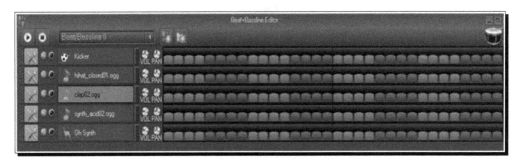

Chapter 3

7. Now let's start with a kick and clap pattern that's just like the previous pattern:

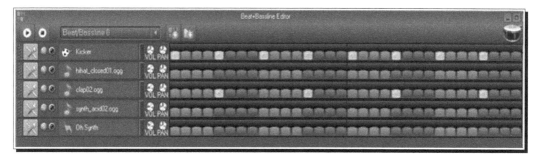

8. Set the tempo of the project to 120.

9. Now let's create a bass pattern that keeps this very simple kick and clap interesting. Double-click in the steps area for the new synth we created. This will open a **Piano Roll**.

10. Write a bass pattern in the **Piano Roll** that looks like the following:

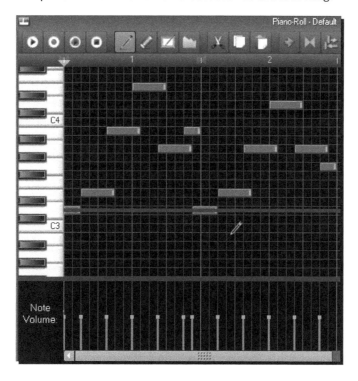

11. Close the **Piano Roll** editor and listen to the bassline playing along to our previous pattern.

What just happened?

We've added a bassline to our pattern that has varying positions and lengths to give us a Larry Heard type of bassline. Notice how there are very few bass notes on the quarter note markers? This is to give the bassline a floating feeling. It keeps the simple kick and clap interesting and leaves room for where they are playing. You'll also notice that the **Beat+Bassline Editor** has now changed from step mode on the bassline to show us that we've created a pattern in the **Piano Roll**.

Creating basslines that do not fall on the kick or clap is an interesting way to create a more complex sound. These techniques were pioneered in the early days of dance music. The kick and clap are usually placed where they are because that induces a trance-like state in the club. It is the heartbeat of dance music. The story gets told in the rest of the music, where the bass is free to roam, the pianos and organs walk around, and melodies are played.

Chicago house music is arguably where house dance music began. Now that we have our roots, let's look at some other patterns.

Have a go hero – create dance music patterns

Here are some examples of patterns in popular dance music styles from the past 30 years. We'll be looking at Beat+Bassline patterns as well as the **Piano Roll** editor. Re-create the patterns you see here and experiment with how you might change them to suit your own personal taste.

New York House

New York House music is also called **Garage House**. It has soul roots and the basslines are usually very melodic. Much of the New York House music elements had a strong sense of funk. Here is an example of a Garage House bassline. Copy this pattern and then make variations for yourself:

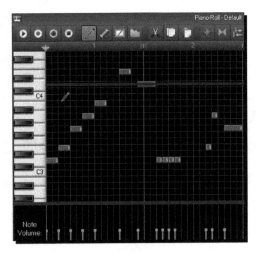

Yes, there's a lot going on there, isn't there? Try experimenting with the notes of this pattern to create a different feel. One cool variation on this theme is to have the line play, and when it repeats, have the second half of the bassline drop out. This can be achieved by using the **Piano Roll** in the Song editor where regions can be repeated and altered without affecting the rest of the beat. We'll explore this in the next chapter.

Artists to listen to: Masters at Work, Junior Vasquez, Blaze, Larry Levan.

Acid House

This style had very strange basslines that were usually short, distorted, and mean. Sometimes the clap of the pattern would be made more complex as well. It was a decidedly less funky sound. Here's an example of an Acid House bassline. Copy this pattern and then make variations for yourself:

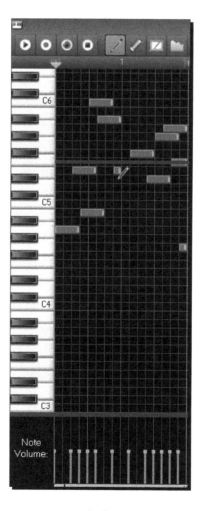

These basslines were often distorted and almost sounded unmusical. They added a dark edge to dance music, and this was when the pattern of the rigid kick and clap pattern began to evolve. This style is decidedly 'underground'.

Artists to listen to: Bobby Konders, D-Mob, Phuture, DJ Hardy.

Breakbeat

A **breakbeat** drum pattern gets its origins primarily from **Hip Hop** music. Its rhythmic patterns are usually a bit funkier, and don't have the straight-ahead, four on the floor kick and clap we've seen up until now in this book. Here is an example of a breakbeat pattern:

1. Go to your sidebar, and open the **My samples** pane.
2. In this pane, open the **Drums** folder.
3. Locate and drag **bassdrum_acoustic01.ogg**, **snare_hiphop02.ogg**, and **ride01.ogg** one at a time in to the **Beat+Bassline Editor** pane.
4. Now, copy this pattern and then make variations for yourself:

See how the Kick (bassdrum) is not on beat five, nine, or thirteen? The snare in this example is where we would usually have our clap. The ride cymbal is also changing up its rhythm in the last five beats. If you find house and trance rhythms boring and repetitive, breaks may be where it's at for you. The rhythmic complexity of the drumbeat can also make the placement of other elements more interesting as well.

Artists to listen to: Junkie XL, Chemical Brothers, Fatboy Slim, Southside Reverb.

Jungle, Drum and Bass, and Braindance

Jungle, Drum and Bass, and Braindance music all arguably stem from the tree of **Ragga Jungle** and **Dancehall** music. This music was originally very aggressive and had roots in Jamaican and Carribean influences. What sets this genre apart is the tempo. It's almost like having a Bob Marley rhythm section on way too much caffeine. The tempo is usually around 165, which may sound crazy. The frenetic drums are usually accompanied by other elements in half-speed, though.

Here is an example of a drum and bass rhythm. Copy this pattern and then make variations for yourself:

Although the kick and snare are relatively far apart, the shaker is giving the sense of frenetic rhythm. Usually in this style of music, the bass is playing in half-time, giving the listener something to hold on to as the beats go blazing by.

Braindance music is a mostly European sound in which the crazy frenetic beats of jungle music is infused with synthesis wizardry.

Artists to listen to: Freestylers, DJ Rap, Photek, Grooverider, Aphex Twin, Squarepusher.

Tasting the ingredients of dance music

As we have explored in this chapter, the most essential part of dance music is the rhythm and the bass. All other elements are important in relation to how they interact with those very essential components. That said, I'd like to list the most commonly used instruments in dance music, so that later on when we are creating our projects, you'll be familiar with them.

Drums

The drums you hear in dance music are related to the drum kit that you've seen rocking on stage with bands of various kinds. When we refer to drums in the electronic music world, we still use terminology from the acoustic world of drums. The surface of the drum that we hit with sticks is called a **head**.

The bass drum

The bass drum is the most important drum in dance music. It has a very low tone that provides the heartbeat of dance music. It's played using a pedal that has a beater attached to it. When the pedal is pressed down, the beater hits the drum. This is what a bass drum looks like from the front:

To listen to what bass drums sound like, we can listen to the samples provided in LMMS as follows:

1. Open your sidebar.
2. Open **My samples**.
3. Open the **Drums** folder.
4. Click through all of the samples that are named **bassdrum**.

Bass drums in the most popular dance music tend to thump along with a steady rhythm that simply provides the pulse of the song. Bass drums usually play on the first and fifth step in a pattern in LMMS. In more aggressive styles, it tends to be used in more complex patterns as we have seen earlier in this chapter.

The hi-hat

A hi-hat is comprised of two small cymbals, one cymbal floating above the other. The cymbals are facing each other, concave sides in, and suspended horizontally. The hi-hat has a pedal on it that causes the cymbals to come together. When using a sample library, you will often see 'open' hi-hats, and 'closed' hi-hats. Here is what a hi-hat looks like:

To hear what a hi-hat sounds like, we can listen to samples of hi-hats in LMMS as follows:

1. Open your sidebar.
2. Open **My samples**.
3. Open the **Drums** folder.
4. Click through all of the samples that are named **hihat**.

The different samples you see are closed, open, and pedal:

- **Open hi-hat** is the hi-hat played with a stick with the cymbals apart
- **Closed hi-hat** is the hi-hat played with the cymbals pressed together
- **Pedal** is the sound of the hi-hat closing together

Hi-hats are usually used more ornamentally in dance music. They are often played both sparsely and very frantically depending on the style of music. Open hi-hats are very commonly used on the off-beat. In patterns that we have seen in this chapter, they would commonly be placed on every third step. This was especially true for early dance music that was still referencing disco from the seventies.

The snare drum

The **snare drum** is a drum that has a top and bottom head stretched to create a high-pitched sound not unlike a gunshot. Snare drums got their name from the wires that cross the bottom head of the drum. When the drum is hit, it has a sizzling sound that is created when the bottom head of the drum vibrates against the wires. The rim of the snare is also played sometimes without the drummer hitting the head. Here's what a snare looks like:

The snare is one of the most important time-keepers in dance music. Sometimes, instead of a snare, dance music will use a clap in its place.

To hear what a snare sounds like, let's visit LMMS again:

1. Open your sidebar.
2. Open **My samples**.
3. Open the **Drums** folder.
4. Click through all of the samples that are named **snare**.

The snare is usually placed on the fifth and thirteenth step of our patterns. More aggressive styles will have the snare doing all kinds of crazy rhythms. Important emotional builds will happen when a snare starts softly and constantly, such as a military march, and gradually gets louder and louder until the main dance beat comes back in. This is called a **build** and we'll be exploring that when we explore transitions.

The tom-tom

Probably the silliest name of the bunch, the **tom-tom** evokes a more tribal sound. They are similar in look to the bass drum, but are half as large and usually ring out a bit longer than the bass drum. They are certainly higher in pitch. In dance music, toms are usually used sparingly, unless you are making tribal house or epic dance music, where they are sometimes used to evoke visions of some kind of epic tribal dance. Here's what a tom-tom looks like:

Name	What this looks like
A small tom-tom	
A large 'floor' tom-tom. (So called because it has legs. The other smaller toms are usually attached to the top of a bass drum.)	

To hear what tom-toms sound like, let's revisit LMMS:

1. Open your sidebar.
2. Open **My samples**.
3. Open the **Drums** folder.
4. Click through all of the samples that are named **tom**.

Tom-toms come in a variety of sizes and if you've ever seen a heavy metal band, the drummer is usually surrounded by toms. Tom-toms are usually played from high to low pitch in between the end of one section of a song and into the next section of a song for dramatic effect. This is called a **fill**. For one of the most epic tom-tom fills in history, listen to Phil Collin's single **In the Air Tonight**. You will hear some electronic drums, then an enormous tom-tom fill, and then the rest of the acoustic drum kit will come in. Trust me. You can't miss the fill in that song.

Basses

Basses in dance music are usually played from keyboards or computers, but sometimes they are real bass instruments. Here are the main types of stringed acoustic and electric basses:

The upright bass

The **upright bass** is pretty rarely used in dance music, but can be heard on some deep house tracks and jazzier styles such as trip-hop (or dub-pop if you prefer), and downtempo styles. It's one of the oldest of the bunch. It is a large wooden frame that has a neck attached to it with four steel strings traveling down that neck to the base of the instrument. In electronic music, it is usually plucked with the fingers. Dance music purists usually turn up their nose to the instrument, but it can be a very full-bodied sound when used correctly. Here's what an upright bass looks like:

LMMS does not have an upright bass in its library, as it is rarely used in dance music, but a quick search for 'jazz bass' on YouTube should return great results of this instrument being played.

The electric bass

The **electric bass** is smaller, lighter, and easier to transport than an upright bass. Dance music has certainly had its fair share of this bad boy. The electric bass differs from its ancestor in many ways. First of all, it's played horizontally across the body and is held on by a strap that goes over the shoulder and around the back of the player. It's also plugged in to amplifiers and speakers, so it doesn't have to be so big to be loud. In dance music, the instrument is often plucked using the fingers, but can also be slapped with the thumb to get a more aggressive, funky sound. The neck of the bass guitar also has **frets**, which are small metal crossbars that make it much easier for a bass player to hit their pitch constantly. Here's what an electric bass looks like:

Chapter 3

To hear what an electric bass sound like, let's revisit LMMS as follows:

1. Open your sidebar.
2. Open **My samples**.
3. Open the **instruments** folder.
4. Click on **basslap01.ogg**.

There are many popular bass libraries out in the world that are compatible with LMMS. You may also want to go searching for your own bass samples. There's always a bass player around. They're everywhere. Waiting. (To play, of course.)

The synth bass

The **synth bass** comes from the golden age of the keyboard synthesizer, which was from about 1973 through 1995. There are several synthesizers that are legendary for their bass tones in dance music and are represented in LMMS. Here are a couple of the most famous:

The SH-101

There are two types of synthesizer keyboards in this world, analog and digital. **Analog keyboards** have no computer chip in them and create their sound via conventional electronics. **Digital synthesizers** create their sound using a computer chip that uses 0s and 1s to compute a sound that is then made into an audio signal by a process that takes those 0s and 1s and converts them into sound. The SH-101 is analog and I love it. Here is mine:

Okay, so it has gotten a little dusty, but it's still my favorite bass synth and in pretty good condition, considering it's been around since 1983!

LMMS has a sample of an SH-101 called **bass01**:

1. Open your sidebar.
2. Open **My samples**.
3. Open the **Basses** folder.
4. Click on **bass01.ogg**.

It is a sample and a short one at that, but it's a fine jack-of-all-trades bass sample. I would suggest trying to find libraries of SH-101 sounds to supplement the already large LMMS library. The SH-101 has made it into most of my productions and I think you could very well fall in love with it too.

The TB303

This is a very special little bassline creation computer that came out in 1981. It was produced by the Roland Corporation until 1984. It had a huge impact on electronic music. This little box allowed a person to record a short bassline into it so that it would play back in a loop. LMMS not only uses this style of step-programming in its **Beats+Bassline Editor**, it also has an actual TB303 emulator included in its instruments! Here's what the TB303 looks like:

Now, if you'd like to hear what a TB303 sounds like, we can visit LMMS!

This time we're going to peruse the presets, though:

1. Open your sidebar.
2. Open **My Presets**.
3. Open the **LB302** folder.
4. Click on the **presets** within.

Now, the difference between a preset and a sample is that instead of playing an audio file from your hard drive, you are hearing an instrument called the LB302 making a TB303-like sound! Remember Acid House that we talked about earlier? It used the TB303 religiously. This little box has been heard in almost every style of dance music and its ability to create little patterns on it changed the way dance music was made. It's a piece of history.

Drum machines

The backbone of any early dance music is the drum machine. Originally, these were drum computers that were about the size of a small television. They gradually became smaller in size, and a particular gentleman named Roger Linn made history when his drum machines were used in some of the most popular songs of the 80s and even 90s. In the 80s, drummers were slightly concerned that they were being replaced, because the advent of **New Wave** and **Synthpop** started becoming insanely popular. Talented musicians and artists such as Prince, Phil Collins (himself a drummer!), and Kraftwerk took the drum machine into the mainstream.

The drum machine's reign was fairly short-lived as reigns go. The 80s ended and rock bands promptly started having the same distain for Synthpop that they had for disco in the 80's. This made old drum machines cheap and that's when the Roland TR909, TR808, and EMUSP1200 started taking over in hip hop, rap, and dance music. These machines sounded great in the hands of the dance community and are still used today.

Here's what an 808, 909, Linndrum, and SP1200 look like:

The Roland TR808

Manufactured and introduced by the Roland Corporation in 1980, it was one of the first programmable drum machines. Originally created as a studio musician's tool for making demos, it did not sound much like a real drum kit. It was, however, popular amongst the hip hop community for its affordable cost and extremely low-frequency kick drum. It has received an iconic status due to the fact that it has been used on more hit records than any other drum machine:

The Roland TR909

Manufactured and introduced in 1983 by the Roland Corporation, the **TR909** is a partially analog, partially sample-based 16-step step sequencer and drum kit. It was the first MIDI-equipped drum machine and became very popular during the beginnings of techno and acid music. Designed with cost-effectiveness in mind, its goal of realism fell a little short due to technical constraints. It sounded synthetic compared to the more expensive, sample-based drum computers available at the time:

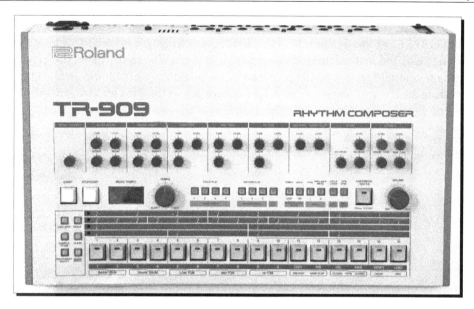

The LinnDrum

Manufactured and introduced in 1982 by Linn Electronics, the **LinnDrum** boasted 15 drum sounds sampled from real drums, a sequencer, a built-in mixer, and individual output jacks for each sound. Used on many recordings all throughout the 1980s, it became very popular in the mid-1980s due to its high-quality samples and affordability:

The SP1200

Released in 1987 by E-mu Systems Inc., the **SP1200** was originally intended for dance music producers. Being the first machine in the industry, which is able to construct the bulk of a song in one piece of gear, it became an icon of the golden age of hip hop. Praised for its gritty texture and "warm" vinyl sound, its characteristics – strengths and weaknesses—alike shaped the vintage New York sound of hip hop.

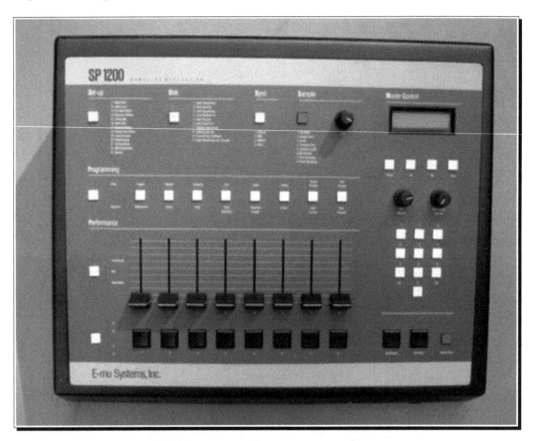

Samplers

The idea of recording audio into a keyboard and have it play back was already around in the 80s, but it wasn't cheap. Most early dance music was recorded to tape and any audio that was sampled was played directly into the tape recorder. When the 90s hit, though, samplers started coming down in price and a couple of samplers really stood out in the crowd for being cheap, reliable, portable, and reasonable fidelity.

Samplers that made a splash were as follows:

- Emu SP1200
- Akai MPC series
- Ensoniq ASR10

In LMMS, we are lucky to have our own dedicated sample playback instrument called the **Audiofile Processor**. How times have changed! Now most computer-based DAWs have samplers built into them.

Other notables

Basically, anytime a synthesizer was going out of style and was selling cheaply, it got snapped up by the dance community. Now that we have LMMS and other software solutions, making music on a computer is nowhere near as expensive as it used to be. I have to admit, though, some of these old machines still have a lot of feel to them. If you see any of the synths on this list for sale, you might consider buying it if only to have it as a collector's item. Here is a list of popular instruments that also helped form the dance music scene:

- Roland TR808, 909, 626, 505, and so on
- Roland Jupiter 8
- Oberheim Matrix 1000
- Any of the Waldorf series synthesizers
- Anything by the Moog Company
- Yamaha DX7IIFD

Have a go Hero – finding your style

Now that you've seen the roots of dance music and played around with some of the most rudimentary patterns, it would be good for you to expose yourself to more of the roots of dance music and electronic music. Here is an ingenious website link to help you on your way:

`http://techno.org/electronic-music-guide`

I would say this individual is objective by any means, but his chart of how dance music has come to be, where it's headed, and the roots of some of the most popular styles is pretty well informed and fun. He offers great examples of the true pioneers of dance music and gives you a clear path to discovery. Go have a listen to these tunes. LMMS is perfect for most of these styles.

Once you have listened to these styles, choose a style that you resonate with:

- Is it a Breakbeat style? Is it house? Trance? What do you like about it?
- I challenge you to listen to just the bass, kick, clap, and hi-hat. Listen to where they are placed. Can you do the same in the **Beat+Bassline Editor**?
- Keep your favorite song open and play it while you have your kick playing in LMMS. See if you can line the tempo up by pushing the tempo in LMMS up and down until the two songs sync.

Good Luck!

Pop quiz!

So, now that we've been to dance land and back, I have some questions for you:

1. What is a four on the floor kick pattern?
2. What is the difference between a four on the floor beat and a Breakbeat?
3. Is a Techno bassline 'on' the beat or 'off' the beat?
4. What are the three types of hi-hat samples in dance music?
5. How do you alter the volume of each individual step of the **Beat+Bassline Editor** without opening the **Piano Roll** editor?
6. How do you add more steps to the **Beats+Bassline Editor**?

Summary

So we've now been exposed to the raw ingredients of dance music and used LMMS to create patterns that we can start getting creative with. We've also explored different styles of dance music to help us decide how we would like to branch out and choose our own path through the dance world. We explored patterns in the **Beat+Bassline Editor** as well as the **Piano Roll** to help us see the patterns and help understand why dance music pioneers decided to place certain kicks, snares, claps, and basses in certain places. We also explored good placement techniques for individual instruments and checked out popular sounds used in dance music.

Expanding the Beat: Digging Deeper into the Art of Beatmaking

We've explored some basic beats from some very well-established styles in the previous chapters. Now it's time to start branching out a bit. It's good to know our roots and be able to create beats, which are the foundation of the most popular dance styles, and now we need to establish our identity.

In order to expand our beat, we are going to dig a little deeper into our **Beat+Bassline Editor** *and get a nice stable of beats together, which will work well for our arrangement.*

In this chapter, we will:

- Explore pattern length and arrangement
- Create a series of beats that will work well in an arrangement
- Explore the **Kicker**, **AudiofileProcessor**, and **TripleOscillator Synth** tools
- Explore basic effects usage
- Learn how to automate the **Beat+Bassline Editor** pattern we created within the previous chapter

Starting fresh

Let's open up a new project, save it as `Advanced Beatmaking`, and get into the **Beat+Bassline Editor** again.

Time for action – setting up long form patterns

We're going to be creating longer patterns for this section. Upon opening LMMS, we need to get set up again. Do the following to get set up:

1. Open LMMS.

2. Create a new project.

3. Save the new project as `Advanced Beatmaking`.

4. Drag the sample **kick_hiphop01** from the side bar **My Samples | Drums** to the **Beat+Bassline Editor.**

5. Extend the editor to 32 steps.

    Now our **Beat+Bassline Editor** is good to go. If you need to review the process of getting the **Beat+Bassline Editor** set up, refer to *Chapter 3, Getting Our Hands Dirty: Creating in LMMS*.

    After this initial setup, we need to decide a couple of things right out of the gate. We've explored some different styles of music and determined that tempo is a big factor for what kind of beat we are going to create. Most dance music lives within the tempo range of 120 and 135 beats per minute (bpm). There are styles that are slower and faster, but the sweet spot is really from 120 bpm to 135 bpm.

    Let's get the decision making out of the way so we can get creating.

6. Set the tempo of the project to 124 bpm:

    The tempo will remain at a 4/4 time signal, as most dance music is four beats per measure. We are going to use a four on the floor kick to start this pattern off. The pattern should look similar to the following screenshot:

7. Next, let's add a closed hihat, snare, open hihat, and clap from our side bar. We are going to create a basic dance beat similar to what we created in the previous chapter:

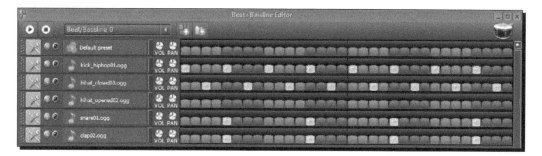

8. Now that we have our basic beat lined up, let's add something a little different. From the side bar **My Presets | TripleOscillator | SBass 2**, drag or double-click on the **SBass2** preset.

9. Let's create 16 extra steps for the new instrument. Remember to right-click on the steps next to the instrument in the **Beat+Bassline Editor** window to make this happen, as shown in the following screenshot:

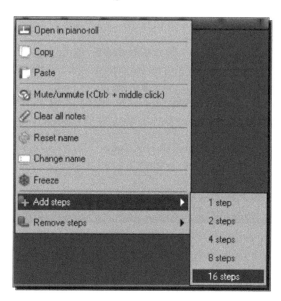

10. Now let's create placeholders for where this synth is going to play. Let's put it at these locations:

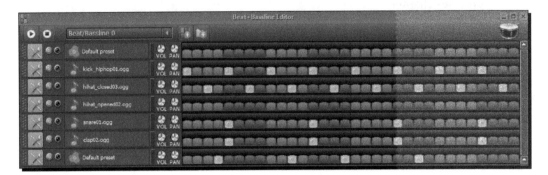

11. Increase the volume for the synth up to about 75 percent.

Now let's hit the Space bar and hear what this beat sounds like, with our new instrument playing as well!

What just happened?

We've created a beat that's identical to the basic beats that we had earlier, but now we are introducing another piece to our puzzle to make things more interesting.

We have explored the foundations already covered in beatmaking, now we need to start adding in other rhythmic elements to keep us from getting bored with what we're working on. We've placed the new instrument on some interesting locations. The placement of the steps for this instrument will intentionally throw the listener off a little bit when it is heard. When used properly, it's supposed to keep the beat from getting too monotonous.

Next, we are going to make this new instrument define the musical movements of the song, by adding a harmony and changing the note pitches a bit.

Time for action – adding harmonies to beats

Now that our new instrument is in the **Beat+Bassline Editor**, let's make it say something. Instead of just droning along on the same note, we want to have each step change pitch:

1. Right-click on the steps' area, and choose **Open in piano-roll**:

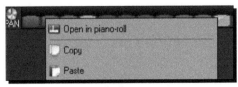

2. Now let's find the pitch of our notes, which are playing the new instrument:

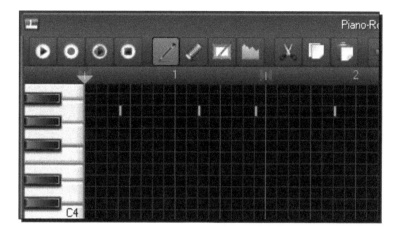

3. The note pitch is A4. Let's move these notes around a bit by clicking and holding on them, then dragging them to the positions we want:

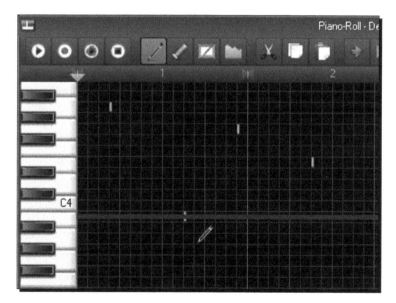

4. Now hit the Space bar, and we'll hear the new pitches playing back.

5. We should now add additional notes above these notes we've just moved around. Place the following notes on our **Piano-Roll** by clicking in **Piano-Roll** with the pencil:

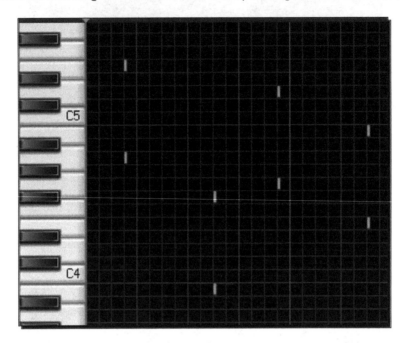

6. Hit the Space bar to listen to the new notes in the **Piano-Roll** editor.

7. Now, close the **Piano-Roll** and click again on the **Beat+Bassline Editor**. Hit the Space bar, and listen to where our new instrument plays now.

What just happened?

We just created a harmony in our beat! The placement of the notes as per the time and pitch are going to keep the beat interesting, offering variation that makes each part of our four-on-the-floor beat different.

 The rhythmic placement of steps in this way is called **syncopation**. Syncopation is beautiful. When we have a strict beat that is fairly unchanging and strong, syncopation is the little deviant that comes in and throws us off a bit, keeping the listener on their toes. It keeps beats fresh when they could potentially get boring, especially with a four-on-the-floor beat.

Chapter 4

Placing the bass

Now that we've made a little syncopated musical line, maybe we should put a nice, simple bassline in there to further root the main beat down. We need to be careful, however. We've started defining where our song can go musically, so we should try and figure out what notes would work for the bass. We've made basslines before, but haven't had to consider what notes to use because there weren't any other melodies, harmonies, or basslines to play off.

In this case, we are using the notes A, E, B, F sharp, G, and D.

Let's create a couple of different basslines, then we'll explore why they worked (or didn't).

Time for action – making the bass pitch friends with our harmony

For our first bassline to go with this beat, we are going to have the bass follow the kick:

1. Grab the sample **bass_acid02** from the **My Samples** | **Basses** folder.
2. Add the sample to the **Beat+Bassline Editor**.
3. Add 16 steps to the new instrument.
4. Use the steps shown in the following screenshot for our new bass pattern:

5. Now hit the Space bar. It doesn't sound great, right? Let's open the **Piano-Roll** and change the bass note.
6. Open the **Piano-Roll** for **bass_acid02**.
7. Change your tool to **Select Mode** by using the *Shift* + *s* keys or clicking on the icon that looks similar to the following screenshot:

[109]

8. Click-and-drag over the notes in the **Piano-Roll**. The volumes at the bottom of the **Piano-Roll** should turn blue:

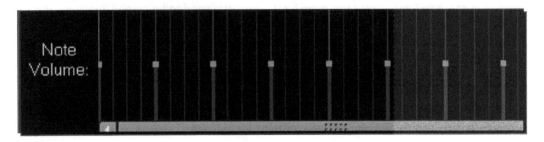

9. Now that the notes are selected, switch back to the pencil tool, and drag the notes down to F sharp 4:

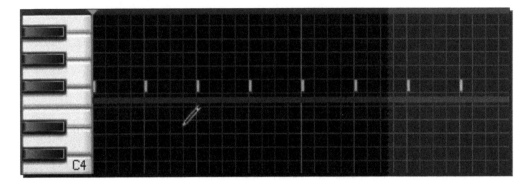

10. Now go to the **Beat+Bassline Editor** and hit the Space bar. This bass note sounds better, right?

11. Turn the volume of the new bassline down to -6 dB, as shown in the following screenshot:

12. Hit the Space bar and listen to the beat again. It's starting to make sense, right?

13. Now let's open the **Piano-Roll** again and try a different pitch for the bassline. This time, move the first two notes and the second two notes:

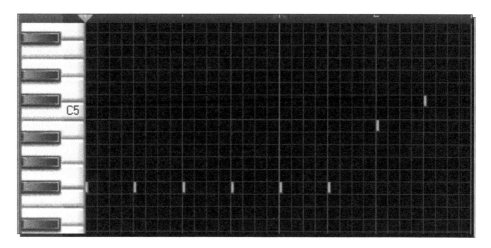

14. Have a listen to this in the **Beat+Bassline Editor**.

What just happened?

We just found the root note of the bassline and added a turnaround phrase at the end of the pattern.

This pattern is in the key of F sharp minor. We can determine this by the notes that were played in our harmonies. At the end of the bass pattern, the note raises to a D sharp before dropping back down to the bass note again. This gives us an indication of where the pattern is coming back around.

Giving the beat a turnaround

Now that our bassline has a turnaround at the end of the pattern, let's reflect it with a change in the drums. Try using the pattern shown in the following screenshot:

Recreate this pattern, and hit your Space bar. Hear where the beat turns around?

So at the end of our pattern, the bass and drums show a little variation. This variation is a clue to the listener that the pattern is starting over again. Some instruments will not change though, namely the kick and hihat. It's good to have some instruments that don't show variation, to give a sense of flow to the song. If everything changes up on the last eight steps of the pattern, then the entire beat can feel like a giant hiccup.

The importance of knowing just a little music theory

When creating beats, you need to have at least a basic knowledge of music so that your basslines and harmonies make sense. We aren't going to go deeply into music theory here, but I want to give you a couple of cheat sheets so that we can create beats, which at least use notes that are in the right key.

First things first. Let's look at a major scale.

The major scale

On a MIDI controller keyboard, there are white notes and black notes.

White notes are called names such as C or D or F.

Black notes correspond to the white note around them. If it is in reference to the white note below it, it would be called a **sharp**. If it is in reference to a white note above it, it is called a **flat**. So the note, shown in the following screenshot, can either be called C Sharp or D Flat:

This all depends on the scale. This book isn't intended to show you too much music theory, just enough to get you going; so now at least you know what I'll mean by sharp and flat.

If you play from C3 to C4 on a keyboard, which are all white notes, that 's a major scale. The gray notes are the notes of a major scale:

Now a **major scale** and a **major key** are the same thing. If I play all white notes, from C3 to C4, the notes will all sound good with each other, and the scale itself (and the key) will sound happy and uplifting. Major scales are hard to take seriously because of their enthusiasm and happy-go-lucky nature, but some dance music likes this kind of thing.

Think of a scale as providing the key to what notes you can use in your song. The key is the code to what you can and probably shouldn't do. Of course, all rules are meant to be broken.

Now let's very briefly talk about whole steps and half steps. These are the distances between the keys on the piano keyboard. If you go from one key directly to the next (this includes the black keys), that is called a **half step**. If you go one extra step, that's called a **whole step**. For example, the following screenshot shows a half step:

Now the following screenshot shows a whole step:

You use half steps and whole steps to figure out how to make scales.

How to figure out a major scale

A major scale has the following code:

Whole step, whole step, half step, whole step, whole step, whole step, half step.

So if we started on D, these are the notes you can use in the key of D Major:

This code for figuring out scales can start on any note on the keyboard. You can write down the notes that make up the scale and go from there.

You can use the **Piano-Roll** editor in LMMS to write in a major scale and listen to it. A C major scale looks something like the following screenshot:

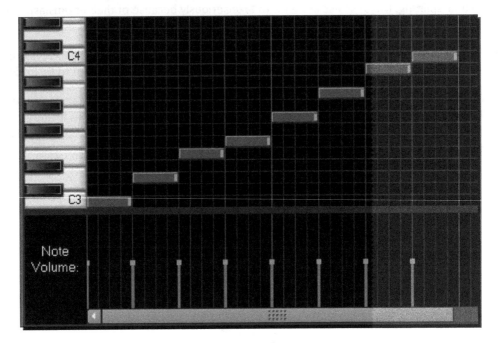

Major scales are the most important scale in music. If you memorize your major scales, you'll have access to a whole lot of musical tools. For now, we can use this method for figuring out what key we want to be in for a song. Of course, we should also include the minor scales.

The minor scale

Don't be fooled. This is not the forgotten orphan of scales, and is in no way less important than the major scale. As a matter of fact, most dance music and electronic music is produced in minor keys, because it can sound a bit more epic and dramatic than major keys. Here's the way to figure a minor scale out:

Whole step, half step, whole step, whole step, half step, whole step, whole step.

So we start from F on a keyboard as shown in the following screenshot:

In LMMS, a minor scale looks similar to the following screenshot:

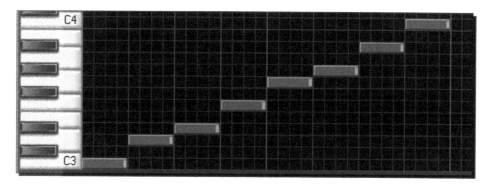

Minor scales sound sadder, but also tend not to sound like a Disney cartoon (which, of course, there's nothing wrong with).

Putting a number to a note

So when we talk about scales, We assign numbers to the notes of the scale. Let's take C Major. C major is the simplest scale to play on a keyboard because it is the only scale that uses only the white keys on the keyboard. Major and minor scales have eight notes in them, so C will be number one, D number two, and so on, until we hit *C* again on the keyboard, and we can call it number one again, and if we play C up high and down low, that's called an octave. (Eight notes, get it?)

Why did we just explore all of this? Well, let's use the rules and find out!

Time for action – using the key of the song

We are going to create a bassline and harmony using the rules we just explored in our **Beat+Bassline Editor**:

1. Create a new **Beat+Bassline** editor by clicking on the button that looks similar to the following screenshot:

2. Add 16 steps to each pattern.

3. Recreate the pattern shown in the following screenshot:

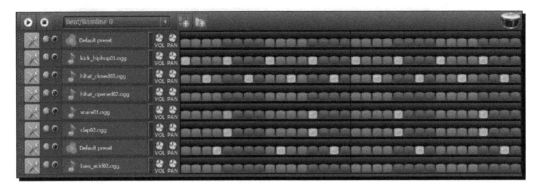

4. Open the **Piano-Roll** editor for **bass_acid02**.

5. Starting from F3, figure out the F minor scale using whole and half notes.

6. Write the notes down.

7. Create a quarter note bassline that follows the kick. To create a quarter note, simply click-and-drag the tail of the note out to the beginning of the next quarter note. Write it on F4:

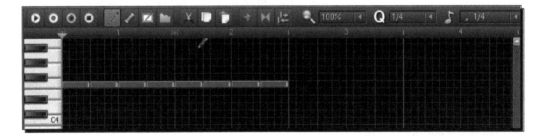

8. Now go back to the **Beat+Bassline Editor**, and hit the Space bar.

9. Let's fix the **SBass2** instrument on the track directly above this one. Let's open the **Piano-Roll Editor**, and use these notes from the key of the scale F minor:

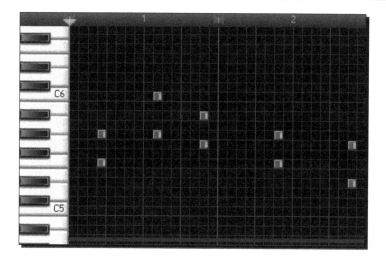

10. Go back to the **Beat+Bassline Editor** and have a listen. Do all of the notes fit?

What just happened?

We figured out what key we wanted to be in and used a minor scale to show us what keys we can and shouldn't use.

Now that we have a cool harmony going along, try this bassline to add a little variation at the end of the pattern, as shown in the following screenshot:

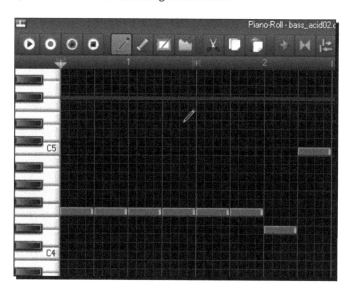

This is a very subtle change, but a good turnaround for the pattern.

Simple guidelines for the bass

Remember those numbers were talking about? Here are some good numbers to remember for making basslines—1, 4, 5, and 6.

It's best to stay on the root note (or the one of our scale) most of the time when creating the majority of dance music. It's a surefire way to keep the song in key and grounded. When moving the bass around though, it can be good to use the numbers four, five, and six to add variation to the end of the patterns. The following cheat sheet is for you:

- At the end of a pattern, have the bass move to number four of the key.
- At the end of a pattern, have the bass move to number five of the key.
- In the bass pattern we just tried, there is a D below the F. This is the number six of the key of F minor. (Remember that F is number one of the scale, no matter which octave F is being played at on the keyboard.) If you have a repetitive bassline, use number 6 in the middle of a pattern to create a cool change in the feel of the beat.
- Have your basslines start on the number 1 of the key. At the beginning of every eighth step, try having the bass go back to the number 1 of the key.

This is a simple cheat sheet to get you started. There are no hard-and-fast rules, but this is a nice map to make basslines that make sense.

Have a go hero – creating your own beat

So now we've made a beat, created syncopated harmonies, and written basslines—all in a specific key. Now it's time for you to make a beat of your own. Do the following:

1. Create a basic beat.
2. Add syncopated drums to the basic beat.
3. Add a bass.
4. Create a simple bassline that follows the previous rules.
5. Add a new instrument.
6. Have the new instrument play notes within the key of the song.
7. Attempt to harmonize those notes by adding one note above the notes you write.

After finishing the beat, listen back to it. Do all of the parts sound good together? Does the bass step on the toes of the harmony? Is everything in key?

Twiddling knobs to set the beat

There are other ways that we can sculpt our beat into something interesting using **Beat+Bassline Editor**. Once we have all of the steps in place, we can actually make changes within the step, which keep the beat interesting.

Automation is a way that we can turn knobs and fiddle with settings in LMMS. We are going to create changes over time and draw in those changes in the **automation editor**. We will be able to automate changes in the song editor as well, when we reach *Chapter 10, Getting the Mix Together*.

Tweaking the bass tone

The instruments in LMMS have a knob built into them that allows you to adjust the tone in an audio file player or synth. Think of it like the treble and bass settings on a car or home stereo.

Treble knobs increase and decrease the highs, and the Bass knob increases and decreases the low end of sound. This process is called **equalization** (**EQ**). We are essentially equalizing the amount of high frequency content with low frequency content. This way, if we're in the car, and a song sounds muddy, we can either decrease the bass or increase the treble to get the sound we want.

The type of EQ in LMMS we are going to use is called a **filter**. This EQ allows us to completely cut off all of the high frequency content above a certain point, and add a little emphasis to our bass sound. Let's have a listen to it and hear what it sounds like.

Time for action – sweeping a filter using automation

We can use the **Beat+Bassline 0** from our previous project to get started. You may also use the included project **Advanced_Beatmaking_pt2.mmpz** that came with this book:

1. Let's have a listen to our pattern. Our pattern should look like this:

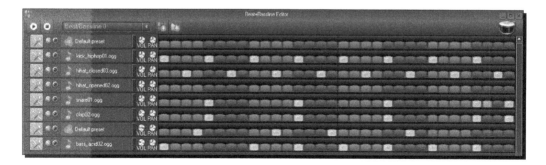

2. Now we need to zero in on that bassline. Let's click on the **bass_acid02** instrument to the left-hand side of the volume knob, as shown in the following screenshot, and have a look at the **AudiofileProcessor**:

3. This is where the bass audio file is playing from. We'll be looking at this plugin in depth in *Chapter 11, Getting into Instruments*, but for now we're going to focus on just a couple of aspects of the processor.

4. Click on the tab that says **ENV/LFO**. It's just underneath the panning knob. This will open up our **Envelope** and **LFO** section tab, which we will go over in more depth in *Chapter 11, Getting into Instruments*. The following screenshot shows the tab:

5. See the filter section at the bottom? It's not turned on yet, so let's click on the **FILTER** LED button to turn the filter section on, as shown in the following screenshot:

6. Click on the **Beat+Bassline Editor**, and listen to the beat again.

7. Click on the **AudiofileProcessor** screen to bring it to the front, and start turning the knob called **CUTOFF** towards the left-hand side.

8. Hear the high end of the sound cutting off? That's what a **LowPass** filter does. It allows the low frequencies to pass through, while the high ones get cut off.

9. Now turn the **RESO** knob to the right-hand side while the **CUTOFF** knob is set at 6800 Hz, as shown in the following screenshot:

10. This knob is taking the very point where the cutoff is happening and applying a little extra energy there. With the resonance up a little bit, we'll be able to hear the cutoff sweeping around more when we automate it.

11. In the **Beat+Bassline Editor**, click on the button that looks similar to the following screenshot:

This will add a special **Automation Track** area to our **Beat+Bassline Editor**:

12. Now we need to choose a knob to automate! Let's go get that **CUTOFF** knob. Open the **AudiofileProcessor**, and hold down control. Drag the **CUTOFF** knob to the **Automation Track**. The following screenshot is what it should look like if you are successful:

Chapter 4

13. See how the lane turns yellow? The name of the knob is now in that lane as well. We should start automating!

    Double-click in the yellow area. Now we should see an **Automation Editor** window:

14. Let's mess with the cutoff! We can see now that the cutoff is up halfway, just like we set it earlier. The range of this filter is 1 to 14,000 Hz. Our ears hear in a range between 20 Hz and 20,000 Hz. Change the cutoff by using a pencil tool to draw a curve in the yellow color:

    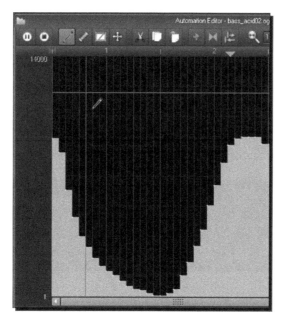

15. Now go back to the bassline and listen for the effect.

16. Let's add some notes to the bass. Create a note on every step, as shown in the following screenshot, so we can hear every move of the automation window:

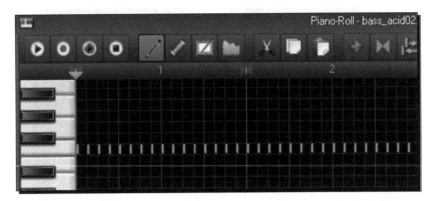

17. Now listen to the pattern by hitting the Space bar.

What just happened?

We've automated a filter on our bass audio file, changing its tone over time.

Using automation in the **Beat+Bassline Editor** is a great way to take a very repetitive sound and make it change gradually over time. There are many ways to use automation creatively.

Next, we're going to explore panning and volume automation, and look at some other aspects of the **Automation** window.

Time for action – panning and volume automation

We can do several different types of automation at once in LMMS. Let's try some panning and volume automation using automation tracks:

1. Create two new automation lanes in the **Beat+Bassline Editor**:

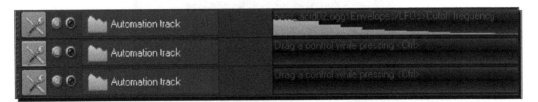

2. Now we need to assign pan and volume. Open the **AudiofileProcessor**, and hold *Alt* while dragging the **Volume** knob to the **Automation Track**. The results should look similar to the following screenshot:

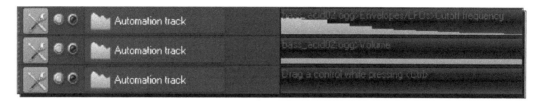

3. And now, add **Panning** as shown in the following screenshot:

4. Let's start with panning. Double-click on the **Automation Track** you selected for panning, as shown in the following screenshot:

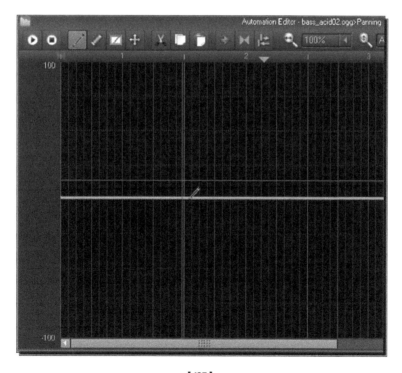

5. Be sure that the automation window is the same length loop as your **Beat+Bassline Editor** by pressing the command button and clicking at the end of bar **2**. You should see what looks like a green bowtie there:

6. When panning, **100** is sending all of the sound to the right-hand side and **-100** sends all of the sound to the left-hand side. The **Automation** window automatically changes values depending on what kind of knob you are twiddling. Let's use our pencil tool to create a pattern that looks similar to the following screenshot:

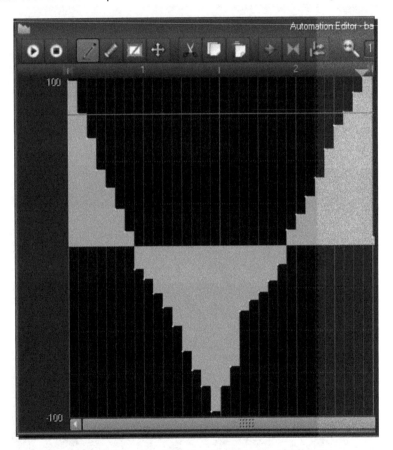

Chapter 4

7. Hit the Space bar and listen to the way our bass is moving from the left-hand side to the right-hand side and back again! We want it to be smoother, so let's change the resolution of our pencil by clicking on the box shown in the following screenshot:

And changing it to the value **1/64** as shown in the following screenshot:

8. This is a much higher resolution. Use the pencil to re-draw the panning curve again. It should look much smoother, as shown in the following screenshot:

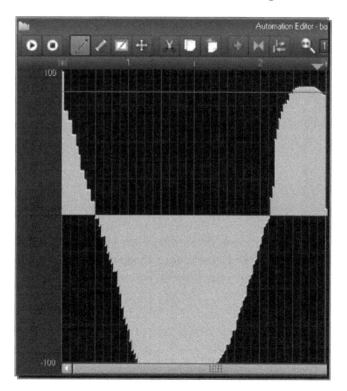

Expanding the Beat: Digging Deeper into the Art of Beatmaking

9. Now for volume. Open the **Automation** window by double-clicking on the **Automation Track**, as shown in the following screenshot:

10. This window gives us a value of **0** to **200** for the volume. Where the yellow line is right now, is where we initially set our volume using the **Volume** knob on either our **AudiofileProcessor** or the **Beat+Bassline Editor**. Let's draw a curve.

> To draw a linear curve, simply click on the desired starting point and press *Shift* and click on the end point. This will draw an equal ramp between both points.

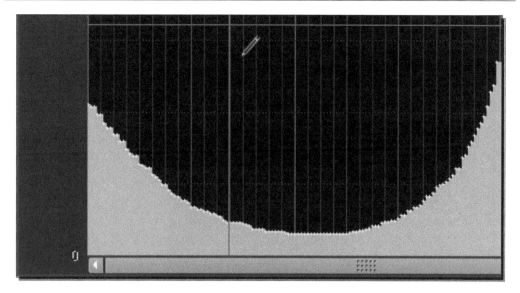

11. Now hit the Space bar, and listen to the volume control.

What just happened?

Now we have multiple types of automation happening at once in the **Beat+Bassline Editor**, such as controlling the filter, panning, and volume of **AudiofileProcessor**.

As you can imagine, there are all kinds of interesting ways that automation can take a beat, which is rather repetitive and dull, and give it some movement and flavor. Automation makes a track breathe. Giving any kind of movement to a pattern can greatly affect its impact on the listener.

Using automation on instrument effects

Instruments in LMMS can have audio effects such as echo, reverb, distortion, and many others applied to them directly. Let's explore how to assign a reverb to our clap using **AudiofileProcessor**, and automate its settings.

Time for action – putting reverb on the clap and twiddling it

Let's open up the **AudiofileProcessor** that's playing the clap and put an effect on it!

1. Open the **AudiofileProcessor** for the clap in our **Beat+Bassline Editor**.

2. Click on the tab called **FX** just to the right-hand side of the **ENV/LFO** and **FUNC** tabs:

3. Now we have the screen looking similar to the following screenshot:

4. Click on **Add Effect**, and choose **LADSPA Effect: Calf Reverb LADSPA**:

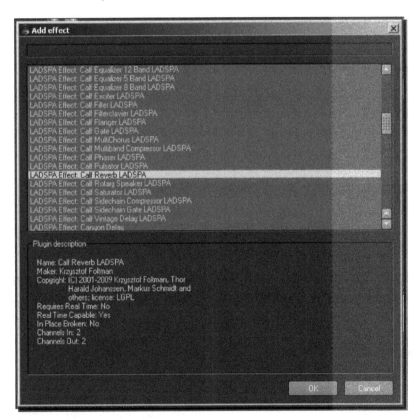

5. Click on **OK**.
6. Go to the **Beat+Bassline Editor**, and hit the Space bar. Hear the new reverb?
7. Now create a new **Automation Track** and drag the **W/D** knob from the reverb to the automation lane while holding the *Alt* key down. If you got it right, you should see something similar to the following screenshot:

8. Now open the **Automation** window and draw some curves. The resolution of the curves will be the same as our previous **Automation** window.
9. Listen to the result in the **Beat+Bassline Editor**.

What just happened?

We've assigned a reverb to our clap, and have varied the amount of reverb on the clap over time using an **Automation Track**.

Reverb is sometimes used in a very static way. After all, if you are singing in a room, does the room change its reverb arbitrarily? Reverb offers us the ability to put the instruments in our song in a space like a concert hall, but automating the way the reverb behaves makes for some really interesting dance music. Some DJs will add reverb on only the thirteenth step of a clap, to add emphasis at the end of a pattern. Doing this changes our beat from a stage play to a sci-fi opera. Manipulating effects in interesting ways gives personality to a beat.

Have a go hero – building your own automations

We've explored panning, volume, filters, and effects. How would you use automation in interesting ways in the **Beat+Bassline Editor**?

Try using other knobs on the instruments in the **Beat+Bassline Editor**, and assign them to an automation track.

Have a listen back to the **Beat+Bassline Editor** every time you change an automation window. Is the new automation bringing life to the track? Or is it just making a distraction? Would automation be a good idea on the kick? How about the hi-hat?

Give it a go and see what you come up with!

Pop quiz

Here are some questions to keep you on your toes:

1. What is it called when you create steps that play outside of a regular beat?
    a. Swing
    b. Syncopation
    c. Jazz
    d. Led Zeppelin

2. What number of the scale is good to use at the end of a pattern's bassline?
    a. Third
    b. First
    c. Second
    d. Sixth

3. How do you build a major scale?
    a. Whole step, whole step, half step, whole step, whole step, whole step, half step from the starting note
    b. Whole step, half step, whole step, whole step, half step, whole step, whole step from the starting note
    c. Whole step, whole step, whole step, half step, whole step, half step, whole step from the starting note
    d. Half step, whole step, whole step, whole step, half step, whole step, whole step from the starting note

4. How do you build a minor scale?
    a. Whole step, whole step, whole step, half step, whole step, half step, whole step from the starting note
    b. Whole step, whole step, half step, whole step, whole step, whole step, half step from the starting note
    c. Whole step, half step, whole step, whole step, half step, whole step, whole step from the starting note
    d. Whole step, whole step, whole step, half step, whole step, half step, whole step from the starting note

Chapter 4

5. How do you create an **Automation Track** in the **Beat+Bassline Editor**?

    a. Hold down the *Ctrl* key and click on the **Add Automation Track** button.

    b. Click on the **Add Automation Track** button.

    c. Hold down the *Ctrl* key and right-click on the **Add Automation Track** button.

    d. Right-click on the **Add Automation Track** button.

6. How do you assign a controller knob to an **Automation Track**?

    a. Click-and-drag the controller knob to the **Automation Track**.

    b. Right-click and drag the controller knob to the **Automation Track**.

    c. Hold down the control key, right-click, and drag the controller knob to the **Automation Track**.

    d. Hold down the *Ctrl* key, and click-and-drag the controller knob to the **Automation Track**.

7. Where is the **Filter** located?

    a. In the **AudiofileProcessor** under the **ENV/LFO** tab, at the bottom just above the **Piano-Roll**

    b. In the **Piano-Roll** under the **ENV/LFO** tab, at the bottom just above the **AudiofileProcessor**

    c. In the **Beat+Bassline Editor** under the **Filter** tab, just above the **Piano-Roll**

    d. In the **AudiofileProcessor** under the **Filter** tab, just above the **Piano-Roll**

8. How do you change the resolution of an automation window?

    a. Click on the **R** box.

    b. You cannot change the resolution of an automation window.

    c. Click on the **Q** box.

    d. Squint your eyes when you look at it.

Summary

Dance beats are built on repetition. The main beat is meant to be like a heartbeat; steady and strong. To make our beats shine a bit more and engage a listener on a deeper level on the dance floor, it's important to have elements changing and moving around like a living thing. Basslines that drone along are okay, but basslines that dare to move around can instantly offer more emotion to a song. Filter sweeps and panning automation are like a good spice rack. They keep things interesting, and the flavor of the music will change over time, like sipping a fine wine. Ahhhhhh!

We've taken the **Beat+Bassline Editor** pretty far, so let's start thinking of other pieces of the puzzle. We can add other editors to add further depth to our project as well. Let's get at it!

5
Making Spaces: Creating the Emotional Landscape

When you have a basic bass and beat going in your song, it's time to start filling out the atmosphere of the track. We're going to be using the instrument plugins in LMMS to create some interesting sci-fi spaces and emotional content for our song. We need to imagine a canvas that we're painting our song on. The ambience of a piece is the emotional background that gives further context to what's happening in a project and glues the piece together.

In this chapter, we will:

- Start using the **Song Editor**
- Explore arranging
- Open and use instruments in LMMS
- Explore using controllers to create control changes over time
- Introducing FX Channels

Using the Song Editor

We're going to use our extended beat in the **Song Editor**, to serve as the pulse that moves above our ambient tracks. Even though pattern-based music making is fun and relatively easy, arranging and creating ambience is going to be the work of the **Song Editor**.

Getting the Beats+Bassline Editor's pattern into the Song Editor

We're going to need our beats in the **Song Editor**, to view how much time they are taking with easy-to-move-around regions. A single region in the **Song Editor** can represent an entire pattern from the **Beat+Bassline Editor**.

Time for action – moving a pattern into the Song Editor

1. Let's get started by creating a new project and saving it with the name `Ambience`. Now, let's use this pattern to get us started:

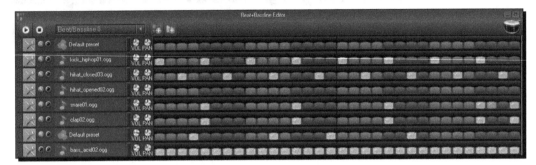

   This beat will be a nice foundation for the project. You can vary it a bit if you like. It's the same pattern from our `Advanced Beatmaking` project.

2. To get this beat into our song, let's open the **Song Editor**, which will be on the left-hand side of our project. The **Beat+Bassline Editor** will show up in the track list of our **Song Editor**:

3. To get our pattern to play in the **Song Editor**, we simply click on the area next to the track, which gives us an element that is the length of the pattern:

4. Now that our pattern is in the **Song Editor**, let's make the pattern play four times as long. Click next to the elements as they are created to have the pattern repeat itself four times:

5. Let's be sure our **Song Editor** is looping the same number of bars and beats. To do this, hold the command key, and click on the button (no command key needed in 64-bit Windows 7) above the **Song Editor**, which looks a bit like a bow tie. This is where you enable the **Song Editor** to loop a specific number of bars, as shown in the following screenshot:

To move the **Right loop-point**, use *Ctrl* + click. To move the **Left loop-point**, use *Alt* + click.

6. Set your loop-points to bar one and bar nine. This will give us an eight bar loop as shown in the following screenshot:

Making Spaces: Creating the Emotional Landscape

What just happened?

We've created an eight bar loop in the **Song Editor** and added our pattern from the **Beat+Bassline Editor**.

The eight bar pattern is very common in dance music. If you were to listen to any popular dance music song, you'd be able to count 32 beats before noticing that the pattern has started to repeat itself. Usually towards the end of a thirty-second beat, (which is an eight bar pattern in a 4/4 time signature), the pattern has a variation, which gives us a hint that the pattern is about to begin again. Using the **Song Editor**, we are going to create that variation and add our ambience.

Different elements for the Song Editor

When we pulled our **Beat+Bassline** pattern into the **Song Editor**, we saw our first element. Following are four types of elements, which we encounter in the **Song Editor**. These elements are containers of activity:

- **Instrument Track** elements: These contain notes and automation data. Double-clicking on this kind of element opens up the **Piano-Roll** editor. It only appears on tracks that have an instrument in them. Refer to the following screenshot:

- **Beat+Bassline** elements: These elements are the parts from our **Beat+Bassline** pattern. Double-clicking on these elements opens up the **Beat+Bassline Editor**, which we can tweak. Refer to the following screenshot:

- **Sampler Track** elements: These elements tell us what audio file to play. Double-clicking on these elements allows us to choose a different audio file, to replace the one that the sampler track is playing. Refer to the following screenshot:

◆ **Automation Track** elements: These elements contain control information for one or more arbitrary controls in an LMMS instrument or effect. Refer to the following screenshot:

Adding new parts to the Song Editor from the side bar

We've explored the **Song Editor** in *Chapter 2, Getting Our Feet Wet: Exploring LMMS*, and now it's time to start using it in the context of a project. We are going to import instruments into the **Song Editor**, which we can use to create atmosphere. For now, we are going to start with the preset settings that someone else made, make slight adjustments, and include them in our project.

Time for action – bringing in instruments

1. Open **My presets** | **ZynAddSubFX** | **Pads** from the side bar.

    Pads are sounds that are usually lush, broad, and are to the electronic music world, what a string section would be to the classical world. Pads are usually slow to come on and slow to fade. They are used to fill out the background of an electronic music piece.

2. Listen to the presets for the **ZynAddFX** instrument by clicking on them with your mouse.

   For our project, we are going to use **0065-Soft Pad.xiz**:

3. Drag the preset into the track area of the **Song Editor**.

4. Now, let's create blank elements in the **Song Editor** next to the preset. Click once next to the preset:

5. Now keep clicking with your pencil tool to the right-hand side of the element, so your instrument elements match the length of the **Beat+Bassline** elements. Your results should look similar to the following screenshot:

6. We now have elements, which will house the MIDI information, that we're going to use to play our preset. Let's test it out by double-clicking on an element to reveal a **Piano-Roll** editor. Add the notes shown in the following screenshot:

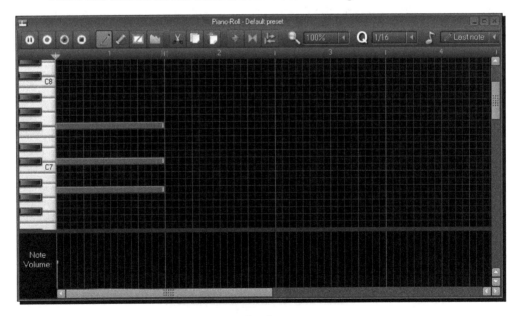

7. Go back to the **Song Editor**, and hit the *Space bar* to play our project with the newly added pad. Please note that this preset is a low frequency sound and therefore may be hard to hear on certain speakers.

What just happened?

We've now successfully imported a preset to our **Song Editor**, and have a set of notes playing over the beat that we created earlier.

The **Piano-Roll** is going to be used, quite often, for making our projects. It allows us more options than the **Beat+Bassline Editor**, as far as being able to express ourselves musically is concerned. We are able to create melodies, harmonies, and adjust our volume per note in this editor.

Inputting notes into the Piano Roll in real time

Writing notes in the **Piano-Roll** with our pencil works fine, but maybe you have piano skills and want to create your own melody using a MIDI controller. Here's how to use a MIDI controller to input notes into LMMS.

Time for action – playing the notes in the Piano Roll editor

It's time to try a couple of different techniques for getting notes into the **Piano-Roll** editor in real time. This means hitting record, and playing the notes along to a click or beat. Please note that the following five steps are unnecessary in 64-bit Windows 7:

1. Go back to the **Song Editor.** Click on the **Track Actions** button shown in the following screenshot:

2. Go to the submenu **MIDI** and choose **Input**. Choose **LMMS:**

Making Spaces: Creating the Emotional Landscape

3. This opens up the **LMMS** port, which will let us use our computer's keyboard for inputting notes! To test it out, double-click on an **Instrument** element, and hold down the number 5, the letter Y, and the number 9 on your computer keyboard. You should hear a chord being played by the current instrument.

    The following screenshot shows how our keyboard is mapped to play instruments in LMMS:

4. Let's delete the notes from the earlier example. By pressing *Ctrl* + clicking on the notes we created previously to delete them (right-click in 64-bit Windows 7).

5. Now hit the **Record** button in the **Piano-Roll**, which is the one that looks similar to the following screenshot:

6. We'll hear a clicking metronome to play along with. Hit the same combination of computer keys we played earlier, but at different times. For example, look at the following screenshot:

    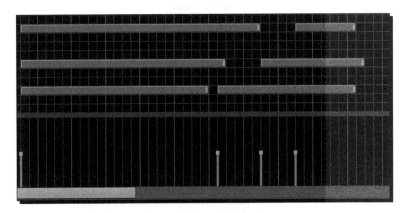

Chapter 5

7. If we want to play along with our beat, we can simply click on the **Record with Accompaniment** button shown in the following screenshot:

8. Now use the **Select** tool to select these notes, and drag them to the beginning of the element:

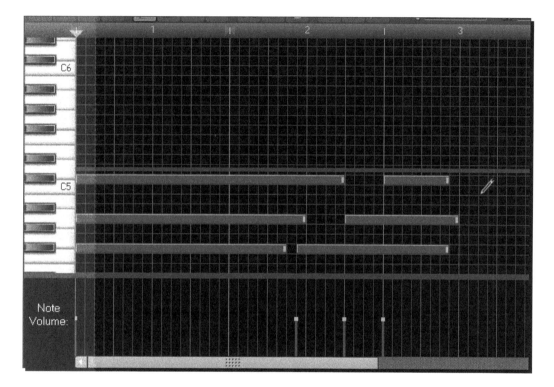

9. Let's set the loop-points for the **Piano-Roll**. Turn on the loop-points, and holding the Windows command button on your keyboard, click on the screen to set the right loop-point.

10. Go to the **Song Editor** and hit the *Space bar*. Have a listen to the pads playing along with the song!

    If you buy a MIDI controller, such as the ones mentioned in *Chapter 1, Gearing up: A Pre-flight Checklist*, the port should show up underneath the LMMS port.

11. Go to the **Track Actions** menu and choose **MIDI** and **Input**, and you should see the port show up underneath **LMMS**, as in the following screenshot:

12. Now open the **Piano-Roll** editor. Your MIDI controller will play the instrument track it is assigned to.

13. For any other tracks that require real-time MIDI input, choose the ports you would like to use. So you can play the instrument in the track actions menu on the track in the **Song Editor**. These ports will become active when you have a **Piano-Roll** editor open.

What just happened?

We just gave ourselves the ability to record MIDI notes in real time, to the **Piano-Roll** editor in LMMS. We explored using the computer keyboard and an external keyboard controller.

We were using a metronome to record to, but we might want to record our beat for inspiration, you know. Sometimes, recording a melody line along to a beat offers more inspiration to the person playing. It can sometimes allow for a more expressive melody.

The **Piano-Roll** editor is going to be the primary tool that we use for creating the musical movement of our project. Beats and basslines are great, but they are the heartbeats of the song. Now we need the emotional context.

Have a go hero

Now that we've explored bringing an instrument into the **Song Editor**, it's your turn to explore using the **Piano-Roll** and **Song Editor** together:

1. Choose a preset you like from **My Presets | Pads**
2. Drag the preset to the **Song Editor**
3. Activate the MIDI ports that you'd like to use with the **Instrument track**
4. Create **Instrument track** elements

5. Write some notes in the **Piano-Roll** editor, or play them using a controller
6. Have a listen. Do the parts fit? Are they too low in volume or pitch?

Time for action – using panning to spread the song out

We're going to create another pad preset in our ambience project, and write in some interesting parts. We can use panning creatively on the tracks to create an interesting sonic world for our listeners:

1. From the same **My Presets** directory that we were in earlier, let's bring in the pad called **0002-sin2x pad.xiz**, as shown in the following screenshot:

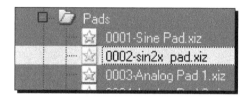

2. Pan the previous pad that we have in the project towards the left-hand side, to -48 percent, as shown in the following screenshot:

3. Pan the new pad that we just introduced in the project towards the right-hand side, to +48 percent, as shown in the following screenshot:

4. Now let's create **Instrument Track** elements in both tracks, as shown in the following screenshot:

Making Spaces: Creating the Emotional Landscape

5. Now open the **Piano-Roll** for the pad on the left-hand side of the screen, and write the notes shown in the following screenshot:

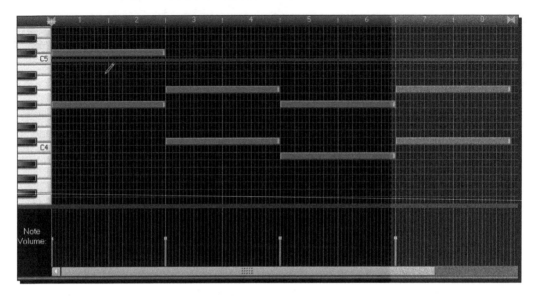

6. Now let's get to the other pad. Try the following notes in the **Piano-Roll** editor for the new pad, as shown in the following screenshot:

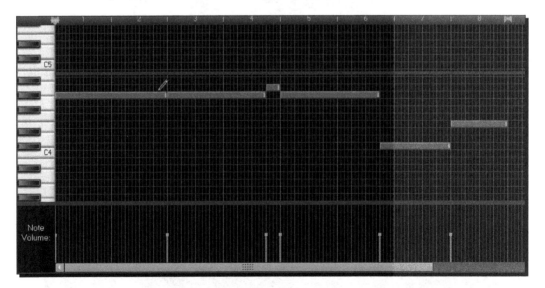

Now, we should hear a kind of melancholic melody wafting from the right ear or speaker.

7. Now, create an automation track in the **Song Editor** using the **Add Automation Track** button shown in the following screenshot:

8. To get panning automation for our lead pad sound, hold *Ctrl* and drag the pan knob from the lead pad track to the **Automation Track**.

9. The **Automation Track** will now have an automation element in it. Drag the right-hand side out until it matches the length of the other elements, as shown in the following screenshot:

10. Now open the **Piano-Roll** editor for the panning automation, by double-clicking on the automation element.

11. Set your quantize to the highest value for your automation element's **Piano-Roll** editor, as shown in the following screenshot:

12. Now let's make an interesting movement for the lead pad we have, as shown in the following screenshot:

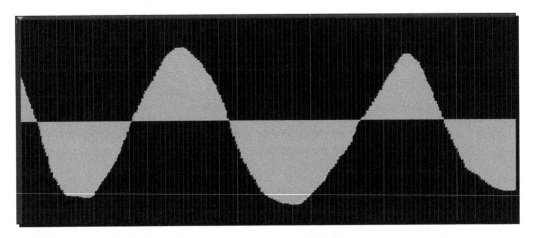

13. Go back to the **Song Editor** and hit your *Space bar*.

What just happened?

Using panning and automation, we've started creating a soundscape the rest of our song can live on. The lead pad sound is panning to keep it from sounding too static, and keeps the part, which is actually only a single note, interesting most of the time.

Now that we have some nice pads and a little ambient melody going on, it's probably time to go back to our original pattern and add a bit of space there.

Blending the old with the new

Ok, our original pattern is hardly old by any means, but it is starting to feel like it has some rough edges that need ironing out.

With our pads, we have used panning to try and add some spaciousness to the mix. They are already set back a bit in space. Now the little synth stabs that were happening in the **Beat+Bassline** pattern are starting to poke out a bit. We are going to use some delay effects to try and blend them a bit with our song's new atmosphere.

Chapter 5

Time for action – delaying those stabs!

Let's get back to the **Beat+Bassline Editor** and look at our pattern. To do this, simply double-click on the **Beat+Bassline** element in the **Song Editor**:

1. First, let's mute the other elements of our beat. We can do this by soloing the stabby synth, which is the preset instrument just above our acid bass. The solo button is just to the right of the green button that is currently turned on, as shown in the following screenshot:

2. Now that the instrument is isolated, let's click on the instrument itself to give us the instrument's editor, as shown in the following two screenshots:

Making Spaces: Creating the Emotional Landscape

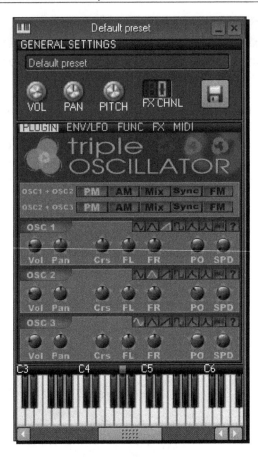

3. Now click the **FX** tab on the instrument editor, as shown in the following screenshot:

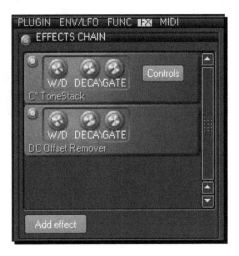

[150]

4. There are effects on this instrument already, but neither of the effects is a delay. Click on **Add Effect**, and choose **Calf Vintage Delay LADSPA**.

5. We now have a sync-able delay. This means it will follow the tempo of the song (as long as our settings are correct)! The following screenshot shows where we need to do our work:

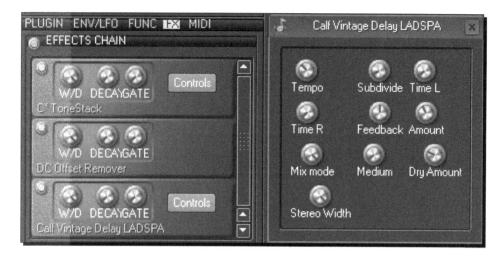

6. The controls for the delay come up when we click the **Controls** button on the **Vintage Delay Effect**. Now double-click on the **Tempo** knob.

7. For fine-tuning controls to our effects, we can press and hold *Shift* + the left mouse button, or enter the amount we want by double-clicking on the control. Double-clicking on a control gives us the following screenshot:

8. We want a tempo of `124`. Simply type the number in and hit return.

9. Now let's be sure to turn the **Amount** knob to a little below halfway up.

[151]

10. Now, we need to alter the **L Time** and **R Time** knobs. Double-click on them, and enter 1 for each, as shown in the following screenshot:

11. The effect controls always give us the range that we can use for each knob. Go to the **Song Editor** and hit the *Space bar*. Return to the instrument's effect section. Experiment with different values for the **L Time** and **R time** knobs to hear the different effects of this delay.

12. Set the subdivide knob to a value of 2. Listen to this delay and hear how it moves this instrument line around.

13. Turn off this instrument's solo button so we can hear the sound along with other sounds.

14. Adjust the volume of the instrument in the **Beat+Bassline Editor** to 2 dbV.

What just happened?

Now that stabbing instrument that seemed very hard and in our face is subdued into the rest of the piece, moving around in interesting ways because of our new delay effect.

Using simple effects directly on instruments can give dramatic results. We can take a sound that was pretty aggressive and diffuse it into a delay, which will help blend the part into our piece more.

Delay versus reverb

So delay has the interesting effect of moving a part of our music further back into the mix, blending it with the rest of our music. What about reverb?

Reverb is arguably the king of setbacks, the great diffuser. It is a way of taking a sound and putting it in a virtual room. In this virtual room, the instrument makes a sound, and the sound bounces around.

So is a reverb different than a delay? Well, yes and no.

Reverb bounces the sound around our ears like a regular delay does, but it also creates delays that are more complex and dense. Standard, delay-based reverbs usually have two modes to them. They have what is called an **Early Reflection** mode and a **Reverb** mode.

Let's say you are in a relatively big room, maybe 20 meters by 20 meters, and you clap. The sound waves that you create are not unlike waves in a pond. The ripples from your clap go out to the walls, where they bounce off them and come back to your ears. This first bounce is called the **first reflection**.

Sound doesn't stop there, though. It travels from wall to wall, but gets quieter each time, because the wall is absorbing some of the sound energy and the solid wave that hit the wall—especially in the corners—has been broken into smaller waves. The breaking up of these big waves into smaller waves is called **diffusion**.

When we clap in a room, the initial **slapback delay** we hear is the early reflections—the waves with the most power. The smaller, broken up waves are the **reverb**. Reverb sounds kind of like a wash. It's the murky sound that you hear in the room just after the reflections go away, and if I were to vocalize the effect, I'd be going 'Haaaaaaaaaa'. With a whole lot of 'h' and less of 'a'. The following screenshot shows a room made specifically to record reverb for music production:

Photo by Henry Mühlpfordt

Making Spaces: Creating the Emotional Landscape

A sound is played into this room, and the resulting delays are recorded. As we can see, this room should make some interesting sounds. Hard, concrete surfaces are good for bouncing sounds around. The concrete doesn't absorb much, so those waves will bounce around for quite some time before losing energy. When they hit the wood, the wood absorbs some of the energy from the echoes, and also splits the waves up a bit, making interesting reverb.

So delay and reverb are the same thing, right?

Well, yes, but we need to be careful. Putting a delay on an instrument directly is not going to overload your CPU. Simple delays are less demanding on your processor, and don't use very much RAM or computer power.

Reverb, on the other hand, is kind of a greedy effect. The delays it produces are still simple, but there are a whole bunch of them. If you are using a fairly large reverb on a lot of instruments, you may experience CPU sluggishness, which means you computer will slow down, possibly to a halt.

So one thing to think about when you are using reverb—how many rooms do musicians sit in when they are recording, say, an orchestra?

Photo by Pedro Sánchez

Well, for an orchestra, the answer is usually one. They play in a big hall, and all of the reverberation that we hear in a recording or performance is the reverb that hall produces. The placement of the instruments is also key to how we experience this ensemble. Instruments are carefully placed according to their sound. (In other words, panning is very important, as we discussed earlier.)

So is the answer to only use a single reverb for our projects?

No way! In dance music, all musical, sonic, and aesthetic norms of the music world have been challenged. Dance music has always created very evocative spaces and used reverb very creatively. You don't want to be limited to a single reverb, but it might be a good idea to be picky about your reverbs.

You see, some producers will use three reverbs—short, medium, and long.

Some will have a longer reverb that they use as a kind of 'glue' to mesh all of the parts of a piece of music together, and then will apply very specific reverbs to the drums, voice, and synths.

The trick to using reverb creatively is to try to be sure every reverb actually has a job. Reverb is kind of like ketchup, (or catsup, whichever you prefer). It tastes pretty good on a lot of things, but if you drown your whole meal in it, you end up with something that tastes like, well, catsup, as shown in the following screenshot:

Photo by Loke Uei Tan, courtesy of Backstage @ Robotics, http://blogs.msdn.com/b/lokeui

In other words, don't drown your mixes in reverb. If you do, then you won't be able to get the punch you need where it counts (namely in the drums and low frequencies).

Making Spaces: Creating the Emotional Landscape

Using FX channels to reduce CPU usage

One way to create interesting reverbs is to use FX channels. One of the issues with having reverb directly on an instrument is that no other instrument in our project can access that reverb. Well, that doesn't make much sense if we are going to have some instruments in the same room together! Let's use an effects channel or two to give us some reverb options for all of our instruments and give our CPU a break as well.

Time for action – setting up reverb on an FX bus

We're going to start using the **FX mixer** to give us reverb options for our entire project, and send various instruments and samples to FX channels:

1. Open up a new preset from the side bar. Open the **TripleOscillator** folder and choose the preset called **The First One**, as shown in the following screenshot:

2. Drag the preset to the **Song Editor**.
3. Now click next to the track to create an instrument element.
4. Double-click on the instrument element to give us the **Piano-Roll** editor.
5. Write in the following melodic line shown in this zoomed out **Piano-Roll** in the following screenshot:

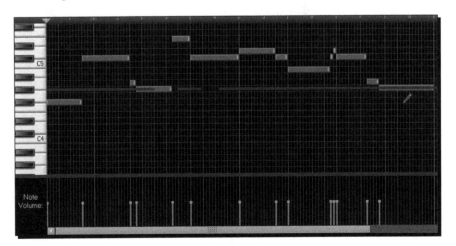

Chapter 5

6. Now listen back to the song with this new melody.

7. We need to set this melody back into the mix so it's not so in our face. Open the **Instrument** editor, and choose **FX channel 1**.

8. Now in the **FX Mixer**, we can see and hear that our new instrument is playing through **FX channel 1**:

9. Be sure to click on **FX Channel 1** so that **FX1** turns green. This assures us that we are working with the correct effect chain.

10. Now go to the **EFFECTS CHAIN** for **FX Channel 1**. It is to the right-hand side of the effects mixer. Turn on the effect chain by clicking on the bubble just to the left-hand side of where it says **Effect Chain**, as shown in the following screenshot:

11. Click on **Add effect**, and choose **Calf Reverb LADSPA.**

12. Solo **The First One** track.

13. Press **Play**, and listen to the effect before we start tweaking it. The reverb is pretty subtle. Let's look at the controls. Here is the **EFFECTS CHAIN** with the controls for the reverb to the right-hand side, as shown in the following screenshot:

14. In the **EFFECTS CHAIN** section, we can see the **W/D** knob. This means **Wet and Dry**. Turn the knob more to the right-hand side to get wet signal (more reverb), to the left-hand side, more dry signal (no reverb).

15. With the **W/D** knob turned all the way to the right, turn up the **Room size** knob in the **Reverb Controls**.

16. Set the plugin to the amounts shown in the following screenshot:

17. Now turn the volume of the instrument down at the **Song Editor**, and take the solo button off to hear the lead with the rest of the song.

What just happened?

We just assigned an instrument to an FX channel that had reverb on it. We tweaked the reverb a little bit, and then adjusted the volume level to further put the melodic sound into the mix.

When using lead sounds, they can become overbearing very quickly. A little melody that was catchy 64 beats ago might be wearing thin by the third repetition of the pattern. Adding some reverb, pushing it back in the mix, and giving it it's own channel on the FX mixer can really help it blend in with the rest of the song.

Have a go hero

So now that we understand how FX channels work, why don't you create some spaces to play in?

- Create **EFFECTS CHAINS** on three FX channels.
- Put two reverbs and a delay on the FX channels, respectively.
- Combine some of the other instruments to the other reverbs.
- Create different reverb dimensions. Play with room size, decay size, wet amount, and diffusion.

Listening to the masters of space

There are several electronic music artists that I personally enjoy for their use of space in their music. The following electronic music artists could give you some good ideas on how to make interesting spaces:

- Brian Eno – Apollo – An Ending (Ascent): Listen to this song at

    `http://www.youtube.com/watch?v=hMXaE9NtQgg`.

    This is a timeless classic by the master of ambient music, Brian Eno. Listen closely as he takes you on a journey upwards, with synths, which are so drenched in reverb that we are given an impression of heaven. This is one of the all-time greats of electronic music, and Brian Eno is considered one of the great masters of using delay and reverb in interesting ways.

- Boards of Canada – Music has the Right to Children: Listen to this song at `http://www.youtube.com/watch?v=B6SiI11qXNs`.

    This song is a great example of pads and panning. Listen to how all of the various elements pan around and surround you. The use of interesting pads, which are sometimes intentionally dirty, creates a very interesting, nostalgic state. This is what happens when pads get old and start breaking down. The process is beautiful.

- Aphex Twin – Selected Ambient Works 85-92 – Heliosphan: Listen to this song at `http://www.youtube.com/watch?v=EPxDpmM2pyU&feature=related`.

    Before Aphex Twin started bending our minds with his psychadelic and menacing glitchfests, he made some very nice, ambient music. His layering of pads and reverb in these early works shows simplicity and a sense of reserve that was kind of uncommon in the dance scene. Many a chillout room had this playing because it not only provided the pads to chill out dancers, but it also had a drive and beautifully hidden melodies that poke out every once in a while.

- Sasha and John Digweed – Northern Exposure: Listen to this album at `http://www.youtube.com/watch?v=Qcum0_NCu1w&feature=related`.

    It's quite a journey to sit down with this piece of music, but you won't be disappointed by it, that's for sure. The use of space on this release is a study in pads, reverbs, and quickly moving mashups. You'll catch glimpses of Tori Amos in here, way in the back, drenched in reverb. Low tones boom away and heavy beats pound away as your head slowly turns into cream cheese. Listen to how panning, pads, and spare atmosphere create a mood.

- Aglaia – Three Organic Experiences: Listen to this album at `http://www.youtube.com/watch?v=7hIEIkDBoYY`.

Last but not least, here we have Aglaia - Three Organic Experiences. This is not something to dance to. It's something to study and experience. Many believe this to be one of the most underrated albums of all time, in the ambient realm. I must admit, there are times during this album that I wonder if I should be getting a massage, but it is undeniable that Aglaia understands space on a deeply profound level. Tweaking parameters of reverb over time can create wonderful effects. Listen for the occasional sounds that emerge from this dense landscape. If you fall asleep, I'll understand.

Making Spaces: Creating the Emotional Landscape

Pop quiz

1. What are the objects in the Song Editor that contain MIDI, sample, and automation information called?

    a. Tracks

    b. Elements

    c. Regions

    d. Instruments

2. What's a pad?

    a. A muted drum sound.

    b. A place where musicians hang out.

    c. A long, sustained sound used as a background instrument, similar to strings.

    d. A tool in LMMS that lets you jot down notes on your project.

3. How can you use the stereo field to create interesting spaces?

    a. Pan different sounds on the left-hand side and right-hand side, and use automation to make sounds move in the stereo field.

    b. Change up the bass line.

    c. Use field recordings in your song.

    d. Use filter sweeps to give the illusion of movement across the stereo field.

4. What are the two types of ports that can be used for external MIDI input?

    a. Firewire and USB

    b. Computer keyboard input and external MIDI controller

    c. Optical and firewire

    d. Headphone and USB

5. What editor allows you to play MIDI notes into the editor in real time?

    a. The Beat+Bassline Editor

    b. The MIDI editor

    c. The Automation Track

    d. The Piano-Roll

6. Are delays and reverb the same thing?

    a. Yes. Reverb is just a much denser delay.

    b. No. Reverb and delay are completely different effects with different processing.

Summary

In this chapter, we used ambience, pads, and panning techniques, which usually don't get the attention they deserve when people start out. Using these elements wisely can put a banging dance track a cut above a stale, static mix. Some people, who make dance music and electronic music in general, go for all of the punch, but don't put it in a space that allows the mix to have more to it than just the ability to give you a bloody nose.

LMMS has some very interesting ways of routing effects to give the kind of space a track needs, but it's the sheer number of effects and the awesome development community that really make some fun effects. Reverb and delay are some of the most popular effects a music producer in any genre will use. Paying attention to your spaces and ambience will give your music a landscape, offer depth, and create something that sounds not only loud and energetic, but profound. Just be careful. Sometimes, people get a bit new age with the verb. I'm just saying.

6
Finding and Creating New Noises

In LMMS, we are provided with a lot of samples, which we can use freely in our projects and songs. The **My Samples** *area in the side bar is a great resource of samples to get our project started. When we start reaching for the next level, however, we should start mining for new sounds and textures from resources like royalty-free sounds found on the Internet, old recordings, and sounds we find around us in the real world.*

In this chapter, we'll explore:

- How to define sampling
- How samples are made
- How to find locations for saving samples
- How to find folders of the previously recorded samples
- How to record sounds in the real world and import them into LMMS
- The audio file player in LMMS

Sampling audio

The word **sampling**, in the dance and electronic music world, has been used to describe the act of taking a snippet of a song and repurposing it in a new song. This technique has been used for a very, very long time, and since the beginning, it's been somewhat controversial. Taking a small section of a song and putting it in a new song sounds like it wouldn't be that big of a deal, but sometimes artists feel that as they have spent the time and resources to get the recording together for that little snippet, they deserve a piece of whatever profits the new song gets. Some sampling artists will argue that sampling actually provides more exposure to the artists they are sampling, declaring a 'rising tide floats all boats' kind of scenario.

Early sampling

Sampling music in the old dance music and hip-hop days was very primitive indeed. In one case, there was a song called *Good Times* by a band called Chic. The song was released in 1979, at the tail end of the disco scene. A group called The Sugarhill Gang used the break section of the song as an inspiration to rap over, and recorded a song that ended up in the New York club scene as a new hip-hop sensation.

Re-recording the instruments for the song didn't bother the original producer (Nile Rogers) too much, but there was a string hit in the song that baffled him. Did the Sugarhill Gang hire a string section?

Nope. The Sugarhill Gang had a DJ scratch in a string hit from the original Chic record. This infuriated Rogers, who demanded some kind of compensation for the string line.

Now this may sound ridiculous, but it isn't, once you determine how much a string section costs to record. Rogers felt that he was giving away a valuable piece of recorded material that he had to pay for himself, and scratching a record into a new recording was kind of like cheating. In the end, Rogers ended up as a cowriter on the song, which in turn meant that a percentage of any money made by the song would come his way.

The lesson here is permission. If you are going to use a piece of someone else's work, they might be fine with it, or they might not. Either way, it's a pretty good idea to ask permission before sampling a whole bunch of songs. The process of obtaining this permission is called **sample clearance**. Sample clearance is absolutely necessary if your song is going to a major label. If the song you are making is just to show friends and family and you aren't making a profit with it, sample clearance isn't as necessary.

The grey area

In 2003, Jay-Z, the rap mogul of America, released an album of his *a cappella* raps. This was called *The Black Album*, and was initially released as a way to encourage others to take his lyrics and make their own creations with Jay-Z as the performer. Many producers and DJs took up the challenge. Heck, even one of my good friends released an album that used these raps. It was tremendous fun, and many folks saw it as a great way to show off their skills as producers.

So there's this DJ who goes by the name Danger Mouse. He decided one day to try a little art project. So the Jay-Z album is called *The Black Album*. Well, there's this little group out of Liverpool that came up with an album called *The White Album* years and years ago. Danger Mouse decided to deconstruct the White Album into snippets, which could be played as an accompaniment for Jay-Z's vocals. The result was called *The Grey Album*.

Danger Mouse released a limited run of *The Grey Album*, and considered it an art project. Little did he know that he was about to light one of the biggest fires in Internet and music industry history. The album was shared virally all over the place on the Internet, and EMI, who had license over the *Beatles* material at the time, came down hard on Danger Mouse. There were cease-and-desist letters flying, threats of lawsuits, and the media attention that ensued put Danger Mouse squarely in the limelight.

You see, *The Grey Album* was good. Entertainment weekly was calling it the best album of 2004. The New Yorker was paying attention. EMI's lawsuit showed Danger Mouse as an underdog, fighting for copyright law revisions for the twenty-first century.

Danger Mouse denies that this was ever the case, but the issues got bigger than him. There were protests online about copyright laws diminishing creativity in the twenty-first century, there were record labels claiming that unauthorized sampling of music was stealing, and then you had Jay-Z and Paul McCartney saying, 'Hey, that album was pretty darn cool!'

In the end, Danger Mouse ended up getting together with Cee-lo Green to create the band *Gnarls Barkley*, and they produced the single *Crazy*. Their album, *St. Elsewhere*, went platinum. This means they made a lot of money.

So there we have it. An album full of unauthorized samples of the Beatles' work thrusts a DJ into the limelight. His little art project, full of unauthorized samples, puts his foot in the door of the entertainment world.

This is the controversy. If you make a lot of samples from works that you don't ask permission to sample, and it ends up being really good, then maybe, just maybe, begging for forgiveness is better than asking for permission...

Finding and Creating New Noises

Either way, I suggest asking first. I find that most artists are eager these days to have their music recontextualized. It broadens their audience and gets them more exposure. Some artists actually have remix contests that are specifically designed to look for talented remixers to re-imagine their original pieces. Make sure to carefully read the legal stuff they throw at you in these contests, though. They may be asking you to sign away your rights to the work.

Ah, the music industry.

Now that we have explored the history of sampling and shown examples of how it can be fruitful, let's start using some samples in an LMMS session.

Getting into LMMS samples

In LMMS, we have the **My Samples** folder that we've explored before. Let's try creating a pattern completely from samples and add a drum loop. A **drum loop** is a recording of a fully produced drum pattern that is used in our work. We're going to encounter challenges getting it to play properly in our pattern.

Time for action – creating a pattern completely from samples, with a drum loop

LMMS already comes with a lot of samples in its library. Let's make a pattern that utilizes them, and then explore using drum loops:

1. Create a new project in LMMS.
2. Save this project as `Samples Project`.
3. Open the side bar.
4. Open the **My Samples** folder.

Chapter 6

5. Open the **Misc** folder and highlight **snaph01.ogg**:

6. Drag the **snaph01** sample to your **Beat+Bassline Editor.**

Finding and Creating New Noises

7. Let's put this snap on the bars two and four of this 4/4 measure, as shown in the following screenshot. Every four beats in this pattern represent a quarter note of time. This 32 beat pattern is four quarter notes long, so here is the proper placement:

8. Now revisit the **My samples** folder, and choose a kick, bass, and hihat to add to this pattern. Use the following samples and create the following pattern:

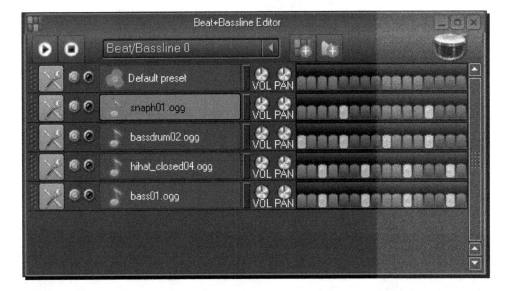

9. This beat is a techno beat, and fits the tempo of 140 very well. Now let's add the following elements:

- From **My Samples** | **Instruments** add **violinpizzicato01.ogg**.
- From **My Samples** | **Animals** add **poor_creature.wav** as shown in the following screenshot. Remember this sample from our previous lesson? If you missed it, then any sample will do in its place

Chapter 6

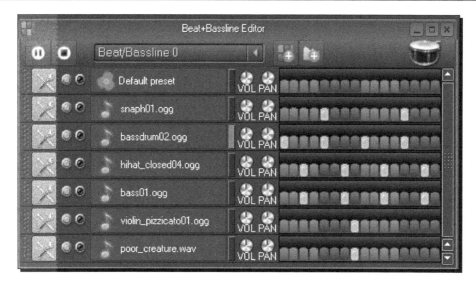

10. Now, we have a little vocal snippet in there. From the **My Samples | Basses** folder, add **techno_synth01.ogg**:

[171]

Finding and Creating New Noises

11. Now we just need to put the synth in the right key. Use the **Song Editor** to edit the pitch of the **techno_synth01.ogg** step to C5. Remember to right-click on the steps for **techno_synth01.ogg** and choose **Open in Piano-Roll**, as shown in the following screenshot:

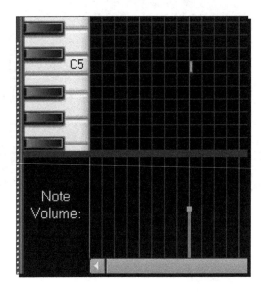

12. Now for the tricky part. Add the sample from **My Samples | Beats** called **break01.ogg**, and activate the first step in the **Beat+Bassline Editor**:

Chapter 6

13. Sounds perfect, right? What? No? Oh, yeah the drum loop was recorded at a different tempo. We need to slow it down to get it to play in time with our pattern. Open the **AudiofileProcessor** for **break01.ogg**, as shown in the following screenshot:

14. First, go to the small, green square above the piano keyboard at the bottom of the plugin and move that square to B4:

15. Now the loop is very close to being in time. To get it even closer, solo the break in the **Beat+Bassline Editor**, and turn on the pitch knob on the **AudiofileProcessor**, as shown in the following screenshot, until the loop sounds seamless. It should sound right if turned for nearly two cents to the right-hand side, or transposed up two cents:

Now listen closely, then turn the solo button off. Now the loop sits within our pattern!

What just happened?

We've created a pattern using nothing but samples, and then added a drum loop on top of what we created. Using drum loops sparingly can dramatically increase the production value of a project. Having a loop that is performed and fully produced will act like a kind of glue that makes a project feel more full and whole.

When using any looping material, we have to keep a few things in mind. First of all, the pitch trick we just performed will not always work on a loop. If a loop has pitched instruments in it, like a bass, keyboard, and so on, pitching the material may not work because the material's pitch might clash with your project. For most non-pitched instruments (mostly drums), this little pitching trick should work well.

The art of sampling

Let's talk a little bit about recording samples. Creating your own unique sample library is a great way to start creating your own musical personality.

Digital recording

To get your samples, we are going to need to record some sound. There are two ways to get sound into the computer. Use a microphone to record sound from the real world, or send sound directly from one device (such as an mp3 player), into the computer. Later in this chapter, we will explore the Internet, but for now we are going to talk about getting sounds from the real world ourselves.

Recording your own sounds outside the studio in the big, real, scary world is called **field recording**. Much like taking a field trip in school, you are leaving the house with a recorder to go capture some obscure sound. Let's explore a couple of the options available for recording.

Recording on the main computer

Granted that this is one of the more limited ways to record sound outside, and it's risky, but some people enjoy recording in their backyard, and will simply use the computer they produce on to record the sound they are trying to capture.

The best way to do this would be to have a team. This team would be one person manning the computer, and another person with a microphone and the stuff to be recorded. If we don't have to move the computer, that will be ideal; but if we have a fairly controlled environment, free of dogs, cats, toddlers, and so on, we can move computers pretty freely these days. All we would need is the main computer tower, a monitor screen, some headphones, and a sound computer interface that pulls in sound from the outside world and digitizes it for use in the computer.

If the goal is to keep the computer in place and have the assistant in the backyard, we're lucky that a microphone cable can be very, very long. We'll be talking about the right cables for the job momentarily. Of course, having a laptop computer makes all of this much easier.

Software for grabbing audio goodies

We talked previously in *Chapter 1, Gearing up: A Pre-flight Checklist*, about using *Audacity* for recording. Audacity is free and can be used for recording audio, and editing that audio so that it's ready to be used as an audio element in LMMS. Audacity runs on Linux, Windows, and Apple OS X. It's a very, fully functional program that allows for a lot of fun audio manipulation. We'll be exploring how to get crazy with audio in Audacity, to get cool samples in a minute, but first we need to clear up some things about the audio cables that we're using to record and play our samples with.

Unbalanced versus balanced cables

Most of the audio cables we use today started out in the telephone industry. It can be fun when you are an audio engineer, to go back to old movies and see old telephone switchboards that have what look like guitar cables sticking out everywhere. Here's a switchboard from 1975:

Photo by Joseph A. Carr, 1975, courtesy of http://joetourist.net.

There are several kinds of audio cables out there, but the majority of what we'd use in the studio and for recording are the following:

Unbalanced cable

Unbalanced cables are great for short distances. If you are using an audio interface that has a jack that fits this cable, you'll want to check the manual out to see whether it is a **balanced input** or **unbalanced input**.

Quarter-inch **unbalanced cables** look similar to the one shown in the following image:

The most common use for this kind of cable is for instruments such as the electric guitar.

Unbalanced cables are really basic. It's essentially a long wire, encased in some insulation (kind of rubbery), surrounded by a metal mesh, and then surrounded by rubber. On the end of the wire is a male plug, a quarter of an inch in diameter, that has two areas on it. One area carries the signal (the black ring). The other area carries some noise captured in the metal mesh (the tip).

Think of the metal mesh in the cable as a kind of armor. Basically, an unbalanced cable could be like an antennae, and acts like one when it is too long. I've heard radio signals picked up by guitars before, because this kind of cable doesn't have a very robust shield to absorb all of the various electrical interference we have going on around us all of the time. If it's only about 10 feet long and plugged between a guitar and an amplifier, the signal is usually pretty good. Running an unbalanced cable longer than 20 feet starts to ask for trouble. Even though they have their suit of armor on, electrical interference (especially power, which sounds like a low humming) ends up getting into the signal. This is because the shielding can't compensate for the antennae-like quality of the cable.

Instruments made to use this kind of cable just inherently have this kind of issue. As noted, if the cable is fairly short, things are good. If very, very long...usually not so good.

Unbalanced cables can also have the kind of familiar plug shown in the following image:

This cable is often used for home stereo equipment. As home stereos usually have their components right next to each other, these connectors are very popular because they are very small.

So in conclusion, if you must use unbalanced cables, just make them relatively short; under 20 feet is a good rule.

Balanced cables

A good example of a **balanced cable** is the XLR microphone cable. XLR cables are used for professional microphones and for the output of high-end audio equipment. They look similar to the one shown in the following image:

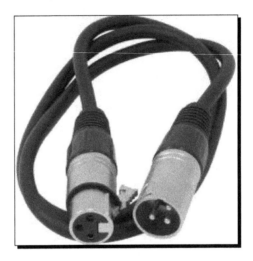

To use this cable with a microphone, you insert the female end into the microphone and the male end into a **microphone preamp**. The purpose of the microphone preamp is to take the very low energy output of the microphone and increase its amplitude (loudness) to the point where there is a good, strong, audio signal going into the computer.

Most audio interfaces these days come with a built-in microphone preamp. External interfaces connect with the computer via FireWire or USB connections. Many computers also come with soundcards that do not take XLR input. Although they might have the ability to increase the gain of a microphone, they may require an XLR cable to be adapted so that its relatively large connector can be shrunken down to something small that fits into the back of the soundcard.

Some audio interfaces also have XLR outputs on them. These require that you hook the end, which you'd usually put in a mic, and jack it into the interface's output. Usually, the cable would then be plugged into some speakers or a mixer that takes XLR input.

XLR cables can be run for miles before they lose fidelity. As you see, there are three wires in this cable. An XLR has three little pins on the male side and three holes on the female side.

What happens on this cable is this; there are two wires in the cable carrying the audio signal. One wire sends a signal in a positive direction, while the other sends the signal in a negative direction or *reverse polarity*. Audio equipment looks at the difference between these two signals and basically ignores anything else. The 'anything else' is noise, hum, and so on that can be picked up by the long metal wires. The third wire in there is a ground wire, so it can take whatever high frequency noise is left over. This leaves a very nice, clean signal.

Balanced cables also come in a quarter-inch variety. They look similar to the one shown in the following image:

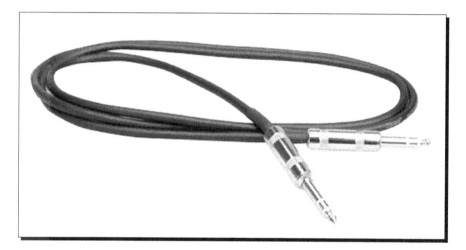

In this case, the tip of the cable acts as the ground, and the two rings carry the positive and negative versions of the audio. It operates exactly like an XLR cable and can be used for very long distances. Again, you can't really use this cable without the proper audio gear.

[Don't mix unbalanced and balanced signals when recording. The result can be noisy, and volumes will be incorrectly represented.]

One-eighth-inch mini stereo cable

We're very familiar with these cables because of all the cool gadgets that use the kind of connector shown in the following image:

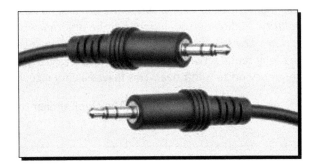

A **one-eighth-inch mini stereo cable** is much like a balanced, quarter-inch cable, but is most often used to transmit and receive stereo data. The channels on the right- and left-hand sides of of audio use two cables, each for one channel. The ground still works the same way even though the cables get divided, as it works for the balanced, quarter-inch cable.

These cables are used all of the time, with inexpensive soundcards. They shouldn't be run for long distances, because they don't have the same noise rejection that balanced cables have. They are actually more likely to get noisy because the audio gear is not filtering out the sound like a balanced system does.

Using handheld recorders

My personal favorite way to capture audio is the small **portable recorder**. These recorders vary wildly in price, but I am very happy with products that are below $300. An example of some companies that make these devices are Zoom and Sony.

Most of these recorders not only have microphones built into them (and usually stereo microphones at that!!), they also have microphone preamps for using your own favorite mics. These units use Flash media for recording, which are tiny cards that store up to 32 gigabytes of data. That is a whole lot of data. Once you get the recordings you need, you simply plug the card into a reader that is very inexpensive, and it loads the information into a computer.

These fun little recorders allow you to really be out in the world and record audio from all kinds of crazy sources. I have been known to stand between two moving trains to get an interesting sound. Please do not try this, but feel free to take your recorder with you the next time you are bungee jumping! (Just be sure to have that recorder zipped in tight.)

Here's what some of my favorites look like:

The Sony PCM-M10

The Sony PCM-M10, shown in the following image, is palm-sized and user-friendly, can record in either `mp3` or `.wav` format. A remote control can be used with it as well:

The Zoom H4n

The Zoom H4n, shown in the following image, uses a stereo condenser microphone pair for recording, has built-in effects, and has a four-track mode that can be used to record audio at a live show, by using one pair of inputs to capture a stereo feed from the mixer and the other pair of inputs to capture the sound from another pair of microphones:

Finding and Creating New Noises

These recorders may not be available to everyone, but these companies have a pretty good distribution network; and hey, there's always the Internet!

Finding sounds on the Internet that won't get you sued

There has been quite a movement in the creative community to build libraries of sounds that people can use freely without the fear of being caught up in a lawsuit with a major record label. An interesting alternative to sampling commercial CDs that are under traditional copyright is to use audio that is classified under **Creative Commons**. Creative Commons licenses are made to give people like you and me access to material produced by others, which we can safely work with creatively. Here are some good sites to check out for audio goodies that won't get you sued!

- `www.freesound.org`: This website, as shown in the following screenshot, has a very eclectic mix of sounds from everywhere and anywhere:

People have contributed synthesizer hits, ambient field recordings, and vocal explorations. It may be slightly chaotic to navigate, but almost all of the work on `freesound.org` is usable under Creative Commons. Be sure to look at the license for whatever you download. Even though Creative Commons does allow for anyone to use the material, it can be important to see what might happen if you make money from the efforts. This is all very clearly explained at `www.creativecommons.org`.

- `www.ccmixter.org`: This has just about everything you could want for music samples. You don't have to join the site to search and use the samples here. The way they organize the site is genius. If you are looking for almost anything, *a cappella* vocals to mad beats, it's all here. Have a look at the following screenshot:

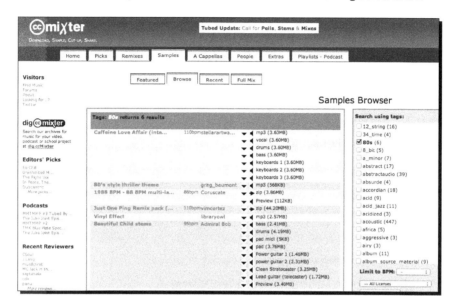

- `www.soundbible.com`: Another cool place for individual sound effects, which are all royalty-free and available to the public. The following screenshot shows you the home page:

Finding and Creating New Noises

We've also talked about various remix contests and the like, but I highly recommend anything that is under Creative Commons. The reason? All of the licenses are easy to understand, whereas in remix contests, many times, record labels are looking to use you for marketing. (Those are just my opinions, by the way!)

Time for action – sound sculpting in Audacity

We're going to explore how to get the most out of our samples by using Audacity to edit, process, and design them:

1. Open Audacity.

2. Go to **File** | **Save Project As.**

3. Save as `Sampling Session 1`.

4. Audacity may give you a screen that says something similar to the following screenshot:

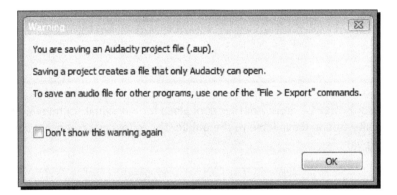

This window simply states that this project will only be able to be read by Audacity. If you want to export this project to another program such as Pro Tools, Logic, and so on, you need to use the **Export** command from the **File** menu. For now, we're just going to say **OK**.

5. Go to `http://ccmixter.org/view/media/samples/browse`.

6. In the **Samples Browser** on the left-hand side, choose the category **80s**:

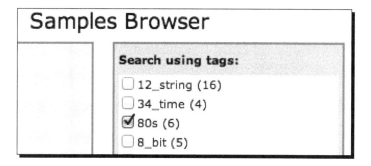

7. Locate the song called **Caffeine Love Affair.**

8. Listen to the drum pattern from this song by clicking on the speaker, as shown in the following screenshot:

9. Now download the drums track by right-clicking on the downward facing triangle next to the drum sample in the browser, and choosing **Save As**:

10. Save the file to your desktop.

11. Go to **File | Import Audio.**

12. Locate your audio on the desktop. It should have the name **stellarartwars_-_Caffeine_Love_Affair_(interstellar_mix_inc_stems)_2.mp3**.

13. Audacity will open the file into its project window.

14. Drag over the audio file between zero seconds and 15 seconds, as shown in the following screenshot:

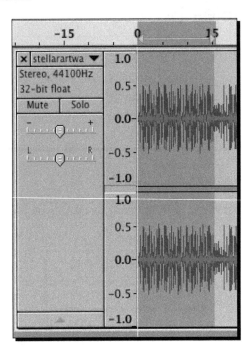

15. Now we need to extract a loop from this. Go to **Edit | Trim**.

16. Now we have the initial drum loop isolated, as shown in the following screenshot. Let's zoom in on it by selecting **View | Fit in Window**:

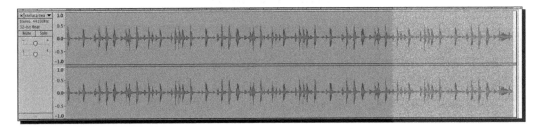

17. Select the area where the loop first comes around, as shown in the following screenshot:

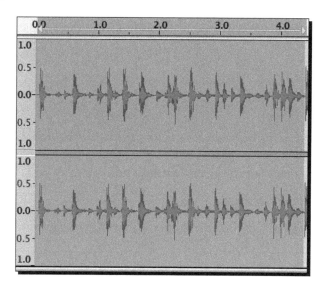

18. Hit *Shift* and Space bar to loop the area you have selected.

19. Zoom in on this section by clicking on the button, as shown in the following screenshot, in the upper right-hand side corner:

20. Now hold *Shift* and adjust the left- and right-hand sides of the selection area until the loop sounds perfect.

21. Now go to **File | Export Selection**. Remember the **Animals** folder? That poor creature? Well now we need a new folder for our new beat. Navigate back a folder, and create a new folder called **Beats**.

22. Choose the format as **Ogg Vorbis files** at the bottom of the save screen.

23. Save this beat here as **80's Caffeine beat 1**. (Names should always be descriptive.)

24. Now in Audacity, let's create a reversed version of this beat. Go to **Effect | Reverse**.

Finding and Creating New Noises

25. Now export this selection, shown in the following screenshot, to the **Beats** folder as **80's Caffeine beat 1-reversed**:

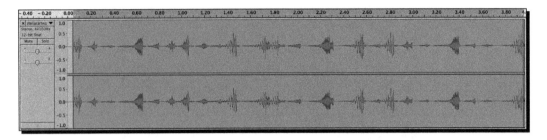

26. Let's reverse that selection again, making it normal.
27. Now go to **Effect | Wahwah**.
28. We'll get a screen that looks similar to the following screenshot:

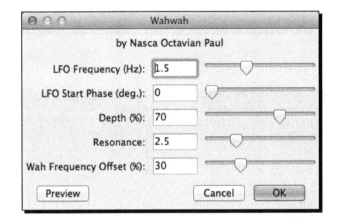

29. Hit the **Preview** button to hear the wahwah effect on the selected area.
30. Now hit **OK**.
31. Export this selection to your **Beats** folder as **80's Caffeine beat 1-wahwah**.
32. Now that we have the beats we've edited, let's put them in our pattern in LMMS. In LMMS, go to the side bar and choose **My Samples**.

Chapter 6

33. Look! A new **Beats** folder! Let's check out what's in it:

34. Drag the audio file from the **Samples** folder to the **Song Editor**.

35. What? It doesn't play! Here's why. We put an apostrophe in the name of the file. Get rid of the apostrophe in the filenames and replace the spaces with underscores, so your names look like those shown in the following screenshot:

36. Now the files play in the sample folder just fine. Drag **80s_Caffeine_beat_1.ogg** to the **Song Editor**.

37. Create an element next to the new beat, and turn the loop on in the **Song Editor**:

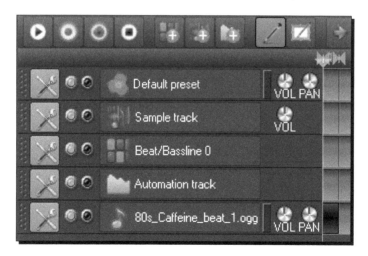

38. Double-click on the element to open the **Piano-Roll**.

Finding and Creating New Noises

39. Create a note on C#5, and drag the right-hand side of the note out so that it is exactly one bar long, as shown in the following screenshot:

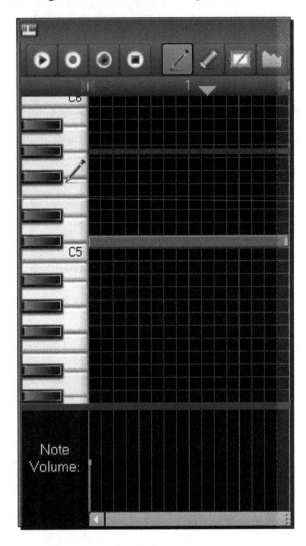

40. Click next to the **Beat+Bassline** track. Now the **Beat+Bassline** should play when the song plays.

41. Go to the **Beat+Bassline Editor**, and mute all but the hihat and bassdrum:

42. In the **Audiofile Player** that is now in the **Song Editor**, set the pitch to 28 cents, as shown in the following screenshot:

43. Press **Play** and listen to the **Song Editor**. Does the loop line up now?

44. Unmute all of the **Beat+Bassline** except for the **AudiofileProcessor** called **break01.ogg**.

45. Adjust the volumes in the **Beat+Bassline Editor** to taste.

What just happened?

We've successfully grabbed a royalty-free sample from the Internet, edited and processed it in Audacity, and added it to our library of samples in LMMS!

When adding new content to your library, make sure that you name your folders in a coherent way. You want to be able to search quickly through your samples. It can be a lot of fun to take samples from Creative Commons and really mess with them in Audacity before shooting them back into LMMS. Audacity should be like the other hand. It is where you have all of the audio flexibility to compliment your LMMS project.

Another very important note—you need to abstain from using spaces, apostrophes, and other symbols in your file names. This can sometimes be the difference between your samples playing or appearing empty in LMMS. A good rule of thumb is to use only letters, numbers, and underscores.

Have a go hero

Now it's time for you to explore recording and editing samples for your own library! Do the following:

- Record a sample in Audacity
- Find samples from the websites listed and import them into Audacity
- Use Audacity to trim selections and export loops and sounds
- Create a file hierarchy in your LMMS folder to store your various sounds
- Bring your new samples into the **Beat+Bassline Editor**
- Bring your samples into the **Song Editor**
- Use **Root Note**, the **Piano-Roll**, and the pitch knob on the **AudiofileProcessor** to tighten up your percussive loops

A note about bits and samples

Without getting too technical, we need to explore bit depth and sample rate as well as file format. When you are recording or using samples in a project, you need to have a basic understanding of bit depth and sample rate.

When a sound wave is represented on paper, it usually looks like a very smooth ripple on the ocean, as shown in the following diagram:

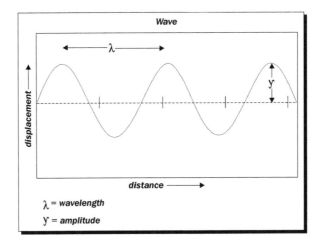

Basically, think of the dotted line as a speaker at rest. The wave moving up is your speaker pushing out, and the wave going under the line is your speaker pulling back in. This pushing and pulling of your speaker makes ripples in the air, which produce sound.

Now, to capture that sound, our computers take very fast pictures of that wave. Each time the computer takes a picture, it records the volume (or the distance from rest) our speaker uses. Instead of a perfectly smooth line, it's something more similar to the following diagram:

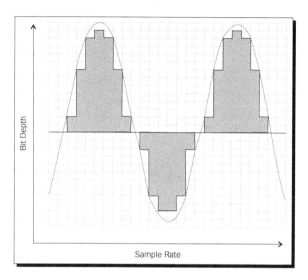

So the **bit depth** records the volume, and the **sample rate** is where the wave is in time.

Sample rate is kind of like a movie projector/camera. A movie camera has to capture at the same rate that it is going to play back to make convincing movement on the screen. Sample rate is the same, just a whole lot faster. Movies play at 24 frames a second. Digital recordings usually play back at 44,100 times per second. Each one of those tiny slices contains a recording of loudness, and we get digital sound!

When recording in quiet conditions or paying attention to really subtle things, recording at 24 bits is really pretty great. You never have to worry that your audio might disappear if it gets too quiet. Most recorders are 24 bit these days.

A good sample rate should be anywhere between 44.1 and 96k. That's 44,100 to 96,000 times a second! This will assure that all of the frequencies are being captured well.

A professionally mastered recording is usually around 16 bit and has a sample rate of 44.1k. This is still the standard now, but as things change, I think we'll be seeing more bits and samples in the next couple of years!

Pop quiz

1. What is Creative Commons?
   a. A place where artists and musicians get together to share ideas
   b. A performance rights organization
   c. An alternative to the copyright law that allows fair use of creative materials under its umbrella
   d. A website where free samples are available

2. Who is DJ Danger Mouse?
   a. A cartoon rockstar superhero
   b. An American DJ, who is most notable for his mashup of Jay-Z and The Beatles called The Grey Album
   c. A character in South Park
   d. An animated character, who gives online tutorials on how to become a DJ

3. What is the difference between sample rate and bit depth?
   a. Bit depth is a measure of amplitude, while sample rate is the rate at which a sound wave is sampled.
   b. Sample rate is a rating of how good a particular sample sounds, and bit depth tells you how many bits are in that sample.
   c. Bit depth measures how many bits are in a sample, and sample rate measures the bpm (beats per minute) of the sample.
   d. Sample rate is the rate at which a sample is played back, and bit depth measures frequency range.

4. What is the difference between a balanced and unbalanced cable?
   a. A balanced cable is taped down or otherwise safely secured, while an unbalanced cable is lying loose on the floor waiting to trip someone.
   b. A balanced cable has a twisted pair of wires and a ground. It rejects noise by having a positive and negative wave flipped in phase at the preamp, where the noise disappears due to being out of phase with itself (1+[-1]=0).
   c. A balanced cable is in good working condition. An unbalanced cable is damaged or twisted, causing noise and dropouts in the audio signal.
   d. An unbalanced cable is too short or too long for a given use. A balanced cable is just long enough, neither too long nor too short.

Chapter 6

5. What is a good way to time a drum loop sample to a pattern?

    a. Count out the beats into a microphone connected to an audio interface and divide the beats by quarter notes.

    b. Record a MIDI keyboard playing a note value that corresponds to quarter notes.

    c. Use the root note and the pitch knob in the AudiofileProcessor for fine-tuning.

    d. Assign a delay to the sound, and turn the feedback setting up and down until you can no longer hear the delay effect.

6. What's a good way to head off getting sued by an artist or label when you sample their work?

    a. Wait until they contact you to complain, then offer them a payout.

    b. Don't worry about it unless you are actually making money on the song with the sample. They have no case against the noncommercial use of samples.

    c. Simply send a letter to the artist or the label letting them know you are sampling their work, then go ahead and sample away. They are obliged to let you know if they have a problem with it.

    d. Ask for their permission to sample their work, and stay in touch with them. Get it in writing if they say yes. Labels are known to be litigious.

7. How do you get a sample to play in the Song Editor?

    a. Drag the sample from the Side Bar to the Song Editor, and create an element next to it. Open the Piano-Roll and create notes there to play the AudiofileProcessor.

    b. Drag-and-drop an audio file into the Piano-Roll Editor.

    c. Open a Kicker plugin and drag the sample into the keyboard area.

    d. Drag the sample on to the desktop, right-click on the file, and choose Add to AudiofileProcessor.

[195]

Summary

LMMS and Audacity are a great complement to each other. Audacity can give you the power to record, edit, and process your audio samples, and LMMS lets you arrange them. LMMS is a great tool for putting together samples in interesting ways using the **Beat+Bassline Editor** and the **Song Editor**. When sampling, remember that there is a huge community out there that wants to share their sounds. Share and share alike! One great example of a music-sharing community is the LMMS Sharing Platform (`http://lmms.sourceforge.net/lsp/`), a central place for LMMS users to share and exchange their works made with and for LMMS, including whole songs, and also new presets and samples. Participating in these new, open communities, where people share their sounds and songs is a great way to see what others are doing, and challenges the electronic musician to think outside the box and figure out how to recontextualize sampling so that they can carve a new niche for themselves. Study the sampling work of the past, and push your sampled ideas into LMMS, where you can arrange a story with them. Study artists like DJ Shadow, Amon Tobin, DJ Danger Mouse, Timbaland, and the artists who influenced them to get new, fresh ideas on how to make fresh, sample-based work.

7
Getting It All Stacked Up

We're going to be exploring a technique that's really popular in dance music called subtractive arranging. It doesn't quite have the same charm as the techniques with more colorful names like chopped and screwed, or glitch, but it is a main staple of the dance music diet.

Now that we know how to make all of the main ingredients for our electronic music stew, it's time to start putting them all together and building the foundation of our song.

The idea is to create a loop, just like we did before, that has all of our basic ingredients, and then layering more and more parts on top of it, until our loop sounds too busy. When we reach this point, we will simply mute the elements that we just created, and build even more parts on the loop. Once we're done, we are going to have all of the parts that we need for the entire song. Later, in *Chapter 8*, *Spreading Out the Arrangement*, we will be discussing how to lay these parts out so that we create a compelling story for the listener.

For now, though, let's get our stack together!

In this chapter, we will:

- Create a looped pattern in the **Beat+Bassline Editor**
- Add the pattern from the **Beat+Bassline Editor** to the **Song Editor**
- Add more elements to the **Song Editor** to flesh out the looped pattern
- Mute and unmute elements in the **Song Editor** to get ideas for arranging new patterns

Get your loop set

To get started, let's get our loop length set. The common length of a looped pattern is 32 beats or eight bars of time. We'll be using the **Song Editor** and **Beat+Bassline Editor** to get our initial patterns together, and start layering from there.

Time for action – setting up the loops

In *Chapter 4, Expanding the Beat: Digging Deeper into the Art of Beatmaking*, we created loops in the **Beat+Bassline Editor**. Now we are going to show how these patterns will be used along with other instruments in the **Song Editor**.

1. Open a new session in LMMS and save the session as `Main Loop Start`; then open the **Beat+Bassline Editor**.

2. Delete the default instrument that shows in the **Beat+Bassline Editor**:

3. Open the side bar and import a kick, snare, clap, and hihat into the **Beat+Bassline Editor** (as we explored before, they are located in **My Samples**):

4. Now extend the patterns out to 64 beats (right-click on each pattern) and zoom out a bit. This is a very long drum pattern, but it's going to be the basis for all of our pattern versions. Let's make a basic beat to start from, as shown in the following screenshot:

5. Before we continue, let's set our loop in the **Song Editor**. Right-click on bar nine of the **Song Editor**. You'll see the green, bow tie icon snap to bar nine, as shown in the following screenshot:

6. Turn the looped section on by clicking the button shown in the following screenshot:

7. Once it is selected, the looped area will be activated along with the loop markers, as shown in the following screenshot:

8. Now that we have our looped area, we need to start using elements. In the **Song Editor**, click next to where the **Beat/Bassline 0** track is, as shown in the following screenshot. You will see the element pop up in the **Song Editor**:

9. Now click in the **Song Editor** next to that element. Another element will show up right next to the first one we created:

10. Now press the Space bar to hear the pattern repeat in the **Song Editor**. Have a listen.

11. Now we can create a new **Beat+Bassline** based on the first pattern. Click on the **Track Actions** menu, and select **Clone Track.**

    Now we see a new **Beat+Bassline** track called **Clone of Beat/Bassline 0**:

12. This pattern will now show in our **Beat+Bassline Editor**. Open the **Beat+Bassline Editor** and select the disclosure triangle next to the pattern's name:

13. Now you can select between patterns. To rename the **Clone of Beat/Bassline 0**, right-click on the track in the **Song Editor**:

14. Let's name it **Beat Variation 1**. The name will show in both the **Song Editor** and the **Beat + Bassline Editor**, as shown in the following screenshots:

Chapter 7

15. Change **Beat Variation 1** so that it is slightly different from **Beat/Bassline 0**:

 Remember that the scroll wheel will alter the volume on individual notes. This is why there are darker green colors in this variation.

16. Now play the **Beat+Bassline Editor**, and switch back and forth between **Beat/Bassline 0** and **Beat Variation 1**. You can do this freely while the patterns are playing in the **Beat+Bassline Editor**. Have a listen to how well they play together.

17. In the **Song Editor**, on the second element in **Beat/Bassline 0**, right-click and choose **Delete (middle mousebutton)** as shown in the following screenshot:

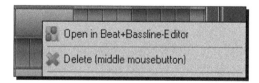

 The middle mouse button is only available on some mouse devices. On Windows computers, the middle mouse button is often simulated by simultaneously pressing the right and left buttons at the same time.

18. Now delete the first element in **Beat Variation 1**:

19. Now press Space bar and listen to the **Song Editor**. The first element should play seamlessly into the second element.

20. Now let's mute elements instead of deleting them. Create elements for our **Beat/Baseline 0** and **Beat Variation 1** again, as shown in the following screenshot:

21. Now mute these elements by either right-clicking and choosing from the menu, or use the keyboard shortcut *Ctrl* and press the middle mouse button. Now the elements are still there, but not playing. Alternatively, we can solo individual elements by using the solo button in the **Song Editor**, which automatically mutes all of the other elements, as shown in the following screenshot:

What just happened?

We've successfully created a pattern, variation, and element in the **Song Editor**. We've also created our loop area for constructing the main loop that we will be using in the song.

Elements in the **Song Editor** are going to provide us with the building blocks necessary in our song. Elements can represent a **Beat+Bassline** pattern, a sample, or an instrument. Elements can be deleted by right-clicking on them, or you can actually mute the element so it will not play back. We are going to use the latter method until we get to arranging the patterns.

Adding instruments

Ok, we've got our main drum pattern now. Time to start putting the other pieces together. We are going to start by getting an instrument for our bassline. Then, we're going to use the **Piano-Roll** editor to create a bassline and variation.

Time for action – making our basses

We need to start adding elements to our song editor to cover our bassline for the song. Instead of using the **Beat+Bassline Editor**, we're going to use the **Piano-Roll**:

1. Go to the side bar, and open up the instruments. We're going to use the **LB302** as shown in the following screenshot:

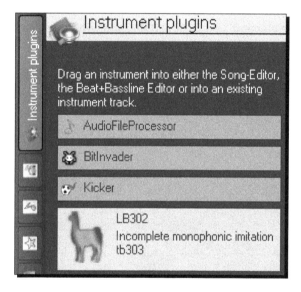

2. Click on the **LB302** and drag it to the **Song Editor**, as shown in the following screenshot:

3. Now click next to the track to get a new element for this instrument, as shown in the following screenshot:

4. Double-click on that element to give us the **Piano-Roll** editor. We will write a basic bassline to compliment our beat.

5. In the **Song Editor**, set the loop area to four bars. Right-click on bar five as shown in the following screenshot:

6. Press the Space bar to hear the four bar loop.

7. Leave the **Song Editor** playing as we create our bassline.

8. Now open the element next to our **LB302**, and write the following notes in the **Piano-Roll**:

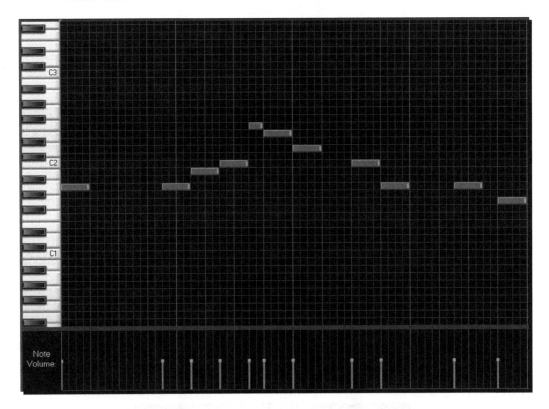

Listen to the beat playing along with this new bassline.

9. Go back to the **Song Editor**. You'll notice that the element is now four bars long, as shown in the following screenshot. The element automatically expanded to fit the notes we put inside:

10. Now hold *Ctrl* and click on the element. You'll see an element that looks like the **+** sign. Drop this element next to the other one, as shown in the following screenshot:

11. Now let's change the last bar of the second element. Double-click on the element and make this adjustment in the **Piano-Roll**, as shown in the following screenshot:

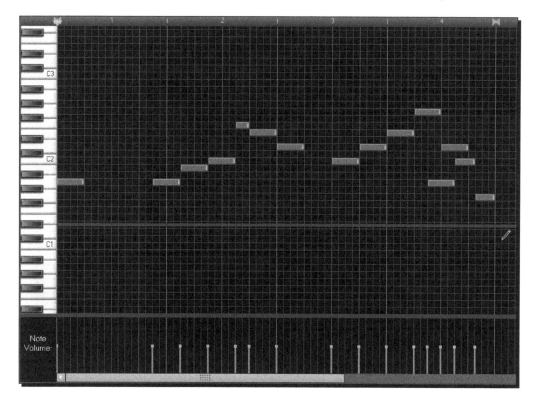

> Remember that you can't trim the front of the note. Hover over the right-hand side of the note with the pencil tool, to adjust the length of the note. Drag the note to adjust where it starts by clicking anywhere in the middle of the note with the pencil and dragging it.

Now we have a pattern in the bassline that repeats, but has a different ending on the second element.

What just happened?

We were able to create an instrument track, and then create two elements for the bassline. Using the **Piano-Roll** editor, we were able to listen to the **Song Editor** in the background as we made our new bassline. We also copied and pasted the elements using right-click, and created a variation on a simple bass pattern.

When creating the parts using the **Piano-Roll** editor, it's good to hear how these parts sound in context with the instrument track. Keeping the **Song Editor** playing while writing in the **Piano-Roll** editor gives context to the parts we're creating.

Making that break dirty

Sometimes, to create variation in an instrument part, we can rely of effects to change the nature of the sound as it's playing along. The idea is something similar to our bass player, when all of a sudden, the beat vanishes for a second, and then drops back in along with our bass player.

Time for action – dirty bass

Let's try this out using the bass line we just made:

1. In the **Song Editor**, use track actions to duplicate the bass line as shown in the following screenshot:

Chapter 7

2. Now mute the other tracks by de-selecting the button directly next to the action button, as shown in the following screenshot:

3. With the other tracks muted, hit the Space bar to playback the bassline. It should sound exactly the same.

4. Now open up the **LB302** by selecting **Default Preset** option.

5. Go to the **FX** tab. Turn the **EFFECTS CHAIN** on by selecting the button to the left-hand side of **EFFECTS CHAIN**. It will light up as shown in the following screenshot:

6. Now click on **Add Effect** at the bottom of the **FX** section, and from the list choose **LADSPA DJ EQ**.

7. The controls for the **DJ EQ** will pop up. Set the knobs as shown in the following screenshot:

8. Now press play and listen to the bass.

9. We need another additional layer to this sound. Go to **Add Effect** and choose the **LADSPA C* Cabinet | Loudspeaker cabinet emulation**. Use the settings shown in the following screenshot:

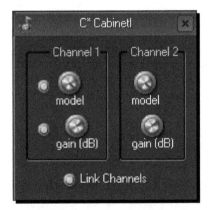

10. Now hit play again. The bass should sound significantly thinner and dirtier.

11. Now go back to the **Song Editor** and turn the other tracks on.

12. Mute the unaffected bass to hear what our new bass sounds like, and vice versa.

13. Now right-click on our new bass track, and choose to rename it AM Radio Bass, as shown in the following screenshot:

14. Go to the first bassline that we created and name that track Original Bass.

What just happened?

We've created an alternate bass that we can use as an alternate for our arrangement. When the music is playing, if the bass suddenly changes character, the thin bass can be used to create tension in the song. We might use automation to change the bass over time, but cutting between the dirty bass and the clean bass will sound good as well. We'll be exploring this in *Chapter 8, Spreading Out the Arrangement*.

Send that sound out to get effected

Now that we have an alternate bass reality, let's see how we can dedicate an effects channel to creating one set of effects that all other instruments (which we add) and tracks (which we clone) can use.

Time for action – sending clones through effects

When we have a **Beat+Bassline Editor**, it can be time consuming to go to each instrument and choose the set of effects we like, then go to the next audiofile processor of the drum pattern, and go through the same process of opening the effects and assigning the settings. So we're going to explore using a dedicated FX bus to give us alternate drum pattern effects:

1. Now let's visit our drum patterns and create clones for each drum pattern.

   The following screenshot shows what will come up at the bottom of the track list:

2. We need to reorder this list so that the clones are next to their parent tracks. Use the textured area to the left-hand side of the action menu on the track, to move the track vertically. The textured area looks similar to the following screenshot:

Now our tracks should be named to reflect what they sound like, as shown in the following screenshot:

3. Open up the **Beat+Bassline Editor** and choose **Main Beat FX 1**.
4. On each **AudioFileProcessor** in the editor, change its **FX Channel** to **1**, as shown in the following screenshot:

Chapter 7

5. This is going to send all of the patterns in this **Beat+Bassline Editor** to the **FX Mixer**. Press play, and open up the **FX Mixer**, **FX1**, which should be showing the **Beat+Bassline Editor** running through it, as shown in the following screenshot:

6. Now select **FX1** in the **FX Mixer**, turn the **EFFECTS CHAIN** button on, and stack the following plugins on:

7. Season these plugins to taste, by adjusting their controls until you feel you have an interesting sound. Keep in mind that not only drums but many other things can be assigned to this **EFFECTS CHAIN**.

What just happened?

We just created a set of plugins that any part of our project can access. Right now we have a drum pattern bussed to this FX chain, but we could send all of the other instruments and any new instruments we have through this FX chain as well.

When you want the whole song to suddenly sound like it's been sent into a radio or delay, using FX channels is a really easy way to have the effect ready and waiting for any elements, new or old. Of course, we have the ability to pick and choose which elements will be sent to these particular FX channels as well.

Adding in the smooth

Smoothing elements or ambient elements should be stacked now that we have a drum pattern and bass line. We are going to create two kinds of ambient elements, which we can switch off in between.

Time for action – adding the ambient elements

We're going to add some ambient elements, which we can choose from, in this exploration. Later on, we can use these parts to establish the mood.

1. Mute the **Main Beat FX** and **Beat Variation FX** tracks.
2. From **My Presets** in the side bar, choose the **Triple Oscillator** folder, and double-click on the **Lovely Dream.xpf** preset.
3. Now let's create an instrument element next to **Lovely Dream** in the **Song Editor**. Double-click on the element to pop open the **Piano-Roll**. Now write this melody:

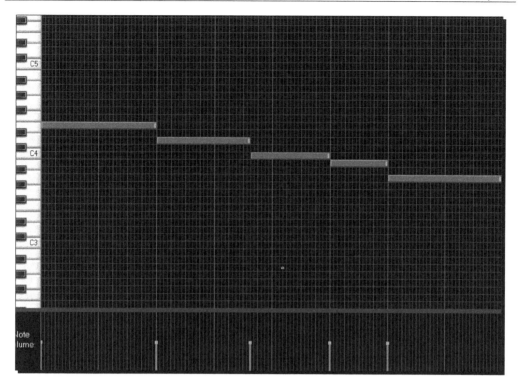

4. Now add the following line to counter the line we just wrote:

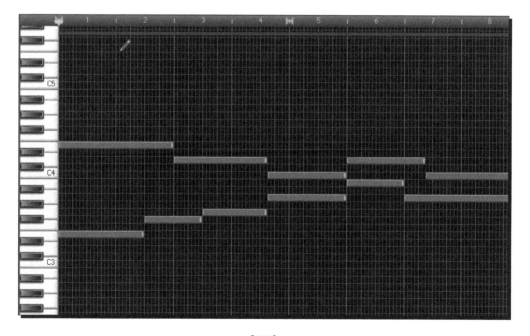

Getting It All Stacked Up

5. Now we have a glittering little background pad. We should bury it in volume. Go to the track volume and set it to **-20 dbV**.

   Let's clone this track and create our alternate track of the same sound. Here's a different instrument line we can have:

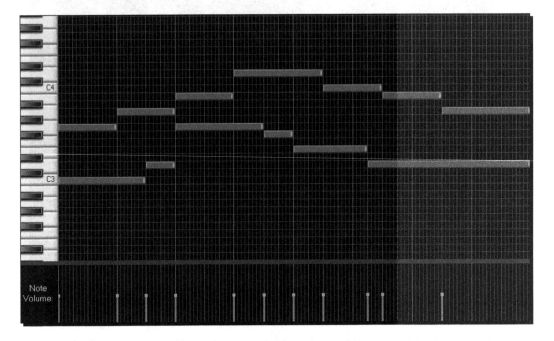

6. Now play this line against the bass. It's sparse and glittery, but it works.

7. Now unmute the other line that we wrote. Press play and listen to what these two parts sound like together.

What just happened?

The two lines that we wrote were complimentary to each other, which means that they play well together as well as make a statement individually. The more interlocking parts we have, the more interesting our song becomes. We have the ability to thin out this idea easily, by muting the elements on either of the tracks when we build this arrangement out in the next chapter.

Have a go hero

So now we have explored making a drum pattern, drum pattern with effects, bass line, alternate bass line, and interlocking keyboard parts. It's time to try this yourself:

1. Create a main drum pattern that all of your drum patterns from here on will reference. Make the pattern 32 beats long.
2. Create clones for these drum patterns and make variations of the drum patterns in the **Beat+Bassline Editor**.
3. Create a bass line in the **Song Editor** using the **Piano-Roll.**
4. Clone the bass line, and add effects to the bass.
5. Mute the parts that are doubled as you go along. Just keep the main beat playing while you get your interlocking parts together.
6. Create a keyboard part with two lines playing off each other.
7. Clone this track and move the notes around so that you have two keyboard parts with interlocking harmonies.
8. Save as you go! This can be the song that you revisit for the arranging part of our voyage.

Using samples in the Song Editor

When you first open LMMS, there is a **Sample Track**. It is different from the audiofile processors that we usually use. On these tracks, we can place an audio file directly on the track, and it will show up as an element. For our requirement, we are going to find some strange sounds on the Internet that are royalty free (see *Chapter 6, Finding and Creating New Noises*).

I like to leave my looped song running in the background, while I browse sites such as ccMixter for a sample that I can use. In this case, we've landed on a sample called **Itty-bitty-tiger-ditty**.

Time for action – adding a sample track

LMMS uses most standard audio files, although for uncompressed files I choose WAV files and for compressed files I use OGG VORBIS. I find these files a bit more cooperative. Let's find a sample from the Internet and add it to our session as a sample track element:

1. Go to `http://ccmixter.org/view/media/samples/browse`.

2. Using the browser, select **a_minor** as a way to whittle our choices down, as shown in the following screenshot:

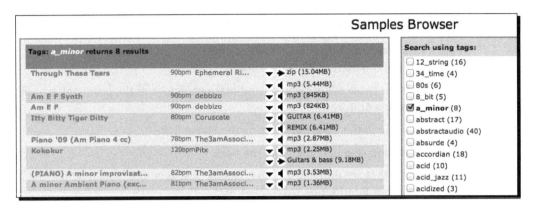

3. Right-click on the downward arrow next to the **itty-bitty-tiger-ditty** guitar part, and choose to **Save File As...** to your desktop.

4. Open **Audacity**. Choose **File->Open...** and navigate to the file on your desktop.

5. When the file is open, select an area to use from within the audio file, as shown in the following screenshot:

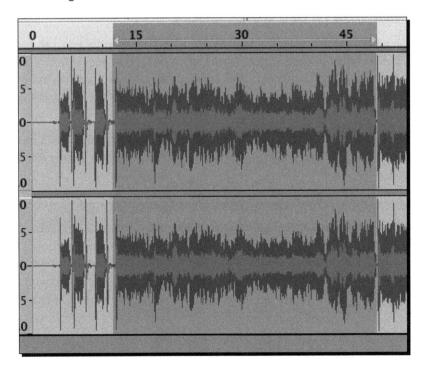

Chapter 7

6. Now choose **File | Export Selection...**.

7. Select **Ogg Vorbis** from the menu at the bottom of the screen, as shown in the following screenshot:

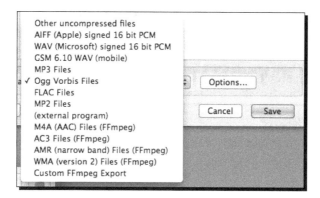

8. Now go back to **LMMS**.

9. Double-click in the area to the right of the sample track, to open up a window as shown in the following screenshot:

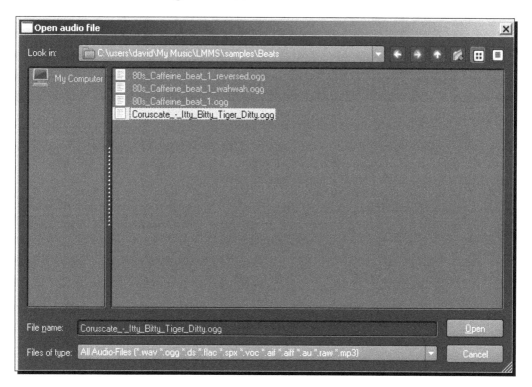

10. Now press the Space bar, and listen to the sample play along with the song. The following screenshot gives an idea of this:

11. Adjust the volume to taste.

What just happened?

Using `ccMixter.org` and Audacity, we were able to find an audio file to use in the **Song Editor** of LMMS. Using the sample track, we can now listen to the audio file play along with the track.

The heavy lifting, when it comes to audio editing, can be handled by Audacity, but we can also adjust the length of the audio using the right-hand side of the sample track element. We can also copy and paste the element, and if we create a new blank element on the sampler track, we can load another audio file into it as well, and place it anywhere within the track. Have moving bass lines, static bass lines, quirky bass lines, and simple bass lines. Make these bass lines work with the main beat by themselves, but also be sure that if they are layered, they can work together as well. Do this with all of the elements, to create a rich set of materials to work from.

Have a go hero

Listening homework:

I'd like to ask you to check out the music video for Daft Punk's iconic music video *Around the World*. Listen to all of the elements that are being used in there. Can you hear them repeating? Hear the stacks? Hear the interlocking parts?

Study how the bass and drums work together, and how the simple little melody talks to the bass. This song is a great way to deconstruct dance music and understand how all of these simple little parts work together with a visual reference!

Enjoy:

`http://www.youtube.com/watch?v=s9MszVE7aR4`

Time to test your brains with a pop quiz...

Pop quiz

1. There are 3 kinds of elements that can be used in the Song Editor; what are they?
    a. FX channel, Sample, Instrument
    b. Instrument, Sample, Beat+Bassline
    c. Piano Roll, Sample, Beat+Bassline
    d. Piano Roll, Automation Track, Sample

2. How do you mute an element?
    a. Right-click and choose mute, or use the middle mouse button on a three button mouse.
    b. Click and choose mute.
    c. Use an Automation Track to turn down the volume.
    d. Just turn down the volume on the volume knob.

3. How do you create a shared FX track that can be used by any element of the song?
    a. FX tracks can't be shared. A single FX track must be created for each element.
    b. Go to the file menu and choose create FX track.
    c. On the instrument that is playing the sound, choose an effect channel on the front panel. The sound will then be routed to the FX mixer, where an effect chain can be applied to the FX channel.
    d. Right-click on an instrument and choose Send to FX.

4. What's a good website to find copyright-free samples?
    a. All samples are copyright-free if you notify the artist or label that you are using the sample.
    b. Any website that uses Creative Commons sample licenses, such as ccMixter.org
    c. Samples are never copyright-free; you can only use a sample when you know who made it and you've notified them that you are using it.
    d. Since SOPA and PIPA were passed, all sampling has been made illegal.

Summary

We created a loop in **Beat+Bassline Editor** and added more instruments with the help of **Piano-Roll** and **Song Editor**. We also used the **Sample Track** feature. The plan is to stack the elements here as deep as possible. In the next chapter, we will be spreading all of these elements out to tell a story, so be sure that you have all of the great characters to tell it. Spend some time making interesting bass lines, melodies, and textures to tell the story. At this stage, bass lines can be stacked deep.

8
Spreading Out the Arrangement

The arrangement is the skeleton of the piece. If there is enough content from the initial loop making, then it may be that we have the main course all ready to go and just need to garnish it. More likely than not, the spreading of the elements out into an arrangement will provide us with additional inspiration, and we'll want to add to what we have. That's ok! That's why a cook always tastes the food while he/she is cooking. If you need more cumin, you need more cumin. Drop it in!

Now that we have our monstrous loop from the previous chapter, we need to start laying out the elements in such a way that we can tell our story. Arranging is one of the most important aspects of creating a good project, as the way that we introduce elements of our song will directly impact how people react emotionally to the piece.

When we listened to the simple song from *Daft Punk* called *Around the World*, we got the idea that there are these very simple, individual parts to the song, but they all fit together flawlessly. The introduction of various melodic phrases on top of the solid bassline and drum beat keeps us interested for what could be coming next in this song, and each set of the eight bars of music brought on a new piece of the puzzle that kept us inspired.

In this chapter, we'll be exploring the following:

- The art of arranging the song
- Spreading our loop out over the length of an entire song
- Adding additional material to fill the song out
- Copying and altering **Beat+Bassline** patterns
- Using subtractive mixing to create our arrangement

The art of arranging

Often when I am teaching students how to remix music, I have them listen to pop music. Really cheesy, middle-of-the-road pop music. Sometimes I'll be sure to add a *Beatles* tune in there, or some other artist that I actually admire, but for the most part I choose what's popular, and not what's great.

The reason I do this is to analyze the structure of the arrangements of music. Music is experienced in movements. These movements are different parts of a story. Some movements are repeated, while other movements stand on their own. In music that we hear commonly on the radio, there are usually three movement types—the **verse**, **chorus**, and **bridge**.

Of course there are other movements as well, but these are the main parts of any pop song. You may have an **intro**, but usually that is derived from the verse or chorus. You might have a **pre-chorus** as well, which is used as a setup, but the verse, chorus, and bridge are the main ways that these stories are told.

The standard pop song arrangement goes something like the following:

1. **Verse 1**: A person explains his/her situation to the listener.
2. **Chorus 1**: The person longingly croons about how much he/she wants out of this predicament.
3. **Verse 2**: The situation gets more strange and the protagonist of the song tries to get out of the situation, but fails.
4. **Chorus 2**: The person longingly croons about how much he/she wants out of this predicament.
5. **Bridge**: Story takes a left turn. Our hero realizes that surrendering to the situation will bring them happiness.
6. **Chorus 3**: The person longingly croons about how much he/she wants out of this predicament, but there is an air of understanding and acceptance.

Okay, so that's really oversimplified, but that is exactly how a lot of songs are structured. The song arrangements will have the **verses** to explain the story. The **choruses** are the anthems that everyone remembers from songs. This is usually because they are higher in pitch, excitement, and repetition than the verses. The **bridge** is a narrative tangent that is supposed to take us to the last revelation of the song, or simply act as a break for a guitar solo.

It's very interesting to take a song and break down the arrangement. Let's take a popular song and break it down.

Analyzing Imagine by John Lennon

The song *Imagine* by John Lennon is among the most popular songs in the world, some arguing that it is the most recognizable song in the world. Well, that may be an exaggeration, but not by much. (The most popular song in the world is most likely *Happy Birthday to You*.)

Time for action – breaking down Imagine by John Lennon

Let's have a look at each section of this seminal work by John Lennon. You can find a video of the song at `http://www.youtube.com/watch?v=-b7qaSxuZUg` if you don't have it already. This song is extremely simple in terms of arrangement, but nonetheless, is a powerful piece of music. The verses and choruses come in two parts, so when we see divisions like 1a and 1b, we are simply stating where the section changes a bit:

1. Piano Intro: This is four bars long, based on the verse. It's only piano.

2. Verse 1a: It is eight bars long - *Imagine there's no heaven…* Lennon describes an imaginary world different from our own. It has piano and Lennon singing.

3. Verse 1b: This is four bars long - *Imagine all the people…* Lennon alludes to the happiness of the people that live in this world. Drums enter with the bass, piano, and Lennon singing.

4. Verse 2a: This is eight bars long - *Imagine there's no countries…* Lennon describes an imaginary world with no borders. It includes piano, drums, bass, strings, and Lennon singing.

5. Verse 2b: This is four bars long - *Imagine all the people…* Lennon alludes to the happiness of the people, who are now living in peace.

6. Chorus 1a: This is four bars long - *You may say I'm a dreamer…* Lennon acknowledges that our current world isn't like this imaginary world, but he is not the only person on Earth who imagines a peaceful world. There is piano, bass, drums, strings, and Lennon singing.

7. Chorus 1b: It is four bars long - *I hope someday you'll join us…* Lennon expresses hope that those who do not subscribe to peaceful ways may someday agree to change their minds. There is piano, bass, drums, strings, and Lennon singing (note the solo piano line that takes us back into the verse structure).

8. Verse 3a: This is eight bars long - *Imagine no possessions…* Lennon describes an imaginary world where there is no idea of ownership or cultural separation. There are piano, bass, drums, strings, and Lennon singing.

Spreading Out the Arrangement

9. Verse 3b: It is four bars long - *Imagine all the People...* Lennon alludes to the happiness of the people who share this imaginary world. Again, there are solo piano, bass, drums, strings, and Lennon singing.

10. Chorus 2a: It is four bars long - *You may say I'm a dreamer...* Lennon acknowledges that our current world isn't like this imaginary world, but he is not the only person on Earth who imagines a peaceful world. There is piano, bass, drums, strings, and Lennon singing.

11. Chorus 2b: This is four bars long - *I hope someday you'll join us...* Lennon expresses hope that those who do not subscribe to peaceful ways may someday agree to change their minds. There is piano, bass, drums, strings, and Lennon singing.

What just happened?

John Lennon's song *Imagine* is simple, but shows us that simplicity does not keep a piece of music from being powerful. In this case, Lennon decides that he doesn't even need the revelation or sonic break of a bridge to get his point across.

Arrangement helps to give the listener a predictable framework, so that he/she can relax into the structure of the song.

Now let's examine a song that has a bridge section in later sections of this chapter.

The purpose of the bridge

Many say that the point of a bridge is to give a guitar player his chance to solo. Some may also say that the bridge is a clever way to offer a break in intensity for the listener, so that they can chill out for a second before the music kicks back in at full force. Others argue that a bridge serves as an important part of the narrative of a song, a kind of revelation that adds depth to a song and gives the listener the impression that the protagonist of the story of the song has had a breakthrough.

All of these observations are correct. Let's take a look at a few popular songs and see how their bridge sections function:

- *Nirvana*: *Smells Like Teen Spirit*: In this song, during the bridge, there's a guitar that simply plays a version of the main melody of the song, but the overall verse structure is intact.
- *Radiohead*: *Creep*: In this song, during the bridge, the character of the song wails as the object of his desire runs out the door, obviously freaked out by this little, obsessed, gnome of a friend.

- *Pink Floyd*: *Comfortably Numb*: In this song, the bridge is not just a guitar solo, it's a supernova. The music modulates its key as well, and it's a pretty clear departure from the rest of the song.
- *Peter Gabriel*: *Don't Give Up*: In this song, the character of the song is in great emotional pain, and has almost given up. He is literally standing on a bridge (clever), and is prepared to jump, but doesn't.

As you see, a bridge can be a great way to add additional, emotional landscapes to a song, and also serve the simple function of breaking the monotony of the verse-to-chorus structure.

The art of the break

In electronic music, we can observe the same kind of structures, but the arrangement of an electronic music piece can be quite radically different from the structure of a pop song. In many forms of dance music, the idea is to have a beat that is steady, a bassline that complements the beat, and a melody that essentially creates a chorus-like section, which serves as the anthem of the song. This is sometimes called **repetitive music**, and dates way back to early civilization and possibly earlier. Sections in repetitive music are not so clearly defined as in classical or folk music. Let's analyze a popular dance music song and see how it breaks down, arrangement-wise.

Time for action – analyzing One

Swedish House Mafia came out with a dance music song called *One* in 2010. It was a pretty big hit in the dance music scene; let's discover why!

First, go to this link, and listen to the song at the following web page, while reading this section:

http://www.youtube.com/watch?v=dg7XO1zgJHA

Here's the breakdown:

1. Intro 1a: This is 12 bars of claps, with the kick drum slowly fading, and the claps slowly fading into reverb. This area is extremely important. The DJ spinning this song cannot have any pitched instruments in this section of the song, because it may make the previous song sound out of key when he mixes it in.

2. Intro 1b: This is approximately 12 bars of the kick slowly subdividing into smaller and smaller bits, then some slight modulation is applied, and the kick no longer sounds like a kick, it sounds like a synth!

3. Section 1a: It is eight bars long. The main melody of the entire song is established using this new synth made from the kick drum.

Spreading Out the Arrangement

4. Section 1b: This is also eight bars long. A new synth counter-melody is introduced with the original melody. There is a drum machine clapping at the end of the phrase.

5. Section 1c: This again is eight bars long. There is a clap happening on the downbeat to add tension to the beat.

6. Break 1: It is eight bars long. The melody and counter-melody play alone, no drums, no clap... What's going to happen?

7. Section 2a: This is eight bars long. The melody and counter-melody are visited by another melody, a very bright, big synth.

8. Section 2b: This is eight bars long. Yet another melodic synth comes in, along with the kick.

9. Break 2a: This is 12 bars long. A single note repeats over and over again. There is a drumbeat, building low in the mix. The repeating pattern slowly filters away while a pitched instrument rises in the background. Two claps, all by themselves, take us into the second part of the break.

10. Section 3a: This is eight bars long. The main melody comes back, but not at its highest intensity. There is an instrument in the background that is very slowly rising in pitch, letting the listener know that we aren't at the most intense part of the song yet. This section doesn't deliver on the break's promise of intensity yet.

11. Section 3b: This is eight bars long. Continuing the slow rise of intensity, there is an additional drumbeat low in the mix that offsets the steady thump of the kick.

12. Section 3c: It is eight bars long. Still slowly bringing up the intensity level, the loudest synth starts to break slightly with the steady rhythm of the other synths, bringing the intensity level up to a crazy degree. An additional sweeping synth can be heard, lifting this section to our final destination, similar to a rocket lifting off. The drums fall out for the final two bars of this section. DJ? You better drop that beat back in!!

13. Section 4: It is eight bars long. We are finally given eight bars of the highest intensity of the piece. The crowd goes wild, people scream, and so on.

14. Section 5: This is eight bars long. Remember the beat that entered in Section 3b? It's back! Oh, and the piano takes more prominence in this part. The energy is dropping a little bit, leading us into Break 3.

15. Break 3: This is eight bars long. Okay, the Swedish House Mafia realizes that, by this point, a break can't be too long (they might make the dancers very angry after whipping them into a froth with that last section), so they limit it to eight bars with a synth sweep in the background, and a beat building underneath this section.

16. Section 6a: This again is eight bars long. We're back to the highest intensity of the song. Everyone dances like crazy.

17. Section 6b: It is also eight bars long. The Swedish House Mafia decide to keep that intensity right where it is, high and mighty. At the end of this section, the melody changes slightly, getting even more intense and high in pitch. The drums drop out at the end of the section for added drama.

18. Section 7a: This is eight bars long, taking it way back down to a reprise of Section 1a.

19. Section 7b: It is eight bars long. The beat that was introduced in Section 3b is added in, establishing that we are likely on our way out with this song. There are no further builds. The Swedish House Mafia are letting us down easy.

20. Rideout: This is where the DJ playing the song gets to mix in the next song. It's important not to have any pitched instruments here so the next song coming on doesn't sound out of key.

What just happened?

We've just explored an arrangement of a popular dance music track. It's pretty different from *Imagine*, right? Dance music is like a very long, amusement park ride. You are taken through highs and lows in intensity, but the emotional content of the song remains pretty much the same. The idea is to create an arrangement that is ecstatic and has the ability to take dancers on a journey without losing a sense of ecstasy.

There are older, more traditional forms of ecstatic music from other cultures, which work much in the same way. Indian classical music is known for not having much of a beginning and end... it's mostly middle. A listener is dropped in the middle of a long form repetition that leads to an ecstatic state. The rhythm may be different from popular dance music, but the sentiment is the same, which is to drop people into a state of ecstasy and keep them there for a good time.

Laying it out for our project

Now we need to get an arrangement together for our project. We've studied pop music arrangement styles and dance music. LMMS works really well for electronic dance music, so we're going to use a dance music arrangement style to get our project going.

We're going to need to open the project we were working on, which is called **Main Loop Start**. As this is the genesis of a new project, we should save this project under a new name. For now, I think a good, descriptive name would be `Poor_Creature_v1_Arrange`. This project has a descriptive name, a version number, and what we achieved on this version.

Spreading Out the Arrangement

Time for action – spreading out the loop

In *Chapter 7, Getting It All Stacked up*, we created a loop and variations. This time around, we need to spread the content of our main loop out for the duration of a song:

1. Mute all of the elements in the **Song Editor**:

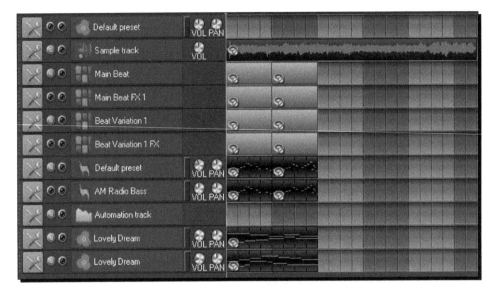

All of the tracks need to be muted. So make sure that all of the mute buttons are lit up:

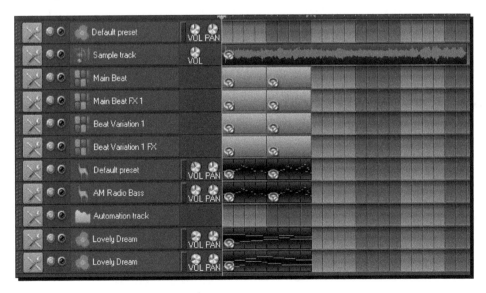

Chapter 8

2. Grab the right-hand side of our sample, and trim the element so that it is only eight bars long. We are going to build this song in eight bar segments. Building a song in repeating eight bar chunks will give nice structure to the song's overall arrangement:

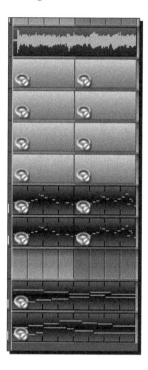

3. Make sure to mute the sample once you're done.

4. Now press *Ctrl* + click on the sample, and click again immediately to the right-hand side of the sample. Repeat this until you have 96 bars filled:

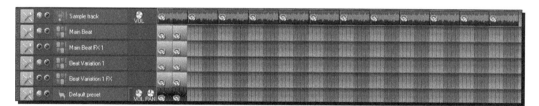

[229]

Spreading Out the Arrangement

5. Repeat this with all of the other elements. Your full arrangement length should be covered by all of the elements:

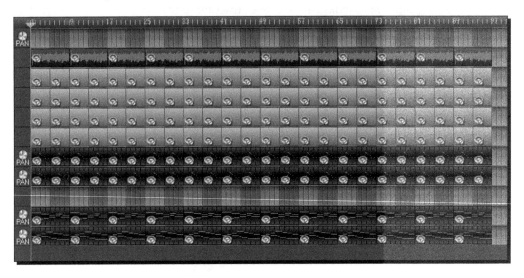

6. Now that we have our arrangement spread out, we're going to create our early draft arrangement. We will start by un-muting the **Main Beat** for the first eight bars.

7. Now extend the loop for the first 16 bars. We're going to unmute the main beat for all the 16 bars and then decide to bring in the **AM Radio Bass** at the second half of the 16-bar phrase:

Chapter 8

8. Now, let's create a little space in the **Main Beat** before the next section. Click-and-drag the lower right-hand side corner of the element to shorten it a bit:

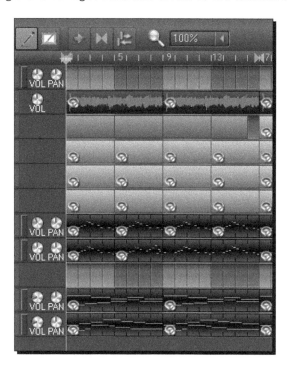

9. Now let's unmute the following elements in the next eight bars:

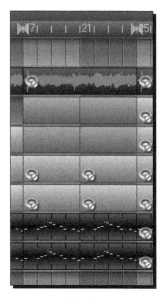

Spreading Out the Arrangement

10. We need to add variation to the **Main Beat FX1**. We need to up the intensity a bit. Alter the pattern to match this example in the **Beat+Bassline Editor**:

11. Now let's set our loop from bar 25 to bar 33. Hmm... Sounds like we need to really up the ante on this song. Alter your **AM Radio Bass** to this pattern in the **Piano-Roll**:

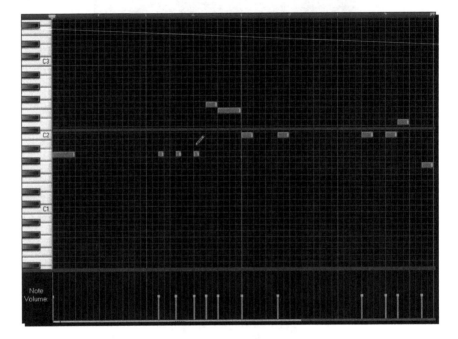

12. Now that we have a more sparse bassline, we can fit other elements around it. Add these instruments and presets from the LMMS side bar to our **Song Editor**: the **Good 'Ol Times** preset and the **STrash** preset for the **LB302** instrument, and the **Fat** preset for the **TripleOscillator** instrument.

13. Create this pattern for **Good 'Ol Times** in the **Piano-Roll**:

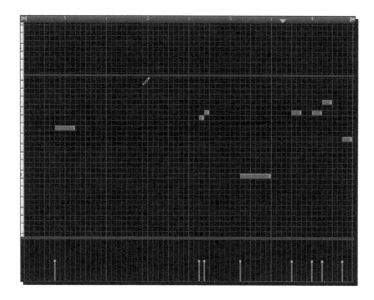

14. Now create this pattern for the preset **STrash**:

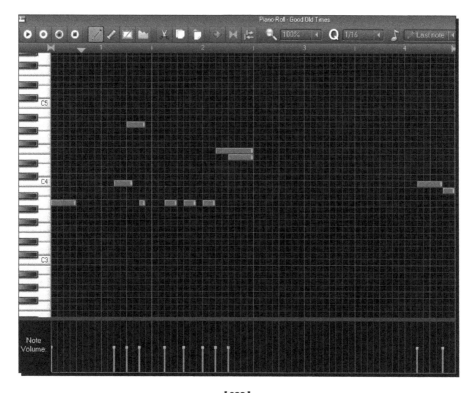

15. And finally, let's add the **Fat** chords on the **TripleOscillator** track:

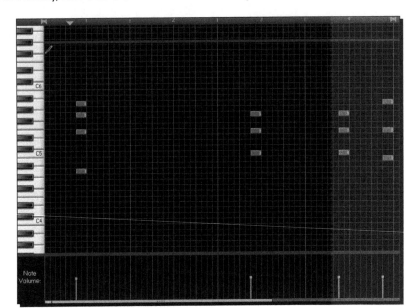

16. Play all of these elements together, and copy the elements to the bars from 29 to 33.

17. Once you have this pattern together, listen from the beginning of the song again. Does everything work?

18. Now let's have the **Fat** chords come in only between 29 and 33.

19. Unmute the sample following 33, and leave only the sample **Lovely Dream** and **Main Beat** in.

20. Listen from the beginning of the song. Does the arrangement appear to be coming together?

What just happened?

We have now created an arrangement template with elements and started un-muting and muting elements to give us an arrangement. This form of arranging in dance music keeps a nice, continuous thread of themes and patterns that keep the listener engaged without taking musical detours, which can throw the emotional and musical center of the piece. This is a tried and true method to keeping our arrangements on a solid track.

Now there are more than enough elements to give us pieces to play with for an arrangement. The addition of new elements, which interlock with the beat, gives the piece more excitement and complexity.

Have a go hero

Now that we've started this arrangement, it's time to get the rest of the piece together. You can use another dance song as a template to determine where breakdowns and high energy points should happen. Copy the new elements out, and try combining these elements in interesting ways to develop new patterns from the elements we have. Remember the big break on the Swedish House Mafia track? Listen to Break 2a of that piece and repeat elements in this song to give a nice area for our build transition that's coming up in the next chapter.

In your **Beat+Bassline Editor**, create alternate beats that can be introduced to the song, but make sure that the song has a consistent feel.

Pop quiz

Now that we've closely studied the art of arranging, we need to be sure we remember the basics that we've laid out in this chapter:

1. What are the main sections of the arrangement of a pop song called?
    a. Verse, Pre-Chorus, Chorus
    b. Verse, Bridge, Outro
    c. Verse, Chorus, Bridge
    d. Verse, Chorus, Breakdown

2. When arranging a dance song, what is the name of the section that interrupts the normal flow of the song and gives the listener a departure from the main beat?
    a. Bridge
    b. Breakdown or Break
    c. Chorus
    d. Takeoff

3. What is the composition type that best describes dance music?
    a. Postmodern Composition
    b. Alternative Pop
    c. Repetitive Music Composition
    d. Trance Music

4. How does subtractive mixing work?
    a. Elements are created in a very large loop, then spread out across the entire length of the song. Elements are then muted and unmuted as needed.
    b. Sections are created one at a time, and then sections that don't sound good are subtracted.
    c. All the possible musical ideas are added, and then the ones that don't work are taken away.

5. How do you copy elements in the Song Editor?
    a. Click-and-drag elements directly to where they are needed.
    b. Hold *Ctrl* first, then click-and-drag elements to where they are needed.
    c. Hold *Shift* first, then click-and-drag elements to where they are needed.
    d. Hold the *Option* along with *Shift*, then click-and-drag elements to where they are needed.

Summary

Arrangement is one of the most important aspects of creating a good song, whether it's dance music, pop music, or any other style of music. I encourage you to listen to as many styles of music as possible, and try to pick out the different sections of music and ponder what they are being used for. Are they projecting higher energy? Lower energy? Do they build, or are they emotionally static?

The different sections of a piece of music are extremely important to telling the story that we want to tell. Having a great beat and bassline are good, but if they aren't put in a larger context, then they aren't really saying anything.

Using subtractive arranging to create dance music is a great way to make sure that the piece feels continuous and doesn't take huge detours when it's rolling along. It also makes it easier to hear how all of our parts are working together over time, and gives us the ability to leave the song and come back to it without having the feeling that we've just dropped off a cliff halfway through putting the song together. Having a beginning, middle, and an end gives us the ability to leave the song and come back knowing that all we have to do is tie all of the pieces together properly. We don't have to worry about taking unnecessary tangents.

In the next chapter, we'll finish off the rough arrangement we have going, and explore different transitions and breakdown techniques.

9
Gluing the Arrangement Together

Now that we've started putting together the bones of our arrangement, we need to smooth out the transitions between the various sections. Transitions are not just used to help smooth out the movement from one section to the next. We will be using transitions to build excitement and augment our arrangement.

In this chapter we will:

- Create transitions using dropouts
- Create transitions using filter sweeps
- Create transitions using reverb effects
- Blend parts using volume automation

The art of the transition

Transitions are primarily used in dance music to merge two sections together, build tension within a section, or provide subtle changes to a monotonous sound. In the previous chapter, we listened to Swedish House Mafia, and how they used a combination of reverb, sweeps, pitched instruments, and dropouts to transition from one section to the next. You may want to revisit the song "One" once this chapter is finished, to understand where different types of transitions work best for different effects.

Gluing the Arrangement Together

Since finishing the last chapter, here is the arrangement I came up with:

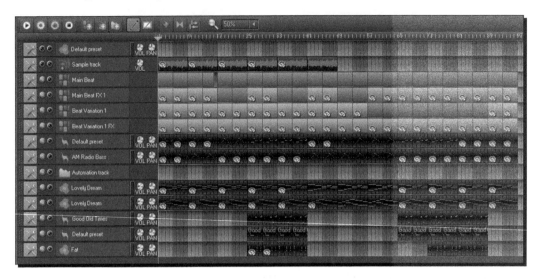

In my arrangement, I decided to leave the sample out for now. I may use it in an audio file processor later, but for now I'm leaving it muted. As you can see, the rest of the tracks are muted and un-muted at will, and the new parts we added in the last chapter have been copied and pasted to the end of the song.

Using dropouts

Remember in the beginning of the piece when we created a little space in the Main Beat before bar 17 (in the *Time for action – spreading out the loop* section in *Chapter 8, Spreading out the Arrangement*)?

This is called a dropout. The idea is that when the foundation of a song is dropped out, the listener is left with a feeling of anticipation. They know where the beat is supposed to fall, and they will be expecting a big change. In the beginning of our arrangement, we have a dropout as the first tonal instrument comes in. Sometimes a dropout can be totally empty. Sometimes a dropout will have a little reverb or a single drum hit. Sometimes a dropout will have a melody or pad continue on as if nothing happened.

Let's see what happens when we transition to a different area of the song. You can either copy the arrangement I made, or you can open the file from the document provided.

Time for action – creating a dropout with the accompanying pitch fall

We are going to create a dropout, and add a pitch fall to the bass instrument that continues playing through the space left by the main beat. The dropout will be happening before bar 49. This song has been saved as **Poor_Creature_v2_transitions**:

1. Find bar 49.

2. Create a looped area between bar 44 and 53, as shown in the following screenshot. This will allow us to hear the pad play through as normal:

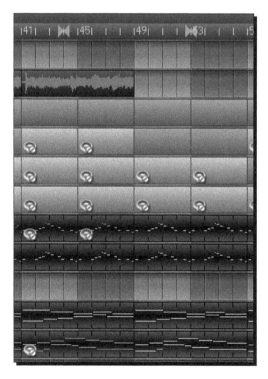

Gluing the Arrangement Together

3. Pull back the right side of the **Main Beat** element so that it stops at bar 48:

4. Now that we have the space, it's time to add a little pitch fall to our bassline! Un-mute the bassline that is doubling the bass line we call **AM Radio Bass**. It is just above the **AM Radio Bass** element.

5. Open the Piano Roll editor for this element, and erase all of the notes except the last one:

Chapter 9

6. Now we need to add a pitch fall. To add note detuning, you need to select **Detuning Mode** at the top of the screen. It looks like this:

7. Using this tool, select the note in the Piano Roll editor. A new editor window will appear that looks like this:

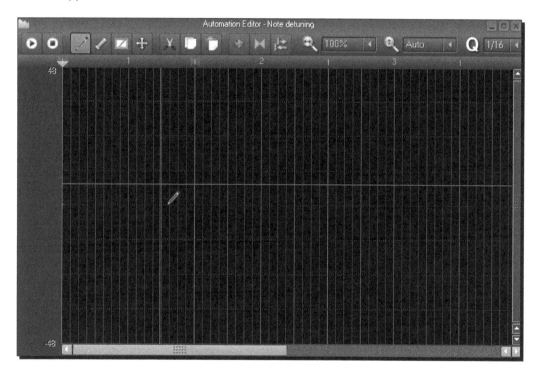

8. On the left side of the screen, you will see tuning values of **48** to **-48**. Start drawing a line in this window starting from the mid-point:

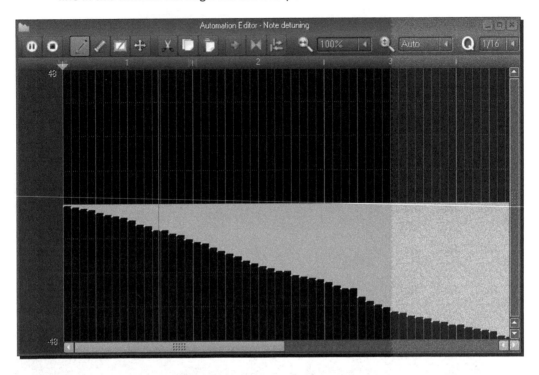

9. Now that bass note will dive down in pitch, un-mute the element in the Song Editor, and have a listen. You should be able to hear it's pitch pulling against the other bass line.

10. Now open up your Piano Roll editor again, and look at the note. You'll see that it now has little yellow dots indicating that it has **Note Detuning** activated:

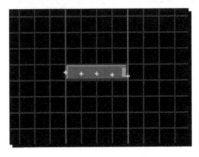

11. The yellow dots indicate that the pitch is going down as the note is played.

Chapter 9

12. Apply the same pitch detuning to the other bassline that is playing:

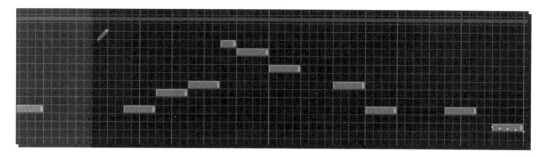

13. Listen to the looped area. Do both basses drift down together?

14. Now that we have the basses detuning together, we need to have the pads stop early. Go to the top-most **Lovely Dream** synth element, and edit the notes to look like this:

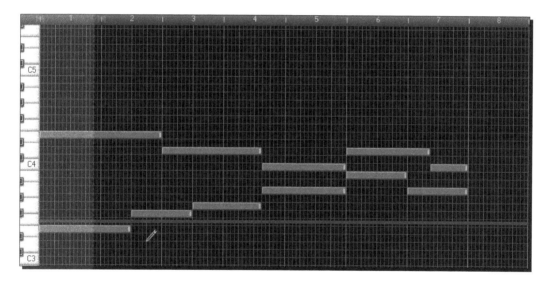

This will make the pad stop in time for the bass to be featured.

15. Now we can let the **Main Beat** play to its first snare hit. Click and hold on the right side to trim the **Main Beat** element, and hold *Ctrl* to fine-tune the edit. It should look something like this:

16. Now listen to the section again.

What just happened?

We've created a small break in the action by using a dropout with a pitch fall.

This kind of transition can be used at almost any time. The only thing to be mindful of with dropouts is that you may distract the listener if they happen too often. When the beat is moving along, sometimes a listener can feel let down if the beat stops too often. It's best to use this technique sparingly.

Creating filter sweeps

A filter sweep is a sound that appears to be rising higher and higher in pitch as a section moves along. Many people think it is simply a sound whose pitch is slowly raised using a technique like we just used. The truth is that most of these tones are single tones, that are being filtered in a dynamic way. Even though the pitch of the original instrument is the same, (usually the root pitch of the song, or a common pitch that works in any section of the song), the filter accentuates harmonics that the sound has in it. This accentuation gives the illusion of pitching the instrument, but often sounds much smoother than a pitch bend.

Chapter 9

Time for action – creating a filter sweep

In this section, we'll be using the **TripleOscillator** instrument to help us achieve a filter sweep. For creating a filter sweep, follow these steps:

1. Open a new **TripleOscillator** instrument from the side bar.

2. Create a blank element at the very beginning of the song.

3. Open the Piano Roll editor, and create a note at A1 that is really, really long—16 bars, to be precise:

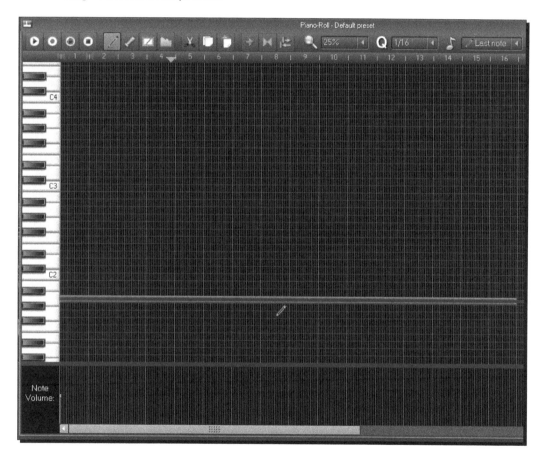

4. Now we need to set the front panel of the **TripleOscillator** instrument. Click on the preset in the Song Editor.

[245]

Gluing the Arrangement Together

5. There are three oscillators. Choose the settings shown in the following screenshot, for each oscillator:

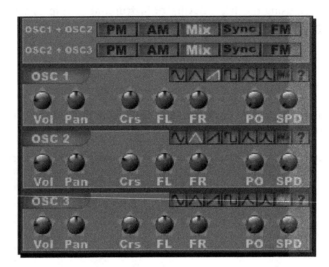

6. Click on **Play** and listen to our new sound.
7. This sound doesn't move at all, and sounds like noise! Let's activate the filter by selecting the **ENV/LFO** tab, and activating the button next to **Filter**:

Chapter 9

8. Now we need to create an automation track for the **Cutoff** knob of the filter. Hold *Ctrl* and drag the **Cutoff** knob to the automation track in our Song Editor:

9. Now we need to double-click on the element in the automation track to open it:

10. The reason the entire area is shaded is that the filter is all the way open. Let's go back to the filter and adjust the settings so that they look like so:

11. Delete the automation element we had open earlier, and pressing *Ctrl*, drag the **Cutoff** knob from the synth to the automation track to replace the previous automation element.

Gluing the Arrangement Together

12. When double-clicking on it this time, it should look like this:

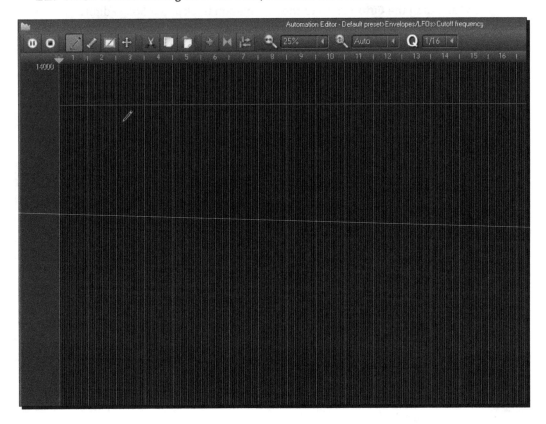

13. This shows that the automation window shows us the current setting of the **Cutoff** knob, which is near zero.

14. Go to the resolution setting, and change it to 1/64:

15. Now draw a line from the lower-left corner of the window to the upper right. Make it straight; but if it wavers a bit, that's okay. Make it 16 bars long:

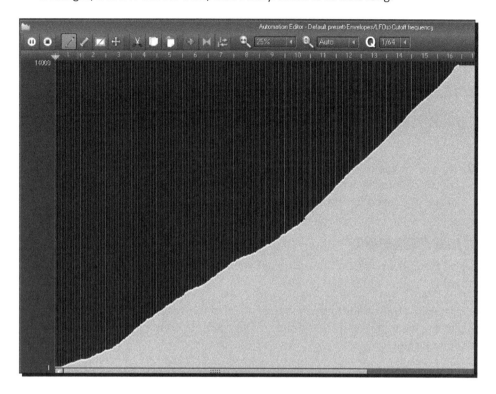

16. Now play back the song from the beginning and listen.

17. Now we have a sweep happening! Let's put some reverb on this instrument. For now we will put it directly in the effects section of the **TripleOscillator** instrument:

18. Now listen again. Adjust the volume of the instrument to -4 dB.

19. For fun, let's copy the instrument and automation to the next section, but reverse the direction of the automation. Move the automation track down to the instrument track as well:

20. Now listen again. The effect should reverse as the next section comes in, and transition into the higher-energy level section. We can now reduce the length of the note used for the sweep if we like. Now copy those elements to bar 65.

What just happened?

Now we've created a sweeping transition between parts, effectively linking one section to another.

Many believe that transitions happen in the course of a measure or 8 beats, or maybe 16 beats at the most, but long transitions are the secret to creating additional atmosphere and tension in a piece.

Next, we'll use the technique of adding effects subtly to a sound to create an almost immeasurable change in a track over time that significantly increases the tension and release of a good transition. Not all transitions need to be obvious. Sometimes the best transition is a slow metamorphosis from one sonic world to another. Adding an effect such as reverb over time can slowly generate a change in mood.

Time for action – adding in effects over time

In the piece *One* by Swedish House Mafia, we heard a section where reverb was subtly added to a clap to create a transition from one section to another. Let's do this on our AM bassline. To do this, follow these steps:

1. Add a reverb to the AM bassline. Use **Freeverb**.

2. Select the **AM Radio Bass** track.

3. Create a new **Automation Track**. Use this button:

Chapter 9

4. Use the settings, shown in the following screenshot, on **Freeverb**:

5. Now, press *Ctrl* and click on the room size knob, and drag it to the new automation track. Place it at bar 9.
6. Open the automation window, and make this shape again:

7. Now listen to the new effect on the **AM Radio Bass**. You should hear the reverb gradually grow. This adds energy to the track, so turn the volume back at least 4 dB on the instrument itself.

What just happened?

Now we are using slow integration of effects on an instrument track as a transition!

Using automation to create transitions will take a static sound and make it appear to change over time, even if the part that is being played is just repeating over and over again. This is the way to keep sections transitioning and moving along, and to keep the listeners' attention. Keep in mind that automation tracks can be used in the Beats+Bassline editor as well as the Song Editor.

Transitions like these should be used subtly, and not too frequently. If a song has too much movement going on, it can sound ungrounded. If it doesn't move at all, it can sound too static and can even get boring. Be very careful using delay based effects in this way, because too much reverb can diffuse the power of all of the interlocking parts that create a groove.

Notice that the parameters in the automation window change when you are using different parameters. Parameters that deal with volume or intensity usually have values of 0-1, where parameters having to do with frequency will have a range of 1 Hz to 14,000 Hz. It's important to be aware of how these values have meaning in a project. We'll be discussing these differences in *Chapter 10, Getting the Mix Together*, and *Chapter 11, Getting into Instruments*.

Have a go hero

Now that we've got a couple of different plans for transitions, look for other opportunities or openings in the song where transitions can be made. Try to keep in mind the arrangement that you've created, and be sure that your transitions never take over the energy of the song.

Pop quiz

Now let's see if we remember what we've done!

1. Which editor has the **Note Detuning** feature?
    a. Song Editor
    b. Piano Roll
    c. The Beats+Bassline editor

2. How do you assign a parameter to automation track?

    a. Press *Ctrl* and drag a knob to automation track.

    b. Option- drag a knob to automation track.

    c. Simply drag a knob to automation track.

3. How do you activate a reverb on an instrument effects chain?

    a. Enter `Reverb On` into the C++ compiler in the project window.

    b. Go to the effects tab, add effect, choose reverb from the list, then set the controls to adjust the wet signal. If the wet signal on the reverb is not turned up, the reverb will not activate.

    c. In Song Editor, right-click on a track and choose a reverb from the contextual menu.

4. Are filter sweeps the same as pitch bends?

    a. No, filter sweeps are accentuating frequencies in a static pitch by sweeping through the harmonics of the sound.

    b. Yes, filter sweeps are the same as pitch bends.

5. What editors can use automation tracks?

    a. Only the Song Editor can use automation tracks.

    b. Only the Beats+Bassline editor can use automation tracks.

    c. The Song Editor and the Beats+Bassline editor can use automation tracks.

Summary

Using transitions in our song creates movement, and gives us the illusion that there is life in that machine. Dance music that doesn't use transitions to glue the piece together can sound disjointed and dead. Transitions create tensions, and music composition is all about tension and release. We will learn in the next chapter how mixing will pull all of this tension and release into a cohesive whole.

10
Getting the Mix Together

We've put all of the pieces in place, and now have a cohesive story with our arrangement sewn up tight. At this stage of the game, we need the elements that we've created in our project to work together sonically. The timbres of individual elements are like colors on an artist's canvas. We need to take this time to carefully blend the different colors we have going on so that every element gets its own space in the mix.

In this chapter, we will learn:

- A little lesson on signal flow and audio energy
- How audio signals flow through LMMS
- The stages of mixing
- Using dynamic, filter, delay-based, and modulation plugins in the FX Mixer
- How to bounce our project out for various media

What is mixing?

We've heard people reference songs, and different versions of songs, by who mixed them or re-mixed them. *Fix it in the mix* is a common expression, and when we see photos of people in a studio, usually it's in front of a mixing desk. **Mixing** is often referred to as a sort of mystical stage of a song, where the song comes alive under the careful supervision of a mix engineer.

A simple definition of mixing – mixing is the art of balancing volume, stereo pan, dynamics, timbre, and depth to allow all of the elements of a song remain clearly defined.

Getting the Mix Together

Audio energy

I like to compare audio signal flow when mixing two rivers travelling towards the ocean. If you think of a river, it has banks that contain the water. Imagine the water as being your audio signal. We aren't going to worry at the moment about how fast the water is flowing. We just want to concentrate on the amount of water that's being channeled through the river.

If we play the included song for this chapter, we can see that the FX Mixer only has one FX Channel playing at the moment. As we haven't assigned any of the instruments to their own FX Channel, all of the audio energy is flowing through the Master FX Channel. As we can see and hear, the Master is getting too much audio energy from our song, and the audio is distorting. Think of this as the river overflowing. The Master FX Channel can only handle so much audio energy before clipping.

Digital clipping and you

Audio energy in the old tape world is way different than audio in the digital world. Tape recorders had a meter that went to **0**, and then a little beyond. 0 dB represented the highest volume acceptable before the tape medium itself started changing the overall timbre of the sound. A tape recorder's meter looked something like this:

Using the meter above, a person recording to tape would watch this meter to be sure that when the audio got louder, the pointer wasn't going too far into the red. In the days of tape, going in to the red occasionally wasn't a bad thing, as long as the signal didn't clip. Going slightly above 0 dB VU would actually make the sound ever so slightly more warm and pleasant to the ear.

Analog equipment had this kind of wiggle room that allowed for pushing the audio slightly hotter than the 0 dB VU ceiling. The little peak light would kick on when the audio was officially clipping. Clipping ended up sounding like a bit of distortion.

In the digital world, we have something called dB FS, and there is no wiggle room. If you go past 0 db **Full Scale**, (**FS**), on a channel strip meter in any DAW, you will get distortion. 0 db FS is also about 18 dB louder than 0 dB VU.

The digital realm doesn't have the same wiggle room as the physical, malleable medium of tape. A digital recording is very accurate and uncolored when you are using very good equipment. Sound in the real world is captured with very little change in the sound, and the hardware basically gives us a 1 to 1 from input to output. You can't make a signal any more pleasant by pushing beyond 0 dB FS. It just ends up distorting.

Now, let's talk a little about clipping. To understand clipping, we should talk about sound waves and speakers.

If you are able to see a speaker vibrate, usually using a low tone of some kind, you'll notice that the speaker can only push a certain distance out. Let's call that +1. Now the speaker also pulls back. Let's call the furthest that it can pull back, -1.

When the speaker is just sitting there, minding its own business, we call that 0. That's the equidistant point between the speaker being fully pushed out and the speaker pulling back in.

When most people look at waves for the first time, the waves are represented like this:

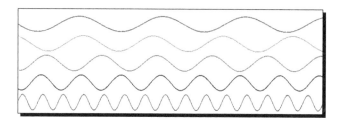

Here we have five different audio waves. The first line is a slower wave, which indicates a lower frequency, and subsequently a lower pitch. The fifth wave has a higher frequency, so it is higher in pitch. We see these waves horizontally passing through time. From left to right, we would have our timeline.

Frequency refers to the number of waves that travel past a given point per second. When looking at a visual representation of sound waves like the one above, think of frequency as the number of full waveforms (from peak to trough and back again) that fit in a given length of space. Frequency is measured in **Hertz (Hz)**.

So at any point, we can see the high point of the wave, and the low point of the wave. The high points would be akin to the speaker pushing out, and the low points of the wave are like a speaker pulling back in. Between those two extremes we have the null point, where the speaker is at rest.

When we record audio or play it back, the audio can only have so much energy before it starts overwhelming the equipment.

Here is an example of two sine waves. The shaded area is the difference in amplitude between the two waves. The upper part of the waves are called **crests**, and the lower parts are **troughs**. The tip of the crest is called the **node**, and the tip of the trough is called the **anti-node**. The top and bottom of the frame represent the physical limits of the amplitude of the gear the wave is being played on. As you see, the top wave is going out beyond the limits of the equipment at the node and anti-node:

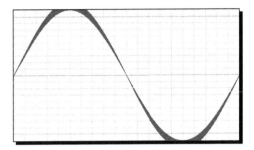

Let's think about our example of the speaker pushing out and pulling back in. If +1 equals as far out as the speaker can go and -1 is how far in it can pull, then what's happening in the upper sine wave of the picture above? Well, the speaker pushes out until it reaches it's outermost point, then suddenly the energy disappears! The speaker then tries to go back to rest, then the waveform comes back into range again. Basically, the speaker then has to go from it's state of rest to +1 with no ramping up to that point. This sounds like a tremendous pop, and the speakers are going to fry if that's how they are being driven.

Clipping can happen at lots of different places in the audio world:

- You can record a sound into your computer too loudly, and the signal will clip when the audio is being converted from analog to digital waveforms.
- When adding plugins to a FX Channel, the plugins can get too much audio energy and clip.
- When mixing, the sum of all of the audio when mixed together can overpower the audio output of LMMS. This clips the audio before it even makes it to your amplifier.
- The audio can clip after it's been sent out from a computer to an amplifier, when the amplifier is driven too hard and it clips the audio before heading to the poor speakers.

So, how do we avoid clipping in these circumstances?

Chapter 10

Time for action – separating audio streams

We need to get our audio separated into individual FX channels and explore the concept of gain staging to get a clear mix. Here's how it's done:

1. Start with the Beat+Bassline editors in the song **Mixing_Start**. You can find **Mixing_Start** at this location:

   ```
   http://www.packtpub.com/sites/default/files/downloads/
   Chapter_10.zip
   ```

2. Open the Beat+Bassline editor called **Main_Loop with CR78**:

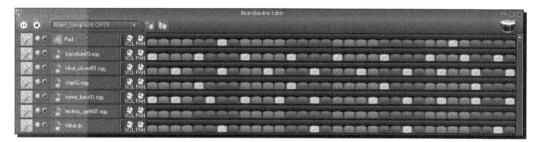

3. Some of the volumes are set to different levels so that the Master FX channel will not clip. Open up the **Pad** instrument by clicking on it.

4. In **Pad**, go to the top where the FX channel can be set:

5. Click and hold on the **FX CHNL** area, and move your mouse up until it says **4**:

6. Now close the editor, and open the FX Mixer.

7. Hit the Space bar. We will see that the **Pad** come through FX channel 4:

8. Now the level on FX channel 4 is very low. We should turn the volume on the **Pad** instrument back to 0 dB:

9. Now the level coming through FX channel 4 is looking more robust, although it still doesn't sound right:

10. The Master FX channel is now clipping because the level of all of the other instruments, plus the level from FX channel 4, are summing together, causing distortion. Let's pull that FX channel 4 back down a bit:

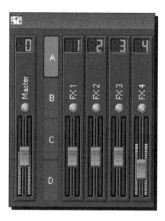

11. Now the Master FX channel is looking better, FX channel 4 isn't clipping, and the balance is correct between the other instruments and the pad.

12. Next we need to go back to the Beat+Bassline editor for **Main_Loop with CR78** and focus on drum sounds. When we assign an instrument to an FX channel, we will be calling that action **bussing**.

13. Bus the instruments **Hihat.ds** and **hihatclosed_01** to FX channel 3:

14. Now let's set their volumes to 0 dB right now, so we don't have to do it later. The quickest way to set the volume to it's default setting is to press *Alt* and click on it:

15. Now that you have the hang of this, assign the bassdrum instrument to FX channel 1, the clap to FX channel 2, and the bass to FX channel 6. Even though there are no notes for the techno synth, assign that instrument to FX channel 7.

16. Adjust all of the volumes to 0 dB.

17. Go back to the Song Editor, hit the Space bar to play the song, and open the FX Mixer.

    The mixer should now show all of the FX channels playing for each instrument that was assigned:

18. Listen to the song clipping. You will hear distortion.

19. Pull all of the sliders down in the FX Mixer.

20. Listen to the song. There are still elements playing!

21. Go to the Song Editor, and assign the remaining instruments and samples to their own FX channels. Use FX channel 7 for the techno synth, so that both instruments can be grouped under one fader.

    There should now be 11 FX channels being used:

22. Double-click on the FX channel names, and give each channel a meaningful name to represent what kind of audio is coming through:

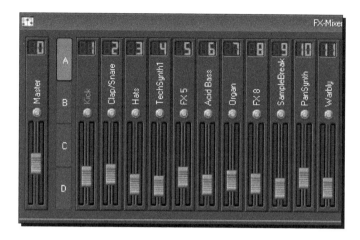

When instruments are grouped together, it may leave some open FX channels. We'll use these later.

What just happened?

We have successfully taken our audio from our instruments and placed them on FX channels in the mixer.

It can be very helpful to view your mix this way, and it's the only way I mix. The reason it's so important is that you need to see the audio on each individual channel, and to see how loud everything is when the audio sums together at the Master FX channel.

If your audio sounds too quiet, turn on your speakers. It's very important that you keep these levels under control, so that your little tributaries, (going with that river metaphor), when they merge into the big river, (the Master FX channel), don't overflow and distort.

ABCs of mixing

When mixing, it's a very good idea to have some sort of system. There are some common rules that help take a mix where it needs to go by breaking the process down into stages.

Volume balancing

Balancing the volume is the most common first step for a mix. We've already accomplished our initial volume settings in the *Time for action – separating audio streams* section. The idea here is to get all of our relative volumes.

The best way to attack the volumes of a mix is to find the most important element and start there. In the case of dance music, the kick is usually going to be the initial focus. We then add in the clap, hihats, and other percussion. Bass would be a good place to start next, then all of the harmonic and melodic sounds.

Once our relative volumes are in place, it's a good idea to be sure that there is still a little bit of range left on the master fader so that we can potentially add more effects. The idea behind this is called leaving **headroom**.

It's a very good idea to not let the Master FX channel go into the red very often.

Panning and stereo separation

The idea of panning is a way of getting sounds out of each other's way, and to create additional horizontal movement in a piece. In this particular song, there are two instruments that are panned hard left and hard right. The effect sounds like a call and response where the synth on the left is saying "Hello there", and the synth on the right answers "Hey yourself".

There are certain sounds that are good for panning, and others that don't do so well with panning.

Low frequency sound

Low frequency sounds should go right up the center. This essentially means that the energy in the right channel and left channel is equal. Low frequency sounds are things such as the kick, the bass, and low-pitched pads. Low frequency sounds don't pan very well because they are omnidirectional. That means that when we hear bass frequencies below a certain value, we can't really tell where they are coming from. This is why people can have a 5.1 surround audio system in a room, and the subwoofer can be placed in many locations without directionality being an issue.

In a mix, we want to keep things focused, for the most part. This is why anything below a frequency of 100 Hz should be right up the center.

Drums

Drums are commonly panned so that they represent either the perspective of listening to a drummer who is playing in front of us, or the perspective of what it sounds like to be sitting at the kit itself.

The common panning for drums is shown in the following diagram:

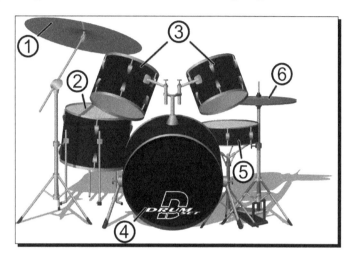

Image attributed to Wikicommons User:Pbroks13

The elements of the drum set are:

1. Ride Cymbal: Left 25 percent.
2. Floor Tom: Left 30-45 percent.
3. Hi and Mid Tom: Hi Tom Right 10-20 percent, Mid Tom – Left 10-20 percent.
4. Kick Drum: Center.
5. Snare Drum: Ever so slightly left or right.
6. HiHat: Right 15 percent.
7. Overhead Stereo Microphones (not pictured): Pan Left and Right 100 percent.

There are many elements in electronic drum kits that bend and even break these rules, but the idea of keeping that kick drum centered is a very, very good idea. Some folks will also keep the clap and snare right up the center as well.

Keyboards, leads, and pads

Keyboards, leads, and pads lend themselves to panning because they are capable of a very wide range of frequency. Higher frequencies are very directional and easy to pan:

Pad sounds are essentially beds of sound that act as a sort of canvas. We explored pads in *Chapter 5, Making Spaces: Creating the Emotional Landscape*. It is suggested to pan the sounds using modulation or LFOs. In the next chapter we will be exploring the use of modulation to make parameters change over time.

Keyboard sounds are usually sounds such as pianos, organs, clavinet, and more percussive instruments. These sounds can usually be spread wide in the stereo field. One trick is to have the sound track the pitch of the keyboard. Low sounds pan left, and high sounds pan right.

Lead sounds are usually monophonic, or have a very tight radius in the stereo field. They are made to stand out, and usually sit only slightly right or towards the left of the center. Using delay-based effects such as reverb and delay, a lead can sound spacious while keeping its place in the stereo field. We will explore this when we get to the delay-based effects stage of our mix.

Vocal samples

Vocal samples can live almost anywhere in the stereo field. Lead vocals should be placed in the center, but backing vocals or vocal doubles can be placed just about anywhere they can fit. A common technique is to have a vocal placed in the center of the mix, and the backing vocals are panned left and right, at a lower volume than the lead.

The vocals are going to be in the same space as the kick drum, bass, and snare. It's important to be sure that the lead vocal is loud enough that the other sounds don't end up drowning them!

Other panning considerations

In the beginning, popular music records were mono. This meant all of the sound you heard from a song was coming from one speaker. There was no stereo separation. The bands were recorded with few microphones, and the sound was mixed down to a single audio channel. My, how times have changed!

If you look at old stereo systems, you may notice that there is a knob or slider called "balance" instead of "pan". When records were first allowed to play two whole channels at once, bands and engineers experimented with different ways to use this novel new device. Some bands would record the entire rhythm section in channel 1, and the vocalists would be in channel 2. The listener would then have control of the mix of band to vocalist by using the balance knob.

Later on, producers and engineers began using the 2 channels as a left and right channel, and around 1958, records started coming out created to be listened to in stereo, as if the listener was at a concert. If you ever listen to these early recordings, it's fun to see just what the engineers were doing wrong, and which recordings sounded like they were heading in the right direction. Some engineers would think of the stereo field as a stage, which is fine. They would pan all of the instruments to their respective locations. A band usually looks something like this:

Image by Keith Crusher of RTFM Records

So we can see the people here... The singer is up front, the bass player to the left, the keyboards to the right, and the drummer behind.

This is fine for earlier recordings, but along came multi-track recording, pioneered by the likes of Les Paul, Sir George Martin, and Tom Dowd.

As artists, engineers, and producers were given more tracks, panning became a way to take all of the newly recorded material and give it a place to live. New problems arose from this technique, (material in one channel could cancel out the material in the other channel when listening through speakers if the engineer isn't careful), but overall the new invention was amazing for its time.

When you create songs in LMMS, keep in mind that after volume balancing, panning is a great way to even out the energy between the channels.

Dynamics

Dynamics are plugins that essentially work like an automated volume knob. When your material gets too loud, a dynamics plugin can take the sound down a bit in volume. One perk to doing this is that you suddenly have more headroom, and can pull the volume of your audio material up without clipping.

Dynamic range is an expression that's used to describe a song's average range of high volume to low volume. If a song has lower volume moments and higher volume moments, it is considered a song with a lot of dynamic range. The less peaks and valleys there are when it comes to volume, the less dynamic range material has.

In modern music production, there has been a strong trend towards material having almost no dynamic range at all. This usually happens as a result of treatment at the last stage of the song, when it is being prepared for duplication in a process called **mastering**. Usually, artists will listen to their beautiful mix, and then listen to another recording. The other recording sounds louder, and to most artists, louder is better. The artists will then obliterate the dynamic range of their recording to try to get their whole song to be as loud as the recording they heard. Using severe dynamics plugins, the mastering engineer will destroy the peaks and valleys altogether, making the whole song loud.

Now I realize that I am getting on a soapbox here, but if you are starting in production, you may be able to stem the tide of recordings that have no softer bits. I urge you to at least consider my plea for preserving dynamic range before I start explaining compression to you.

Compressors and limiters

The following image is of one of the most simple to operate and legendary **compressor/limiters** called *1176* by Universal Audio. It has four knobs and eight buttons. Let's talk about these to get ourselves familiar with compression:

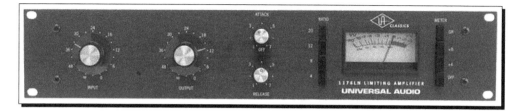

The Input knob is basically feeding the compressor audio energy, and as it is turned up, the compressor begins turning the volume down on the material. Essentially, once the audio energy reaches a threshold, the compressor hears it and says, "Well then, turn down!"

The Output knob is also called **make-up gain**. We used to have audio material that got loud in bits, but now it is softer when those loud bits come in. Why not increase the volume on the entire audio energy? This will accomplish a couple of things: The overall sound will be louder, and material that was previously too soft will now be audible.

The Attack knob is how fast the compressor is going to react once the audio energy goes past its threshold. A very short **attack** will turn the volume down quickly, and a slow attack will turn the volume down slowly. If we were using this compressor on something very snappy, like a snare, we would likely want a quick attack, since the snare is a quick, sharp sound. If we are compressing a kick, we may set the attack to be slower so that we get more of the initial attack, and the compressor pulls the volume down on the boom that comes immediately after. This way the kick can be snappy, and the booziness tamed a bit.

The Decay knob is how long the compressor takes to release its grasp of the audio energy. When the **decay** (release) is set to be short, the compressor lets go as soon as the audio energy goes below its threshold. If its long, then the compressor will keep the volume down for an extended time. If we had a bass guitar and wanted to add sustain, we would have a fairly long attack to let the initial picking of the bass come through, then a long release so that we could turn the whole bass guitar up and even out the pick of the bass to the sustain, giving it a nice warm sound.

The Ratio buttons are the "how much" area of the compressor. So let's say the compressor is set with a **ratio** of 4:1. This means that the audio energy beyond the threshold of the compressor is going to be one-forth of what it would be normally. That seems pretty extreme, right? Well, 4:1 compression is still considered to be on the lighter side. As we go up in value, the compressor ends up at 20:1. The sound is one-twentieth of the volume it would normally be past the compressor's threshold. This is what we call **'limiting'**.

Getting the Mix Together

Limiting is the "you cannot pass" of compression. Any audio going past the threshold of this setting is reduced to almost nothing. This can sound good to complex content, such as a drum mix, but must be carefully used.

The last four buttons on the right side of the 1176 are used to change the view of the meter.

Let's see how compression is applied in LMMS.

Time for action – using compression in LMMS

The various dynamics plugins in LMMS are very useful. We're going to start with compressing the kick using the Effects Chain on FX channel 1 of our mixer:

1. Locate the effects chain for FX channel 1 of the mixer in our project.
2. Choose **Add Effect**, and select **LADSPA Effect: Simple Compressor [Peak: Envelope Tracking]**.
3. Turn off all of the FX channels except for the kick:

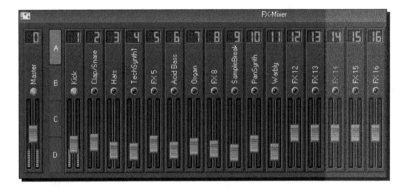

4. Now set the controls of the effect plugin, as shown in the following screenshot:

This effectively sets the compressor so it isn't compressing at all.

5. Turn **Compression Ratio** to the far right. This will make the compressor act as a limiter.

6. Listen carefully with the ratio turned to value **9**. Do not alter any more settings.

7. Now start pulling the threshold down by turning the threshold knob to the left slowly. The sound energy will begin passing the compressor's threshold, and you will hear the compression start to kick in. Move the knob to the far left, far right, then settle on this setting: **.24**.

8. Now we can hear that the kick is obviously being compressed. Start turning the attack knob up and down to hear its effect.

9. Turn the decay knob up and down to hear its effect.

10. Now turn the attack and decay knobs to this setting and listen:

11. Listen carefully to the kick.

12. Now listen with the effect turned on, and off. Use either the On/Off button of the effects chain, or simply turn only the compressor effect off:

13. Listen carefully. Can you hear the difference? The kick sounds harder and less boomy with the compressor on.

14. Now adjust your attack and decay to the following settings:

15. Listen to the kick now.

16. Adding more attack time is letting in more of the booming after the initial attack.

What just happened?

Using a dynamics plugin, we shaped the amplitude of a kick drum in our project.

Compression is supposed to be a subtle art. Most engineers who use compressors are trying to compress the signal so that nobody knows there is compression on it.

In dance music, compression is often used as a special effect. Tracks such as the kick and bass are over-compressed as a special effect to give a pumping effect to the low end of a project.

Using compression both subtly and intensely are both good ways to use compression. The trick is to be deliberate, and know when and when not to use compression.

On material that doesn't peak very much, compression is usually unnecessary. This would be ambient sounds, and keyboards.

Drums and bass can be highly transient. This means that there is a big difference between the attack of the note and the sustained portion of the note played. For example, a snare drum hit looks like this before compression:

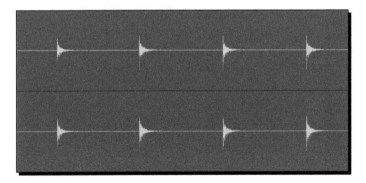

Now, after compression using a fast attack and slow release:

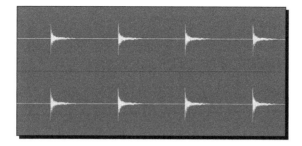

Note how much longer the tail is on this snare? It will sustain longer, and the difference between the decay of the snare and the attack in volume is more similar.

Now check this out:

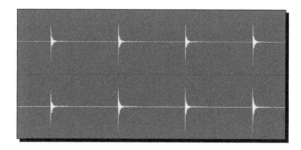

We have a radically different effect. Now we have a slow attack and fast release, which gives us the initial pop of the snare, but then the compressor backs off suddenly, so that the snare decays quickly like it did before processing.

If you are working with a vocalist that gets really loud, then really soft without warning, it may be a good idea to compress them. Be very mindful of your attack and release settings, though. You don't want them to sound crushed.

Work with varying compression ratios for different effects, and start learning compression by overusing the plugin first with radical settings, then back off and get more subtle with it. You are going to need to train your ears to hear the differences in amplitude over time.

Getting the Mix Together

Filtering

You've used a filter before, and maybe not even known it.

The filter pictured below is a hardware version of a studio-grade audio filter:

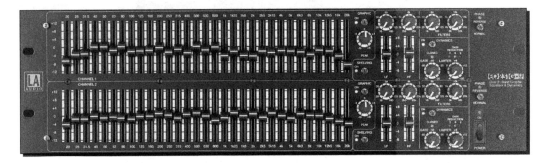

Here's another example of a filter:

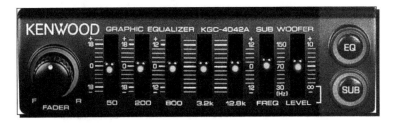

Yes, that's a car stereo equalizer. Do you see a similarity between the studio filter and the car stereo? That's right; both of them have the ability to boost or cut amplitude of certain frequency bands of sound.

Most people like to hop in their car, turn the stereo on, and turn up the bass and treble. Those are the two widest bands available in car stereos. When you boost or cut the low end on a car stereo, the filter is basically saying "turn the volume up or down, below the frequency of 200 Hz". On the high end, or treble, the filter is set to cut or boost above, say, 8 K. This all depends on the manufacturer, of course.

Filters were originally used to help balance out the energy of the various frequency bands. Maybe your music is weak in the low end; just boost the lows and your music sounds correct! Maybe the vocals in a song are a little harsh; try taking the mid-range down a bit!

This is called the process of **Equalization (EQ)**.

After adjusting the volume, panning, and dynamics of our mix, EQ is the next logical step. EQ is how we can keep elements with similar frequencies from stepping on each other's toes, and change the timbre of different elements.

Chapter 10

Time for action – using EQ

We are going to use EQ to try and make our sound sample a bit sweeter:

1. Turn the FX channel for the **SampleBreak** on, and turn the **Kick FX Channel** off.
2. Listen to **Sample Break**.
3. On the **Sample Break FX Channel**, add this EQ: **LADSPA Effect: C* Eq2x2 – stereo 10-band equalizer**
4. Open the Control Panel. You will see rows of knobs:

5. Press play in the Song Editor.
6. While the **SampleBreak** is playing, turn each knob of the plugin controls. Listen to how it changes the timbre of the sound.
7. Use the setting, shown in the following screenshot, for the **Eq2x2**:

8. Turn the plugin on and off while the song is playing to get an idea of how the EQ is affecting the sound of the **SampleBreak**.

9. Now turn the other channels in the FX Mixer on and off to get an idea of how the **SampleBreak** fits with the rest of the mix.

10. Make your own adjustments to the EQ settings, and turn the rest of the FX channels on in the mixer.

What just happened?

We just used equalization to help shape the timbre of a sound.

Using EQ creatively is a way to add subtle colors to a mix, as well as solve potential problems. EQ allows an engineer to create sonic spaces for each element of a song, so that instruments in different frequency ranges can be heard clearly.

One of the reasons that we do volume changes before we mess with EQ is to try and solve issues by first simply creating volume differences between material. We shouldn't reflexively grab for dynamics plugins or EQ to try and solve problems, because if there is too much EQ going on in a project, it can sometimes make the overall material sound weak, or muddy.

A good general rule for EQ is to first try and decrease the energy of frequency ranges that cause issues, instead of boosting the energy to try and overcompensate for those frequency ranges. Once the **carving** is done, apply subtle boosts to get the sound where it needs to be.

Types of equalizations

Let's explore some of the most common types of EQ that we use. EQ types are usually defined by the range where they are most effective.

Shelf EQ

Shelf EQ is what is most often found in car stereos. When we see an EQ that simply adjusts **Bass** or **Treble**, the EQ is essentially indicating that a frequency range is going to be boosted or cut below or above a certain point. On professional EQ plugins, this point is defined. On car stereos, the manufacturers will decide upon a certain range that they think sounds best on the widest range of material.

Here is a photo of a shelf type EQ that has a cut at 200 Hz, and a boost just above 1000 Hz:

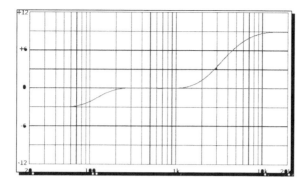

Low and high pass EQ

Low pass and high pass EQ types are also often referred to conversely as **high cut** and **low cut** filters. These types of filtering are most commonly used in synthesizers that have integrated filters. The point at which the filtering begins is called the **cutoff**.

There is a phenomenon that happens when a filter is fed back into itself so that it begins to resonate at the cutoff point. The point at which this happens, and the ensuing bump in audio energy is called **resonance**.

The rate at which frequencies are attenuated over time is called the **slope**. The slope is usually expressed in 6 dB increments. These increments are also frequently called **poles**. This is due to the old days where you could look at a hardware EQ and count the resistors and capacitors used for every 6 dB of attenuation over time. One capacitor and one resistor meant you'd have 6 dB of attenuation over an octave. Two capacitors and two resistors would be a 2-pole filter. As the capacitors looked like little poles, that's where 2-pole, 4-pole, and names like these came from.

Here's a visual representation of a low pass filter:

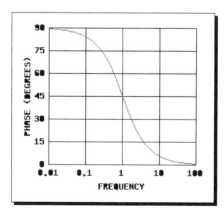

And, here's a visual representation of a high pass filter:

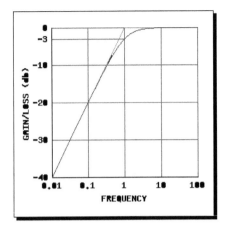

These filters are very helpful in mixing. Low pass filters can be used to get rid of high frequency noise, and help define bass frequencies.

High pass filters can be used to keep instruments from muddying the low end of a song, and taking out low frequency hum resulting from bad power, where 60 Hz hum is introduced into a signal from badly grounded power outlets in a building.

Low pass filters sound very cool when you add a bit of resonance to a low pass filter and turn the cutoff knob. This causes a very audible emphasis where the cutoff is, and gives a nice sweeping sound to any synths that it is applied to. We will explore this in the next chapter when we talk a bit about programming synthesizers.

Parametric EQ

Parametric EQ allows us to sweep through the entire frequency range of an audio signal, pinpoint an area we wish to boost or cut, and decide how many frequencies around that area we would like to affect as well.

Parametric EQ is the most flexible type of EQ. The area around the frequency that we affect can be widened or focused depending on the **Q (quality)** setting, or as it is called **Bandwidth** in some filters.

A technique that some engineers use parametric EQ for is called "seek and destroy" EQ. If there is a problem area in a piece of audio, you boost the amplitude of a frequency in an EQ that sounds close to the offending frequency, and hunt around with the frequency knob until you hear the offending frequency get a whole lot worse. When it sounds totally awful, you then leave the frequency knob alone, and turn the amplitude knob down until the sound is pleasant again.

Parametric EQ leaves alone the frequencies outside of its range. It's great for surgical EQ that is capable of great precision. Here's what a parametric EQ curve looks like:

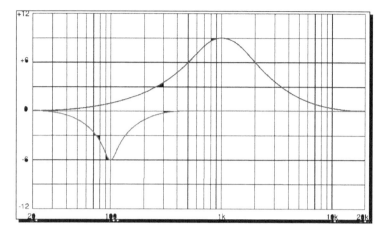

Band pass EQ

Band pass EQ is a combination of a low and high pass EQ that essentially limits the entire frequency bandwidth of our audio, so that only a narrow sliver of audio makes it through. Band pass EQ is great for creating telephone-like effects on a voice, or making a wheezy, thin sounding synth. A bandpass EQ's frequency spectrum looks like the following (note the different Q settings, and how they change the bandwidth of the EQ):

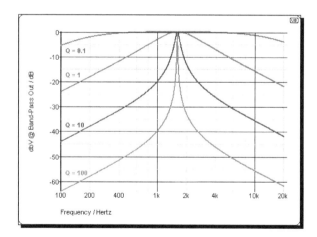

When using a filter to cut instead of pass a select number of frequencies in a small range, the term is called **notch filtering**.

These are the major types of filters you will find in just about any mixing situation. Learn to use them well, and your mix will sound very clear and pleasant. Just be mindful not to overdo it!

Getting the Mix Together

Delay-based plugins

We explored reverb and delay in *Chapter 5, Making Spaces: Creating the Emotional Landscape*, but it's time for a quick refresher.

Delay-based effects are effects that give the impression of a sound bouncing around in our ears. Delay was one of the first special effects used in music production. It was originally created by arcane techniques like using a tape machine that had a gap between the record and play to create a short delay à la Elvis. Rooms were built of reflective materials so that engineers could play their music into the room and re-record the sound to get the source content to sound like it was recorded in a spacious room, even though it was not.

Delay is now mostly digital. There are simple delays, which repeat the same sound back in iterations that go down in volume over time; and reverbs, which have a short delay component that emulates the first couple of reflections in a room, and a more diffuse, complex delay to emulate the dispersion of sound over time in a room.

Delay-based effects are extremely helpful for adding depth to a song. Depth is perceived as the sounds taking place in a virtual room. The instruments are placed in such a way that the listener will feel that they are in a room with the artists and their band.

When delay is used creatively, spaces can be made that don't happen in the real world. The amount of control that an engineer can have over the properties of the reverb and delays is pretty awesome. At this stage of the mix, it is important to be choosy about which delays and reverbs are going to be used in our song. Delay and reverb are providing the space that our music is playing in.

Time for action – exploring echo and simple delays

LMMS has a lot of delays and reverbs, but the categories can be broken down so that they are easier to understand:

1. Mute all FX channels in the **Mixer** except for **TechSynth1**.

2. Go to the effects chain for **TechSynth1**, and click on **Add Effect**.

3. Select **LADSPA Echo Delay Line (Maximum Delay 5s)**.

    This is a very simple delay, called an **echo**. Delays like this do not incorporate reverb. They simply repeat whatever signal they receive. Adjust the delay knob to get a longer or shorter delay. Use the **Dry/Wet Balance** knob to adjust the level of the delay to the original signal. Play around with these settings and listen to the result.

4. Click on the **Link Channels** button to make **Channel 1** and **Channel 2** independent of each other.

5. Now set **Channel 1** to 2550 ms and **Channel 2** to 800 ms:

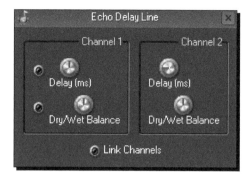

6. Now listen to this simple echo. It should sound as if the sound is bouncing from the left to the right speaker.

7. Now go back to the effects chain and disable the echo.

8. Add the **LADSPA Effect: TAP Stereo Echo** effect.

   This will bring up the following controls:

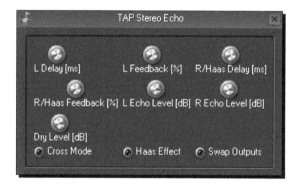

9. Adjust the **L Delay** and **R/Haas Delay** settings. Adjust **L Feedback** and **R/Haas Feedback** to change the amount of delay over time. Adjust the L and R echo levels. Listen to the results.

10. Click on the **Swap Outputs** button. That will switch outputs.

11. Now turn on **Cross Mode**.

12. Turn on **Haas Effect**.

13. Use the settings shown in the following screenshot:

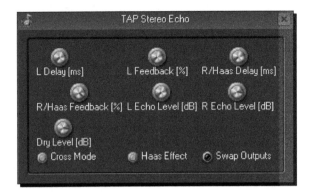

14. Listen to the effect.

15. Change the **R/Haas Delay** knob and listen to the effect.

What just happened?

We introduced feedback into our delay, causing a delay over time that gradually dies out. We also used the **Hass effect**.

The Haas effect

The Haas effect is a great cheat for those who would like to take a mono sound and spread it to the left and right channels of a mix, without the listener being aware that the stereo image is being created from a mono source.

In 1949, Helmut Haas was very interested to know how the human auditory system perceived localization of sound. To simplify, he wanted to learn how humans hear where sounds are in space. He conducted an experiment where he had a single human voice played through two speakers that were equal distances from a listener's head. He then started delaying the signal to one of the speakers by about 12 ms. The listener suddenly heard what sounded like a stereo signal. The same sound was playing through both speakers, but the listener assumed that the sound was recorded in stereo. Once the signal was delayed by about 30 ms, the effect vanished, and the signal sounded more like a stereo delay.

This effect is great for mono distorted guitars that want to be more stereo, or laser-beam, boy band vocals. I hear this effect all of the time on the radio as a kind of sheen that is applied to certain instruments in pop music to give the impression of a wider sound.

The **TAP Stereo Echo's Cross** and **Haas** settings take one of the channels and turn it off. The remaining channel is then subjected to the Haas effect.

Time for action – exploring Freeverb

Reverb is nothing more than a fancy delay, but it's important for us to understand and hear the properties of reverb and how it is different from simple delays:

1. Disable all other plugins on the effects chain for **TechSynth1**.
2. Add the **Freeverb (Version 3)** effect.
3. Now open the controls:

4. Turn the **Wet Level** knob up about halfway.
5. Adjust the **Room Size** knob and listen to the resulting effect by hitting play in the song editor.
6. Adjust the width to create a wider stereo image, and listen to the effect.
7. Turn on the Freeze Mode. Listen to the effect.
8. Turn Freeze Mode off, and adjust the damping knob. Listen to the effect the damping has on the reverb.

What just happened?

Freeverb is a reverb plugin. It is nothing more, and nothing less. It does have an interesting freeze function that takes a snapshot of the reverb as it is happening, and loops it out so that it never decays. This can be really fun with transitions! The knob that we haven't played with yet in our delays is the **damping** parameter.

Damping is what happens to sound as it travels through air.

Believe it or not, air isn't the best thing for sound to travel through. Water is better. Crazy, huh?

When sound travels through air, higher frequencies are gradually attenuated. Lower frequency waves travel better. That's why if you hear shrieks of kids on a playground, it doesn't hurt as much when you are across the street as it does when you are in the middle of them. Sure, volume goes down over distance as well, but we must remember that higher frequencies are lost in air over distance.

If you are ever in a pool, snap your fingers underwater, or hit two pieces of metal together. You'll be amazed at how clear the sound is. This is because there are more molecules closer together for the sound waves to excite. Interesting, huh? Damping is a part of many plugins, and if you want to imply distance in your delays or reverbs, use damping to emulate distance from the source of the sound.

Plates, springs, and convolution

Now that we've discussed damping in reverb, it's time to talk about how people made cheap reverbs back in the day when reverb was pretty hard to record and control.

We've discussed how engineers strived for great reverbs by building rooms and recording in great halls. Reverb chambers were sought out by high end producers making music for triple-A artists to create huge sounds. Insecure artists like nothing better than a slathering of reverb on their voice.

Other engineers were trying to find ways of getting reverb from unique sources, and were also trying to save space. Not everyone has the real estate for a concrete room dedicated to reverb in their house.

Some crafty engineers started coming up with space and pocketbook saving reverb techniques using surfaces that naturally reverberated and got nice, compact reverb devices.

Plate reverbs

Plate reverbs are large sheets of metal that have a transducer vibrating them, and some kind of contact mic or regular condenser mic recording them. Here's what a plate reverb looks like:

Image by sknote Software Sound Synthesis Company

Yes, this was the length that some people would go to get good reverb tone from a relatively smaller footprint. The large sheet is suspended, as you see, and the transducer, which is not unlike a small speaker, is placed near the center of the plate. Sound would be sent from the mix engineer to the plate, and the reverberated signal would come back through the mixer to be added to the original sound. Although smaller than an echo chamber, you weren't going to haul this kind of plate reverb around with you if you could help it!

Spring reverbs

Have you ever played with a slinky? It's a popular children's toy that is nothing more than a loose spring coil. When I was a child, I noticed that if I hung a slinky from a doorknob and played my trumpet at it, the slinky would reverberate for a little while after I played. That's essentially what a spring reverb is. A transducer plays at one end of a wound spring, and the spring would reverberate. The Hammond Company was the first to include this kind of reverb into their organs, and it was wildly popular. Remember how large that plate reverb was? Well here's how small a spring reverb can be:

Yes! A reverb that you can almost carry with one hand! This was revolutionary, and allowed amplifier manufacturers to incorporate reverb into their amps for guitars, keyboards, and anything else the travelling musician desired. Spring reverbs were also tremendous fun to kick around, and I mean that literally. The spring would knock around inside its casing, and you would get a crashing, reverberant sound.

Many vintage reverb plugins now include this type of reverb as an emulation.

Vintage reverb sounds have a lot of character, and can sound very interesting when used in the context of dance music or any other kind of electronic music. There are websites where enthusiasts have created their own VST plugins for free download to those that want to explore these and other vintage reverbs.

Time for action – exploring vintage reverb

For this section, we're going to use an emulation of a plate reverb in LMMS:

1. Disable the plugins that are on the effects chain for **TechSynth1**.

2. Click on **Add Effect** and select **C*Plate2x2 – Versatile plate reverb, stereo inputs**.
   The following controls will pop up:

3. Adjust the **bandwidth** knob to control how many frequencies are going to be reverberated. Listen to the result.

4. Adjust the **tail** to create a longer or shorter reverb. Listen to the result with the bandwidth set about halfway up.

5. Use **blend** to adjust the amount of dry to reverberated signal. Listen to the result.

6. Adjust **damping** to emulate how many high frequencies will be attenuated. Listen to the result.

What just happened?

We just had listened to the plate reverb included in the LADSPA plugin suite included with LMMS.

The plate reverb emulation included with LMMS is a pretty wonderful sound. Reverbs like this work very well on vocals and realistic instruments, but I find myself using plate reverbs on more and more material as time goes on. One artist that I really enjoy for his use of vintage reverbs is Squarepusher. The cover for his album, *Music is Rotted One Note*, even features one of his favorite reverbs—a small plate reverb, with the album title and track list written on the plate reverb for a nice touch.

Automation

Okay, so we've balanced our volumes, panned our instruments in the stereo field, added compression and EQ, and applied our delays and reverbs. Now we can add life to the mix.

In *Chapter 9, Gluing the Arrangement Together*, we talked about the importance of using automation in transitions. The application of automation is a way to feature different aspects of the mix at different times to feature different elements. Some sounds can be slowly faded out while other sounds take over, and the arrangement can be highlighted, using automation on plugins, volume, and panning. As we have explored how to create automation, I would like to pose a challenge!

Have a go hero!

Now that we have the recipe for mixing success, it's time to have a go for it!

- Finish the arrangement of the song included with this chapter
- Use subtractive arranging to lay the song out for at least three minutes
- Add at least two additional elements to the song
- Assign those new elements to two open FX channels
- Follow the mixing stages laid out in this chapter to get the mix for the entire song
- Use compression on at least one track
- Use EQ on at least one track
- Use at least two reverbs and one delay
- Place a plugin on an instrument as well as the FX mixer.
- Use automation for transitions, buildups and breakdowns of elements of the song
- Use automation in mixing to create high points and low points in the mix

Good luck!

Exporting the mix

Welcome back!

Now that we have a song that's pretty much ready for consumption, it's time for the final stage of mixing, and that's exporting the pre-master for mastering.

Here's what that means, exactly:

When you finish your mix, make sure that the levels at the Master FX channel aren't clipping. If the Master FX is clipping, but only once in a while, (and I mean very, very rarely), you can use a built-in limiter on the effects chain to simply keep the "occasional" peaks from clipping the mix. I would suggest placing **Fast Lookahead limiter** on the Master.

This plugin is interesting... Is it looking into the future?

No, not really.

Fast lookahead means that the plugin actually delays the signal. The signal that comes into the plugin is analyzed, and the plugin decides what kind of attack is going to be used to make the limiter sound smoother. The delayed signal is then the result, which we hear. It's is okay to do this at the end of our mixing process. Having delayed tracks on FX channels could cause big problems.

The following screenshot shows the plugin controls:

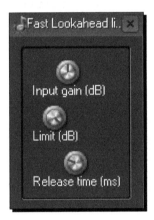

Now that's what I call simple.

We can attenuate the signal before it gets limited, decide how much limiting should be applied, and then decide on a nice release amount to smooth the plugin's effect.

> This is only to try and limit the occasional peak. Don't get greedy and start limiting the heck out of the track. You are just shooting yourself in the foot. If this were my mix, I might even bring the volume down a couple more dB to allow room for a mastering engineer, (more on that in a minute). For now, this is for our listening pleasure, so we can let it peak ever so slightly.

Now, let's export! Go to the **Project** menu and select **Export**, or use the *Control + E* key command.

When exporting, you'll get the following screen:

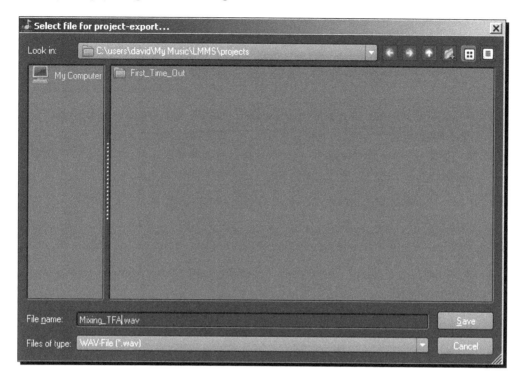

Let's name the song `Mixing_TFA.wav`.

There are two file types to choose from in this screen—WAV and Ogg Vorbis.

Ogg files are compressed to take up less room. This is achieved by removing frequency bands from the sound that our ears cannot perceive. This works pretty well for files that are going to be listened to on an iPod or computer, but to get the highest quality sound, I would suggest using an uncompressed PCM WAV file.

Now our song is bounced! Open it in the music listening software of your choice and listen for potential mix changes we may want to perform before mastering.

Mastering

Mastering is the final stage of a song before it is released out into the world. Essentially the two track mix is given some last bits of sweetening and timbre control so that the song will play well on any system it is played on. I highly recommend finding a local mastering engineer who has experience in mastering to take the song to it's final stage of completion for two reasons:

- When you've spent all your time producing and mixing a song, it can be hard to have an objective view of what needs to be done in mastering
- It's good to have the master completed on a system that is made specifically for mastering by a person whose profession is mastering

There are other reasons too, but the ones mentioned above are the main reasons.

If you'd like to master your own track, I would suggest opening the audio file in **Audacity** and applying effects there for the final stage. The chain of plugins could go something like this:

- Basic light dynamics processing with a compressor to take out offensive peaks in the material.
- Very light parametric EQ to adjust the timbre of the entire song. Frequency ranges to be mindful of 200-300 Hz, 40-80 Hz, 1500-3000 Hz, and 8000-12,000 Hz.
- Digital limiter with look-ahead processing.

If you decide to master your own material, maybe for your listening pleasure, or to save budget, make sure to play other songs and reference them. Listen to see if your song sounds good in cars, headphones, and speakers similarly to how the reference songs play. Choose material that is similar to yours. Having reference songs that sound like they are in the same family as your music helps to ensure that your audience is going to feel good when your song comes on in the middle of a playlist.

Pop quiz

1. What is mixing?
    a. It is the art of balancing volume, stereo pan, dynamics, timbre, and depth to allow all of the elements of a song to remain clearly defined.
    b. It is the process of rearranging elements of a song into a new version.
    c. It is balancing the volumes of all the different elements in a track.

2. What is clipping?
    a. It is trimming the length of an audio file.
    b. It is when the amplitude of a signal is louder than the audio system permits.
    c. It is shortening the length of a song.

3. What is a good workflow for mixing?
    a. It is to balance volume of one instrument at a time, but it doesn't matter which instrument you start with.
    b. It is to balance the following, in order: panning, dynamics, filtering, delays, and finally, volume.
    c. It is to balance the following, in order: volume, panning, dynamics, filtering, and delay-based plugins.

4. What is the threshold setting of a compressor?
    a. It is the amplitude level that a compressor will stop compressing at.
    b. It tells you how much gain the compressor will add.
    c. It is the amplitude level that a compressor will begin compressing at.

5. What is a high-pass filter?
    a. It rolls off frequencies below its cutoff point.
    b. It rolls off frequencies above its cutoff point.
    c. It boosts frequencies within a specific range.

6. Where should a kick drum be panned?
    a. Most commonly panned to the center.
    b. Usually panned slightly left.
    c. Should be doubled and panned hard right and left.

7. Where are the two locations you can place an effect?
    a. On the main output channel or directly on an instrument.
    b. Directly on an instrument.
    c. On an instrument, or on an FX channel in the mixer.

8. In which medium does sound travel better:
    a. Air.
    b. Water.

9. What's the difference between an Ogg Vorbis file and a PCM audio file?

   a. An Ogg Vorbis file is compressed. A PCM audio file is the highest quality audio file that can be exported.

   b. A PCM audio file is compressed. An Ogg Vorbis file is the highest quality audio file that can be exported.

   c. An Ogg Vorbis file is normalized. A PCM file is not normalized.

10. What is the purpose of mastering?

    a. Mastering is simply the process of making a song loud enough for radio.

    b. Mastering is the process of taking a two-channel audio file and processing it so that its mix translates well no matter what it's played on.

    c. Mastering is just about evening levels between songs.

Summary

Mixing is something that gets better and better every time it's done. Like a chef cooking a signature dish, the more you mix, the better you get. It's important to mix all kinds of music if you can, but remain focused on the style that you resonate with most. You've been listening to music that inspires you, so be sure that when you are mixing, the elements that excite you in other music are there in your mix to inspire you as well. Try hard to be very deliberate about the changes you make in the mix. Listen closely to EQ and compression settings so that you are mixing with your ears and not your eyes. Many people can get stuck in a rut where they mix in such a way that they are boosting levels, adjusting EQ, and compressing everything in sight just because they can. Make decisions because they are the right things to do. Play around with settings to experiment, but at the end of the day compare your mixes to mixes of those that you admire. The better your music sounds when played alongside their music, the closer you are to your goal of having an awesome mix.

In the next chapter, we'll be getting into some of the more geeky settings and programming techniques that can help you be deliberate in your programming of instruments as well!

11
Getting into Instruments

We've been through a lot in this book, and had a good bird's eye view of how to realize an electronic music production. In this chapter, we're going to learn the language of instruments and how to bend them to our will using synthesis techniques. Having the ability to deliberately create a new instrument setting is a cool way to differentiate your sound from others, whether it's with pads, lead sounds, or drum tones.

In this chapter we will learn:

- The language of synthesis
- The different types of instruments included in LMMS
- How to use modulation
- How to save and retrieve preset settings
- How to use Chords and Arpeggios

The instruments of LMMS

In LMMS, we can load audio samples into our session, but the main ingredients of our project will be software instruments, which I will occasionally be calling **synths**, which is shorthand for synthesizer (except for the Audio File Player; I will explain why later).

Getting into Instruments

The LMMS instruments all have very similar layouts, and they also each have their individual personalities. Some instruments are better at creating pads, some are better for leads, some emulate strings, and some emulate old computer chip synthesizers from ancient computers. We're going to first explain the language of synthesis so that we have a good foundation for programming instruments, then we will explore the differences between the instruments built into LMMS.

The language of synthesis

Most software-based instruments that we encounter in the world speak a similar language that has been developed for over decades. To break things down, we are going to learn the following:

- The main parts of an instrument
- The parameters that can be changed on each section
- How to change parameters over time using modulation techniques

The main parts of an instrument

To learn how to program a synthesizer, we are going to use the **Triple Oscillator** synth. Create a new project, and drag a **Triple Oscillator** instrument from the sidebar to the song editor:

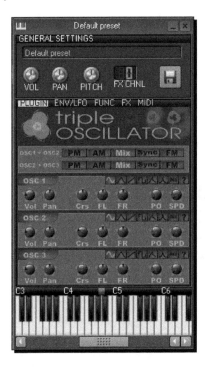

Most instruments will have three main sections—the Oscillator section, the Filter section, and the Amplifier section. Let's explore them, starting with the Oscillator section.

The Oscillator section

When we first open the **Triple Oscillator** instrument up, we are presented with the oscillator section. The oscillator section is simply the part of the instrument that is generating sound. In an instrument like the **Triple Oscillator** synth, we have the ability to create three different sounds at once.

On most instruments, the oscillator section has the ability to create several different kinds of sound waves. The most common waves produced are:

- Sine waves
- Triangle waves
- Sawtooth waves
- Square waves
- Noise

If the instrument is more complex, then it can also create other waves, but these basic waves are the most common building blocks of synthesis.

Sine waves

Long ago, a fella named Jean Baptiste Joseph Fourier came up with a theory that all complex waves can be broken down to fundamental components. The building blocks of these complex waves are **sine waves**:

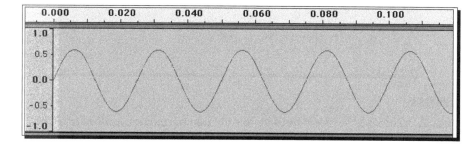

Sine waves are the purest tone you can get. It sounds a lot like someone whistling. A sine wave can be used with other sine waves to create more complex waves used in synthesis. When we start stacking sine waves on top of each other, we start to get really rich sounds. No other wave is like a sine wave. Many sine waves playing together can theoretically create any more complex wave possible. They are truly the building blocks of sound.

Figuring out the harmonic series

The waves that we are going to explore after sine waves are all going to contain multiple harmonics. Think of harmonics as being additional sine waves that are playing at specific frequencies. What defines the fundamental frequency is simply the loudest sine wave. After that, the sine waves happen at predictable frequency intervals to create sawtooth, square, and triangle waves.

This series of frequencies can be predicted easily by taking a sine wave's frequency, say 100 Hz, and multiplying it by 2, 3, 4, 5, 6, 7, and so on. The resulting frequencies would be:

- Fundamental, or 1st Harmonic: 100 Hz
- 2nd Harmonic: 200 Hz
- 3rd Harmonic: 300 Hz
- 4th Harmonic: 400 Hz
- 5th Harmonic: 500 Hz

The harmonics will gradually decrease in volume as they reach higher and higher.

Sawtooth waves

Sawtooth waves are very strong, buzzy sounds. They also happen to contain the entire harmonic series. Having all of those frequencies makes these waves very rich, loud, and proud. Sawtooth waves are used quite a bit to make everything from string sounds to thick bass sounds:

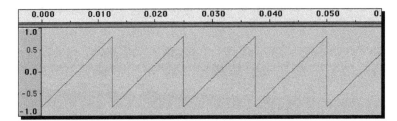

Square waves

Square waves occur when we have nothing but the odd harmonics, and we leave out the even harmonics:

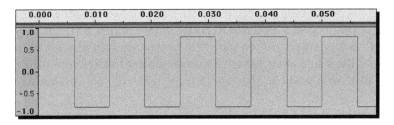

These waves sound a bit-like the hollow pure tone of a clarinet. Square waves are extremely popular for bass lines in dance music. A combination of square waves can sound very pure, but still aggressive because they still have harmonic content.

Triangle waves

Triangle waves are related to square waves. These waves are created by taking the odd harmonics of the harmonic series, and gently rolling off a more of the high frequencies:

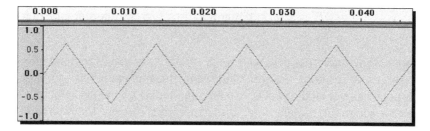

This results in a tone that sounds remarkably similar to a sine wave, but there is some harmonic content, so triangle waves are richer because of it. These waves are mellow and pleasant, rather flute-like.

Noise

Now... why noise?

Well, noise can be fashioned into all kinds of things. We get noise by having all frequencies that we can possibly get, with randomized volumes. The waveform looks totally random as well:

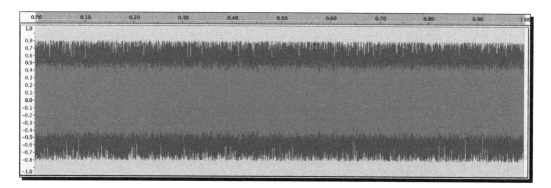

Noise can be filtered and mangled to create everything from bass drums and snares to wind sounds. It can be used to make an instrument sound aged. It can be used to create giant drops in the middle of a song. We will explore the possibilities of the noise generator when we talk about filtering.

Other waves

In the **Triple Oscillator** instrument, there are some other waves that can be used. One wave is a variation on a sawtooth wave that is meant to emulate a popular synthesizer by the Moog company. Another wave called **exponential** has a slightly different look to it than a sawtooth wave.

Most instruments you find these days will create variations of waves that are more complex than the essentials we see here. We aren't limited by the analog physical world, so we can theoretically get whatever kind of wave we want, depending on the instrument. We will always have sine, sawtooth, triangle, and noise generators, though. They still remain the building blocks of synthesis.

Parameters of the Oscillator section

Now, when we say **parameters** we should be thinking, "what knobs can I turn, and what do those knobs do in this section of my instrument?" In the case of the oscillator section, instruments will give the following parameter options:

- Type of wave produced
- Pitch
- Wave offset

Now in this particular instrument, the **Triple Oscillator**, we get a couple of additional parameters:

- Phase Offset
- Phase Detune
- Volume
- Pan

Although you can find volume on many other instruments, the ability to adjust panning and make phase detuning adjustments is less common.

Offsetting **phase** simply means that instead of starting the wave from the 0 amplitude part of its cycle, the wave starts at a different point in the wave's cycle. The waveform doesn't clip or anything because the end of the cycle still matches the amplitude of the beginning of the cycle. We will explore these parameters when we explore the oscillator area in our next exercise.

Chapter 11

Time for action – exploring oscillators

Let's have a listen to the different waves our instrument can create, and adjust some of the parameters of the oscillator section:

1. Turn the volume down on oscillator 2 and 3:

   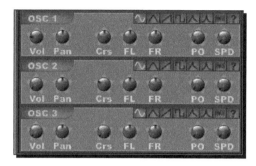

2. Now hit the *Y* key on your computer keyboard. You should hear the instrument play the note value of A. This oscillator is playing a sine wave.

3. Select the Sawtooth wave in oscillator 1:

4. Hit the *Y* key on your computer keyboard again. Listen to the difference some harmonics make!

5. Now select the Square wave:

6. Hit *Y* again on the computer keyboard, and listen to the Square wave.

7. Choose the Triangle wave:

[299]

Getting into Instruments

8. Hit Y on the computer keyboard and listen. Compare this wave to the Sine wave, and the Square wave. The Triangle wave sounds like it is somewhere in-between.

9. Choose the noise oscillator. Be sure your volume is down before listening to the noise:

10. The last three remaining waves were created specifically for this synth. There is another sawtooth-like wave, an exponential wave, and a curious wave that looks like a question mark. Mouse over the waves to get their descriptions.

11. When you mouse over the question mark, you are told that you can input a user-defined wave. These waves can be created in another program as an audio file and imported.

12. Now double-click on the question mark. You'll get a dialog box, as shown in the following screenshot:

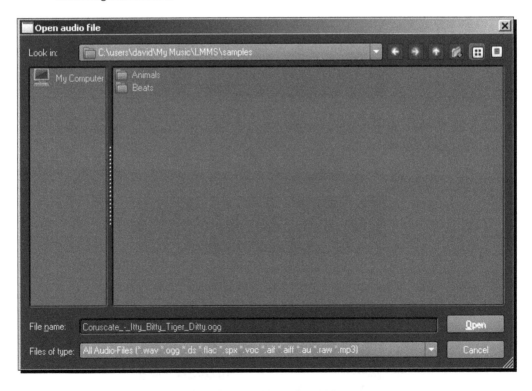

13. This is where you can import an audio file that will be used as an oscillator. Keep in mind that the audio file would have to be a single cycle of a wave; a single peak and trough. You would have to use another program to do this, so we'll come back to this later.

14. Now go to this section, press Y, and adjust the parameter called **FL**, as shown in the following screenshot. Press Y again when you are done:

15. Listen to the result, then adjust the knob labeled **Crs**. This stands for Coarse **Tuning**.

16. Adjust **PO (Phase Offset)**, and **SPD (Stereo Phase Detune)**

17. Listen to these parameters. **Crs** obviously tunes the entire oscillator, while **FL** and **FR** adjust the fine pitch of the right or left side alone.

18. Listen to the effect of **PO** and **SPD**.

19. **PO** appears to do nothing. **SPD** is shifting the phase between the left and right side, so that when one wave is travelling down, the other is going up, and vice versa.

What just happened?

We've explored the sounds of the different waves we can use in the **Triple Oscillator** instrument, and then adjusted various parameters related to the oscillator.

These waves are certainly the building blocks of synthesis. The **Triple Oscillator** synth has some great additional parameters besides the simple ones, but the basics are still there—type of wave, tuning, and phase offset.

Why didn't phase offset seem to do anything? Well, this parameter takes effect when we combine more than one oscillator together.

Have a go hero

Now that we've explored a single oscillator, it's time to mix it up! Take a moment to do the following:

- Listen to Oscillator 2 and 3.
- Turn the volume up equally on each oscillator and listen to different combinations of waves from different oscillators.

Getting into Instruments

- Change the coarse tuning on oscillator 2 and 3, and adjust the volume on each oscillator to achieve more harmonic content.
- With all three oscillators set to sawtooth waves, use the phase offset parameters on each oscillator and listen to the sound. The pitch will not change, but listen to the subtle shift when the phase is adjusted.

Types of synthesis

Check out the buttons shown in the following screenshot:

What do they mean? Well, they are different ways in which we can make these waves relate to each other. These relationships are different forms of synthesis—ways to combine different waves in interesting ways.

Mix

Mixing waves together is the oldest and arguably most powerful form of synthesis. The earliest synthesizer ever made was arguably this:

The pipe organ

Pipe organs work by taking different waves that are being created by the pipes, and mixing them together. See all those white knobs in the photo? Those are called **stops**, and they control the different mixes of waves coming from the pipe organ.

Remember earlier when we said that Fourier had developed a way to break down any complex wave into sine waves? Well, this beast did the opposite. By combining pure tones created by the pipes, the organist could make the organ sound like reed instruments; make it sound brassy, or very mild and flute-like. Any time we mix waves together with volume, we are performing **additive synthesis**. It is simple, extremely powerful, but hard to achieve great sounds. See how big that organ is? Kinda hard to move around, right? In the digital synthesis world, additive synthesis is very expensive. To have your computer cranking out the waves needed to make a complex sound, you may find yourself maxing out even heavy computer brains.

This is because of the sheer number of waves you would have to have per note to make a cool sound. Maybe 128 waves generated per note is on the conservative side. Now imagine a computer churning out a five-note chord. See where I'm getting at? Lots and lots of waves and heavy burdens on the computer's brain.

The **Triple Oscillator** synth has very basic additive synthesis (three waves play at once), but there is another instrument in LMMS called **Organic** that is especially made to perform additive synthesis. As it is fairly simple, it doesn't tax the computer too much. It does, however, sound remarkably like an organ.

Phase modulation synthesis

Phase modulation (our **PM** button) synthesis essentially takes the wave shape of one wave, and distorts the phase of a second wave when you apply volume to the first wave. In phase modulation synthesis, we get rich harmonic content from only two waves. The wave being affected is called the **carrier**, and the affecting wave is called the **modulator**.

Just to refresh—waves have a peak and trough to them, right? Well, altering phase is changing the way the peaks and troughs are relating to each other. To flip phase is to make a peak a trough, and vice versa. Distorting phase causes anomalies between the peak and the trough that alter the phase of the waveform.

This form of synthesis is a cheap way to get lots of extra harmonics. We don't need oodles of waves to get what we want—we can use as few as two waves to get there. As you adjust the pitch of the modulator wave, you will hear the higher frequency spectrum affected in the carrier.

Getting into Instruments

If you'd like to hear examples of phase modulation in action, simply enter *DX7* in YouTube's search box. The Yamaha DX7 was the most successful synthesizer in history. It came out in 1983, and blew the music industry away. Not only was it the first digital synth, It also was the first instrument to ever use **MIDI**. Here's what a DX7 looks like:

Phase modulation is the less brash, less extreme cousin of frequency modulaton.

Frequency modulation synthesis

The **FM** button stands for **frequency modulation**. The difference between phase modulation and frequency modulation is that instead of distorting or altering the phase of a waveform, we are altering the frequency of a waveform.

FM is best known for its use in radio broadcast. Essentially, a waveform containing speech or music would be incorporated with a very high frequency wave. This wave's frequency would be modulated by the music or speech, and broadcast from a radio transmitter. A radio receiver in someone's car or home would be set to detect the high frequency waveform. The receiver could then detect the changes made by the voice or music, and play the music or voice back at very high quality.

In FM synthesis, the technique is the same , but slightly different. Here's how it works.

A carrier is playing along, minding its own business, when a modulator wave comes along. The modulator wave will start altering the frequency of the carrier with its own wave, making very rich harmonics called **sidebands**. Phase modulation and frequency modulation sound very similar, but we end up with richer tones from FM and subdued effects when using PM. Early keyboards that were marketed as FM synthesizers were actually using the PM technology. Phase modulation tends to come up with more easily controllable and smoother harmonics than FM.

Many folks think that the Yamaha DX7 was the first FM synthesizer, but others argue that it was actually using phase modulation. If I was to explain the difference between the two technologies, I would need to start talking pretty serious math, so I am going to leave the difference between PM and FM up to our ears instead of trying to give a thorough explanation on the differences.

If you're a math guru, and want to know the definitive truth, check this site out:

```
http://moinsound.wordpress.com/2011/03/04/frequency-modulation-or-
phase-modulation-synthesizer-technologies/
```

Yeah, that's pretty heady stuff, but it will give you the absolute answer when it comes to FM versus PM synthesis.

We'll explore these two types of synthesis momentarily... Let's move on!

Sync

Sync happens between two oscillators. The first oscillator is restarted every time the second oscillator restarts. This means that instead of the first wave going through its natural cycle of peak and trough, it is rudely interrupted and told to start again if the second wave tells it to. The second wave would do this only if its frequency was higher than the first wave. In other words, higher frequency are shorter waves, so they restart faster than lower frequency waves. This can lead to some pretty interesting effects that we'll explore momentarily.

Amplitude modulation

Amplitude modulation is yet another way that we can mess with a carrier wave. The wave will be playing along, doing its thing, when another wave comes along at a different frequency. The second wave's peaks and troughs will alter the amplitude of the carrier. This effect sounds a lot like the old-timey sound effects used in early cartoons and science fiction.

Now let's get into these different modes and see what's up!

Time for action – exploring different synthesis methods

Now that we've heard the mix of different oscillators together, it's time to explore using the oscillators of the **Triple Oscillator** instrument to affect each other.

1. Put a new **Triple Oscillator** instrument in the **Song Editor**:

2. Be sure that only the new instrument is playing. Mute other tracks, and turn the volume on the new **Triple Oscillator** instrument that you just put in the **Song Editor** down to approximately -18 dB:

3. Now click on the instrument to open its parameters. Set the volume of Oscillators 2 and 3 to **0**.

4. Hold *Y* down on your computer keyboard. You will hear the note value of A. It should sound like a very simple sine wave.

5. Click on the **PM** tab:

6. Record a note playing in the song editor so we can hear the changes we are making in this instrument. Start to adjust the volume of Oscillator 2. Listen to the result.

7. Now set the volume of Oscillator 2 to **25%**.

8. While holding down the *Y* key, start adjusting the **Crs** knob.

9. Listen to the effect of changing the tuning of the second oscillator.

10. In this mode, Oscillator 2 is the modulator and Oscillator 1 is the carrier. Select the **FM** tab next:

11. Now repeat steps 6 through 9.

12. Listen to the difference that frequency modulation makes on Oscillator 1.

13. Click on the **AM** tab:

14. Repeat steps 6 through 9
15. Listen to the effect of amplitude modulation on Oscillator 1.
16. Now click on the **Sync** tab:

17. Now set Oscillator 2 so that the **Crs** knob is at **0**.
18. Change the volume on Oscillator 2. Check if there is any effect.
19. Leave the volume parameter of Oscillator 2, and start adjusting the **Crs** parameter on Oscillator 1.
20. Listen to the effect that this has on the phase of Oscillator 1.

What just happened?

We have explored all of the synthesis types available to us in the **Triple Oscillator** instrument!

We've covered a lot of ground here. In listening to these various synthesis techniques, we are getting a nice foundation in synthesis basics. There is a major synthesis technique that we haven't covered yet, though. This is because it requires a filter; but we'll get to that momentarily.

Have a go hero

Now that we're familiar with **getting the different types of synthesis in the Triple Oscillator** instrument to work, it's time for you to experiment:

- Experiment with Oscillator 1 and 2 synthesis techniques
- Use different waves in each oscillator to get different harmonic content
- When you have a sound you like, turn the volume up on Oscillator 3

- Select **OSC2 + OSC3** synthesis techniques, and listen to how this changes the sound
- Try using the **FL** and **FR** parameter knobs to add stereo separation to your new sounds

Experimenting with subtractive synthesis

One of the simplest forms of synthesis is **subtractive synthesis**. Subtractive synthesis is simply taking a complex waveform and filtering certain harmonics out of that waveform.

We've used the oscillator section to create complex sounds. Now we will switch to the filter section to listen to different filter types and listen to how they affect the sound.

We explored filtering already in *Chapter 10, Getting the Mix Together*, so we have a good idea of filter types. Now we just need to put those filter types into action in our synth.

Time for action – activating instrument filters

It's time to leave our oscillator section and move into the other sections of our instrument. You may use the sound you created recently, or use a simple sawtooth wave in a single oscillator to perform the next task. As long as you don't have a sine wave, the filter should work just fine (remember that sine waves have no harmonics to filter!):

1. Select the **ENV/LFO** tab on the **Triple Oscillator** synth:

2. Turn the filter on by clicking the button just to left of the name **FILTER**:

3. Hold *Y* down on your computer's keyboard, and start turning the **Cutoff** knob.

4. Listen to the effect the filter is having on the sound. Turn the **Reso** parameter and listen to the emphasis that is placed at the cutoff point.

5. Change filter type to **HiPass** by clicking on the disclosure triangle next to the cutoff type:

6. Use the **Cutoff** parameter and listen to the effect of the filter. You will hear the low frequencies of the sound being filtered starting at the cutoff point.

7. Now choose the **Moog** filter from the disclosure triangle menu.

8. Listen to this filter by using the cutoff and resonance parameters to get an idea of the character of it.

9. Toggle back and forth between the **2x LowPass**, **LowPass**, and **Moog** filters. There are subtle differences in each filter. Listen to each one, and get familiar with their characteristics.

Getting into Instruments

What just happened?

We've successfully assigned different filters in the **Triple Oscillator** instrument.

These filters are available in all of the instruments in LMMS. There are several filter types available, and I will give you brief explanations of each, but for subtractive synthesis, **LowPass** and **HighPass** filters are most commonly used. As you can hear, the cutoff parameter effectively cuts out and carves the timbre of the sound, giving us something that sounds deep and rich.

Using modulation

So we've explored the **Oscillator** section and the **Filter** section by this point. The last major part of any instrument is the **Amplifier**. This section is really pretty simple. We are simply adjusting volume, and deciding how much of our sound is going between the left and right channel of our instrument's output by using panning.

We've already discussed panning and volume. I'm going to take this opportunity to start talking about modulation.

Modulation is a way to change the parameters of our instrument over time. This happens within the instrument, unlike using automation. In LMMS, there are a number of different modulators that we can use on an instrument. Let me give you a quick run-down.

Using envelopes

Envelopes basically alter a parameter in stages over time. For instance, the sound we play may come on slowly in volume, dip down a bit, hold at another volume, then when we let go of a key the sound will gradually die out. This is one of the most common envelopes, and it has the following stages:

- Attack
- Sustain
- Decay
- Release

The instrument envelope section looks like this:

Most instruments in LMMS have an envelope assigned to volume, the cutoff of the filter, and the resonance of the filter. These envelopes can be selected in the **Target** area:

In LMMS, each instrument actually has an envelope assigned to volume with six stages:

- **Delay**: This delays the onset of the envelope
- **Attack**: This is the stage at which the volume rises to the hold stage
- **Hold**: This will hold the volume of the instrument until the volume raises to the decay stage
- **Decay**: This parameter determines how long the sound will take to reach the sustain stage volume
- **Sustain**: The sound will hold at this stage's volume until the note is released
- **Release**: This parameter determines how long the sound will take to die out

The stage knobs look like this:

The visual representation of how this envelope is going to behave is shown in the viewer above these parameter knobs:

Turn the amount knob up and down, and the viewer will become brighter or dimmer to represent how much the envelope is affecting its associated parameter. Twiddle the knobs to see the viewer change, and since we are assigned to volume, we should hear the effect immediately, as long as our amount knob is turned up a bit. If the amount knob is assigned to 0, then the envelope has no effect at all. If it is turned to a negative number, then the envelope has a reversed effect (the attack stage will turn the volume down not up).

All of the instruments in LMMS give you these envelopes, in addition to any additional modulation that might be built into the instrument.

Using envelopes creatively gives us tremendous dynamism to instrument sounds. We'll be exploring this shortly.

Using LFOs

LFO stands for **Low Frequency Oscillator**. LFOs are used to affect parameters over time similar to an envelope, but using a repeating low frequency wave.

I know when you hear Low Frequency Oscillator, it sounds as if we are going to have a very low-pitched sound. That's not the case. What an LFO does is oscillate a pattern up and down according to the shape of a wave. So instead of the peak and trough of a wave representing compression and rarefaction, it is representing the range of a parameter value. For example, if we had a sine wave LFO assigned to panning, the top of the sine wave could be the left speaker, and the trough of the sine wave would be the right speaker. The sound would slowly oscillate between the left and right speaker.

If we were to use a square wave LFO, then the sound would abruptly jump between the left and right speaker.

Let's put these two modulators to work for us and explore their effects on our instrument.

Time for action – assigning modulators in LMMS

Now we're going to put our envelopes and LOFs to good use, starting with volume:

1. In the envelope section, click on **VOLUME** as the target.
2. Set the parameter knobs, shown as follows:

3. Be sure that the **AMT** parameter knob is turned up all the way.

4. Play the *Y* key on your computer's keyboard, and listen to the how the envelope affects volume.

5. Now turn the **AMT** parameter knob all the way to the left to hear the same envelope reversed in effect.

6. Now click on the **CUTOFF** target:

7. This envelope and **LFO** are assigned to adjust the cutoff of the filter. Turn on the filter if it isn't already on, and select **Low Pass Filter**.

8. Now turn the amount knob up on the envelope, and adjust the parameter knobs so that they read like this:

9. Hit *Y* on your computer keyboard. Do you hear any effect?

10. Try reversing the effect of the envelope by turning the **AMT** knob all the way to the left.

11. Now the sound appears to be filtering. Turn the **AMT** knob all the way to the right again, and turn the filter **CUTOFF** knob all the way down:

12. The filter is now opening properly. This is due to the fact that the envelope was set to have a positive effect, and the cutoff knob was already all the way open. When we closed the filter down by turning the cutoff all the way to the left, the positive value of the envelope was allowed to have effect again.

13. Now turn the **AMT** knob for the envelope to **0**, and let's assign the **LFO**.

14. Turn the LFO **AMT** knob up a bit, and hold down *Y* on the computer keyboard:

15. Listen to the effect.

16. Turn the filter's cutoff up to 980 Hz, and gradually increase the amount as the sound plays.

17. Listen to the LFO affect the filter cutoff.

18. Now increase the speed of the LFO by turning the **SPD** knob up and down.

19. Watch the visualizer to get an understanding of the frequency and amplitude of the LFO. The brighter the line is, the more effect the LFO has. The more waves you see, the higher the frequency:

20. Now click on the **FREQ x 100** button:

21. Switch this button on and off to get an idea of how increasing the frequency of the LFO by 100x affects the LFO.

22. Listen to the **FREQ x 100** setting both on and off.

23. Turn off the **FREQ x 100** setting, and turn on the **MODULATE ENV-AMOUNT** setting:

24. Listen to how the envelope and LFO are now affected by this setting.

25. Adjust the delay and attack to change the rate at which the LFO's influence comes on.

26. Hold down Y and listen to the attack and delay settings on the LFO.

27. Turn off the **MODULATE ENV-AMOUNT** parameter so the LFO stops adjusting the envelope amount.

28. Right-click on the LFO **SPD** parameter.

29. Choose the **LFO** to synchronize to the tempo of the project:

30. Listen to the synched LFO!

What just happened?

We have successfully applied modulation to our instrument, using both an envelope and an LFO.

Using combinations of LFOs and Envelopes on a sound breathes life into an instrument preset. By changing the amounts between the filter, volume, and resonance settings for the LFO and Envelopes, we are given a lot of different ways to add color and dynamism to a sound every time we hit a key.

We have also synced the LFO to the tempo of our project. This is extremely helpful when making basses for dance styles such as dubstep, where an LFO assigned to tempo is essential to get **wobble** type basses.

Have a go hero

Now it's your turn to experiment with modulation settings! There are three targets that you can shoot for:

- Adjusting the settings of the volume envelope and LFO

- Adjusting the settings of the cutoff envelope and LFO
- Adjusting the settings for the resonance envelope and LFO
- Getting creative with your filter choices
- Using different wave types below the visualizer to explore different LFO waves' influences on the sound.
- Tempo sync LFOs to different values

Using the Function tab

LMMS instruments have a nifty tab called **FUNC** that gives the LMMS user wondrous tools to make music making easier.

Pop a new **Triple Oscillator** instrument into the song editor, and mute the other instruments in the song editor so we can focus on it.

When you click on the **FUNC** tab on our new **Triple Oscillator** instrument, this is what we get:

As you can probably imagine, this section just might let us get away with not having to memorize scales and chords. Tricky little tab it is!

Getting into Instruments

Chords

When we click on the **CHORDS** button, we are going to allow LMMS to play chords based on the notes that we hit on our keyboard controller or computer keyboard. The list of chords is extensive. If we turn on the chords section, and click on the disclosure triangle for the chords, this is what we get:

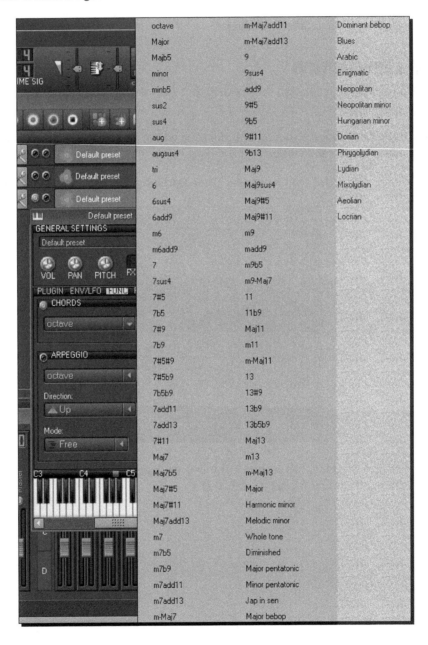

[318]

That, my friends, is an extremely comprehensive list of chord types! Beyond just major and minor chords, we are given chord types such as **Enigmatic** and **Major Bebop**. These chords styles and types are a great shortcut to getting us in the right direction when it comes to creating chords on the fly. They can be played live using the computer keyboard or MIDI controller.

Let's turn the volume down on the instrument to **-17**, and choose the **Maj9** chord:

When we play our computer keyboard, we are greeted with one of the happiest dance chords ever made, the Major 9 chord.

Adjusting the range of the chords spreads the chords out even wider. Considering how thick this chord already is, it's probably going to just get bigger. Playing with the range knob creates new Major 9 chords. This is cool, but might take up too much space in the mix, so use sparingly.

Using different chord types gives a lot of emotional content to a project. Try experimenting with different chords within the context of a project. Learning a little music theory can go a long way towards getting really nice chords to play together—**Major** and **Minor**, **Diminished** and **Bebop**—all of them have very distinct personalities and will require a little practice to understand which chords work together.

Arpeggio

An **arpeggio** is made when you take a chord's notes and play them in a row. Classical arpeggios are simply running up and down the chord tones, but you can also change it up and have the notes play out of sequence. The **ARPEGGIO** section in LMMS instruments does all of this for us, and it has a TON of options.

Getting into Instruments

Let's turn off the chord section and focus on the arpeggio section for a minute:

The **ARPEGGIO** section as the following parameters:

- A list of chords that can be played:

- The range of the arpeggio:

- The direction of the arpeggio:

- The time between notes of the arpeggio, (we can right-click on this to sync the arpeggio to tempo):

- The length of each note of the arpeggio:

- The mode of the arpeggio. This selects how the arpeggio is going to behave when holding down notes:

Remember that **Maj9** chord we picked for the **CHORDS** section under the Function Tab? Select that same chord here, and then hold a note down on the computer keyboard. Then use *Y* on the computer keyboard to hear the arpeggio.

Nice little arpeggio screaming along... Now let's try these settings:

Hold down *Y* on the computer keyboard, and we have a nice little arpeggio!

The arpeggio travels up and down the chord note values, each note is fairly short, it's got a 2-octave range, and it's certainly a Major 9 chord...

Arpeggio modes – Sort and Sync

Now let's see what **Sort** means.

Hold down *Y*, and *I* as well on the computer keyboard. Now the arpeggio goes up in one chord, and down in the second chord value. This is what sort mode is all about. If we were to choose **Sync**, then the notes we are playing would both travel up and down the arpeggio together!

Arpeggios are great in dance music; they can really move a piece of music along. Free-flowing arpeggios are more rarely used than tempo-synced arpeggios, but free-flowing arpeggios can sometimes provide a nice atmosphere for a piece.

So there you have it... these sections, parameters, modulation types, chords and arpeggios are available in every instrument in LMMS. Now we also know how to program them effectively. Although these parameters are common among all LMMS instruments, not all LMMS instruments are alike. We should explore these various instruments types.

The different instruments of LMMS

LMMS has quite a host of instruments to help us on our way to making music. Let's take a second to figure out what the heck each of them do! The instruments are located in the "instrument plugins" area on the left side of the song editor. If you would like to listen to them, simply drag them to the song editor.

Bit Invader

This instrument allows you to create your own waveform by dragging the mouse within the display:

Here is an overview of the main functions of the Bit Invader instrument:

- **Interpolation**: It smoothes out the waveform by plotting out more points between the points on a curve
- **Normalize**: It sets the maximum volume possible for the given waveform.
- The Knob at the left increases and decreases the sample length
- The **S** button smoothes the waveform by averaging out points on the waveform curve
- The buttons to the right are preset waveforms that are good to start from

These low resolution sounds are a lot of fun when making styles such as electro, and even sound good in dubstep due to their brash and buzzy nature.

Kicker

Kicker is extremely simple. We've covered it already, but let's brush up on it:

Kicker is a very simple noise generator that sounds a lot like a kick when programmed correctly. Here's what we get on the front panel:

- **START:** This parameter determines the frequency the kicker starts at.
- **END:** This is where our frequency ends up. When this is set low, the kick drops. We can also reverse the effect.
- **DECAY:** How long does the frequency take to reach its end point? The length of our kick is determined here.
- **DIST:** This adds distortion to the kick. Sometimes this is good for thickening the kick up.
- **GAIN:** We rarely need to add gain, but we can also attenuate the gain here so our instrument doesn't clip.

To create long bass drops, this instrument works really well. Just turn **DECAY** up, **START** up, and the **END** down to achieve a nice long drop transition.

The kicker has a nice pure tone to it. Adding a Low Pass filter with high resonance can also help further to define kick sounds.

LB-302

Remember the TB-303 we talked about in *Chapter 3, Getting Our Hands Dirty: Creating in LMMS*? Well, this is the emulation LMMS has built in. The **Beat+Baseline** editor works best with this bad boy. The original TB-303 was a pattern-based bassline synthesizer as well:

Here's what the LB-302 parameters mean:

- **Slide**: When different pitches are played, the pitch will slide between the notes. This parameter determines the length of time a slide takes.
- **VCO**: VCO stands for Voltage Controlled Oscillator. The name is a throwback to when instruments like this weren't digital. This is the type of wave the LB-302 is going to use. It's a single-oscillator synth.
- **VCF**: Ah, so here's something interesting... The filter in the LB-302 has been specially re-created to mimic the filter of the original TB-303.
- **Slide**, **Accent**, and **Dead**: These buttons dictate how notes played in the LB-302 behave. **Slide** will slide in pitch between a note and the next note played. Accent will apply additional volume to a note played. Dead will mute a note.
- **Dist**: This adds distortion to the sound.

Remember when we explored Acid House? This is the synth at the heart of acid house. Its patterns would circle around and add the nervous energy to acid house. Using distortion and varying the velocity of the notes can help to have some notes be more distorted than others.

Mallets

Mallets is an interesting sample-based instrument that makes three categories of mallet sounds:

- **Percussion**: These are tuned percussion instruments such as marimba, vibraphone, and other pitched percussion sounds.
- **Tubular bells**: These are long tubes that are struck with a mallet. Kind of giant doorbells.

- **Bars**: These are simple metal bars and—strangely enough—bowls.

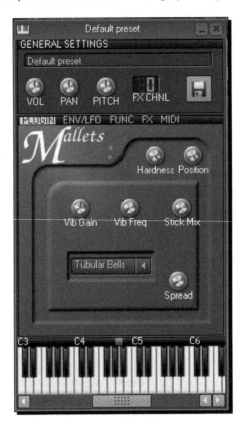

Each instrument type has different parameters assigned to it. These are the options for **Percussion**:

- **Hardness**: This is the hardness of the stick used for striking
- **Position**: This is the position where the mallet strikes the instrument
- **Vib Gain**: This is for vibrato intensity, which is a warbling in the pitch
- **Vib Freq**: This is how fast the Vibrato warbles
- **Stick Mix**: How much of the striking sound do we want?
- **Spread**: This spreads the instrument across the stereo field according to pitch

These are options for **Tubular Bells**:

- **Modulator**: This is adding a little bit of frequency modulation to the sound, causing a more bell-like tone in the higher frequencies.
- **Crossfade**: This parameter decides how much FM we want to add to the tone.
- **LFO Speed**: This is an LFO that is assigned to amplitude. So the volume will oscillate up and down at a speed determined by this parameter.
- **LFO Depth**: This parameter determines the intensity of the LFO on the sound.
- **ADSR**: This is a special envelope applied to the sound. It's preset, so we are only going to be able to adjust the intensity of this envelope with this parameter.
- **Spread**: This spreads the instrument across the stereo field according to pitch.

These are the options for **Bars**:

- **Bowed on/off**: Solid bars can be bowed with a violin bow. This causes an eerie tone that has a very undefined attack.
- **Pressure**: When bowed, this determines the pressure of the bow on the bar when it is travelling across the edge of the bar.
- **Motion**: This provides variation to how the bow is crossing the bar.
- **Speed**: This is how fast the bow is moving across the tone bar.
- **Vibrato**: Unlike the LFO used for the Tubular bells, this LFO is affecting pitch. This knob adjusts intensity.
- **Spread**: This spreads the instrument across the stereo field, determined by pitch.

These mallet instruments can sound very interesting when the various parameters and modulation are applied so that the sounds aren't just vanilla marimbas and vibraphones. Adding an attack stage and using bowing techniques can take a jazzy mallet sound and convert it into a deep Tibetan singing bowl with a bit of experimentation.

Organic

The fact that its icon looks like a carrot should not keep you from checking this instrument out. The eight banks you see are individual oscillators, playing at different pitches. The method of synthesis is additive. Remember additive synthesis? We talked about it earlier. One of the simplest synthesis techniques, it simply involves adding waves together of differing pitches that are usually related to the harmonic series:

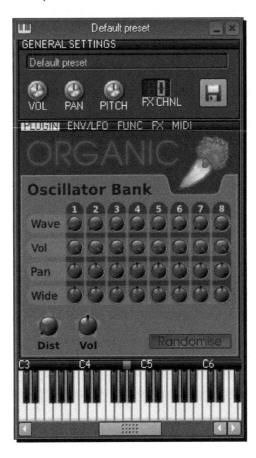

Here's what we get with the front panel of the **ORGANIC** instrument:

- **Wave**: This determines the wave generated by each of the eight oscillators. All the way left, we get a sine wave. As we turn to the right, we get a sawtooth, pulse, triangle, moog triangle, and exponential wave.
- **Vol**: This is the volume control for each oscillator.
- **Pan**: This determines the wave's placement in the stereo field.
- **Wide**: This detunes one side of the wave in the stereo field.
- **Dist**: This applies distortion across the entire instrument.
- **Randomise**: No matter how you spell it, you get a completely random set of parameters to work from.

Let's explore the **ORGANIC** instrument:

1. The best way to start with this instrument is to turn the wave parameter to **0%**, Turn all of the volumes down, pan all oscillators to center, and turn the width down for all of the oscillators too. This way we can start fresh. While holding Y on our computer keyboard, we can slowly add in the volumes of the different oscillators.
2. The pitch of each individual oscillator has been chosen from the harmonic series. As we turn the volume up on each oscillator, we can hear our tone turn more and more organ-like.
3. Mess up that bland organ sound by mixing different wave types together. Make the tone sound twisted by altering the width of a couple oscillators.
4. To get really crazy, use **Randomise**. This parameter completely randomizes the settings on the front panel. Using this function gives us a great start in a direction we may never have taken before. The rest of the synth is untouched, so we can still filter this additive synth, which technically means Organic is both an additive and subtractive synth.
5. Using the volume envelope with a very short decay and longer release time can make for some interesting percussive organ instruments. Experiment to taste!

FreeBoy

A new type of music has been emerging over the last five years out of our nostalgia for old videogame systems and their charmingly limited palate of sounds. The **Game Boy** was the most popular handheld system of all time, and it was very challenging to score for. There were four channels that played together to create not only the music, but the sound effects as well:

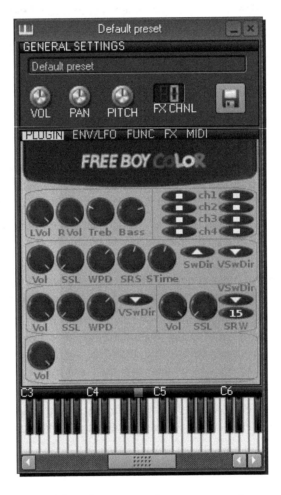

The FreeBoy is an emulation of the infamous gaming system, and we are given the same limited palate of sounds to choose from. Here's how the parameters work for this instrument for the top row:

- **LVol**: Left side volume
- **RVol**: Right side volume
- **Treb**: This gives more high frequency presence to the overall sound

- **Bass**: This gives more low frequency response to the sound
- Channel buttons: These buttons decide which side the four waves are going to occupy, and when deactivated, they basically mute the channel.

Row 2 is dedicated to the parameters of Channel 1, which is a square wave oscillator. The parameters for row 2 are:

- **Vol**: This is the volume for this square wave.
- **SSL**: This is the sweep step length. This oscillator has the ability to sweep up or down in pitch and volume. Each step of that sweep can be lengthened here.
- **WPD**: This stands for Wave Pattern Duty. A square wave is created by a simple on and off command for each cycle of the oscillator. This parameter shortens the "on" portion of that cycle, leaving more "off" than "on". The result is a change in the timbre of the oscillator.
- **SRS**: This parameter is Sweep Right Shift. That means the sweeping sound will travel to the right speaker when this value is turned up.
- **STime**: This determines how long the sweep will last.
- **SwDir**: This determines the direction of the pitch of the sweep.
- **VSwDir**: This button determines whether the volume will fall off, or grow louder as the sweep happens.

For fun, you can create a video game jump sound by using these settings for this square wave:

To play the square as a normal musical wave simply turn the **STime** parameter to **0**.

Row 3 is dedicated to the parameters of channel 2, 3 and 4. All of the settings have the same meanings as Channel 1, with the added noise oscillator on the far right. The two types of noise are determined by the **SRW** parameter, which shifts the frequency of the noise.

The FreeBoy is a lot of fun to experiment with. Now we can make Nintendo scores with multiple FreeBoys if we wish, and have a Game Boy symphony. Now, that may be a mixed bag among music purists, but I'm all for it!

PatMan

Nothing gets quite as esoteric as this instrument. Will you use it? Well, probably not, but hey, I can still tell you what the heck it is!

PatMan opens files from the now long defunct IBM Gravis Ultrasound soundcard. This soundcard was around when soundcards created all of the sounds we needed to hear for games. The built-in synthesizer was crude, but sounded better than the sound blaster equivalent of the time (around 1994).

There are two modes for this instrument—**Loop** and **Tune**. Loop mode plays all of the sound elements of a GUS file in sequence, and Tune mode allows a user to play each of the 180 sounds that are located in the .pat file included with the soundcard resources.

This is a truly esoteric instrument, but for those die-hard retro gamers I suppose it has some hipster appeal.

SF2

Soundfonts aren't quite as old, but are similarly retro-chic. You can find SoundFont 2 files on the Internet, and from the file area you can load these soundbanks in SF2:

SF2 emulates the reverb and chorus settings used with old soundfont players of yore. They can be turned on by selecting the **Reverb** and/or **Chorus** button.

SF2 loads a default library of useful sounds, and we can switch between the different sounds by turning the **Patch** number up.

Getting into Instruments

Vestige

Vestige is very useful for loading up third-party plugins into LMMS. Many popular manufacturers of software instruments and plugins have VST compatibility so that users of popular digital audio workstations can use their wares:

Vestige is very simple. Click on the folder icon to find your VST plugins. **Show/hide GUI** shows the interface for the said plugin. **Turn off all notes** is a panic button for when MIDI notes might stick and play incessantly.

Chapter 11

Vibed

This instrument warrants some attention! Vibed is basically a nine-stringed instrument. Unlike a guitar, which we play a combination of strings and positions on the guitar neck, this instrument can have up to nine strings vibrating simultaneously:

Each string can be edited individually by selecting the string in this box:

The **Imp** button shows the shape of the pluck as it propagates up and down the string in the graph just to the right of this area. If it is turned off, then the graph will show the string shape itself once it has been plucked.

Below this area we have our pitch in octaves, and the length of the string as parameters.

Directly under the graph we have this area:

In this area, we have some familiar parameters. **S** stands for smoothing of the waveform in the graph, and **N** is normalization. Then we have:

- **V**: Volume of the string.
- **S**: The stiffness of the string. The higher the number, the stiffer the string and the shorter the release of the string.
- **P**: This is the pick position. When we pick this string, where on the string are we picking it? We can excite the string to the far left, middle or right, and the ensuing waveform that travels up and down the string will be affected by this.
- **PU**: This is the pickup position. Just like an electric guitar, where we are listening to the sound will make a big difference in how our string will sound.
- **Enable/Disable**: This is where we can turn the string on and off.

Each string that we choose can have a completely different set of parameters. Including **Panning**, **Detuning**, and **Slap**, (a kind of fuzziness applied to the string sound).

This type of synthesis is called **physical modeling** and was developed in the 70s, but wasn't used commercially until the 90s when Yamaha started using the technology in their synthesizers. Basically, we are creating a mathematical model of the way a string actually behaves in real life. We aren't using oscillators or samples. We're using an equation that is able to create all of the various parameters needed to recreate the properties of a string. This technology has been used in almost every software instrument we use today that emulates strings without the use of samples or oscillators.

Using nine virtual strings with various modifications to pitch, tuning, stiffness, type of wave (the wave types are on the right-hand side), and pickup position, we can create our own bizarre nine-stringed instrument that doesn't exist in nature. This is one of the most complex and interesting instruments built in LMMS. Take your time with it and explore its possibilities.

ZynAddSubFx

Okay! A fellow named Paul Nasca created this innocuous looking synthesizer, and he is some kind of genius. I could write a whole book on this instrument alone, but we don't have room for that here now, do we?

I am going to suggest to you this link:

http://zynaddsubfx.sourceforge.net/index.html

This website has every last lick of information that you could possibly need to know about this incredibly deep and beautiful sounding instrument.

I had not played with ZynAddSubFx before writing this book, and I am pretty astounded at the depth of programming Mr. Nasca has put into this bad boy. If you go to the sidebar and check out the presets made for this synth, I think you'll agree that this is one powerful, versatile instrument.

Be sure to contribute to this guy. He's got a heart of gold for allowing us to use his creation for free!

Summary

This chapter of the book is dedicated to helping you understand the palate that you have available to you for creating just about any sound you need in LMMS. In previous chapters we have laid out LMMS' interface, various editors, and talked about making arrangements in different styles, but I wanted to give you some synthesis chops so that you didn't have to go to presets every time you felt inspired to start a project.

Entire projects have bloomed from nights where I've been sitting with an instrument, exploring and making dynamic sounds. The process of synthesis is inspirational to me, and I hope that I can instill the same passion in you that I have for making interesting timbres that have never existed before. It's like cooking with ingredients that you made from scratch instead of buying a box from the store. Using these instruments to their potential, you can create a unique voice for yourself.

I hope that after this exploration into the instruments of LMMS and the basic foundations of synthesis, you get your hands dirty and make your own noises. Making your own instrument patches gets you one step closer to being deliberate about your music. Every tone and timbre crafted and thought out to express who you are as an artist.

You should also check out this piece of work:

```
http://soundcloud.com/macrowave
```

This was a piece of music created using LMMS and mostly ZynaddSubFx. It's pretty wonderful.

Have a blast!

12
Where to Go from Here

This chapter will explore various agencies, groups, and communities in the music industry. The purpose of this chapter is to find outlets for your music, now that you have a way to create it. We will also explore music distribution and social networking.

So here we are. The end. Nope! The beginning.

It's my sincerest hope that after you've finished this book you are hungry. You are starving to create, inspired, and ready to push LMMS as far as you can push it. I hope that you feel empowered and unafraid to finish songs and get yourself out there with your music.

So the question is, once you've walked out your front door, blinking in the light of day, where do you put your music? Where is it going to live? How can you find an audience? Can you make money?

Well, I have some suggestions for you.

Guilds, societies, and such

I love the sound of it—'I'm part of the _____ Society'. Or 'I'm in the _____ Guild'.

Harkens back to older, simpler times. Remembering olden times when 'times' was spelled with a 'Y', where jousts happened, and peasants were really, really muddy. Kind of makes me feel special, like a knight or something...at least a page.

There are some societies that you should consider joining, if only to have someone looking out for you and your music. Different countries have different organizations for such things. I live in the United States, so I chose to first join **ASCAP**.

ASCAP

It is the **American Society of Composers, Authors, and Publishers (ASCAP)**. It's their job to make sure that if my music is bought, sold, licensed, or published, I get my fair share. They are like bloodhounds, who are always sniffing around to make sure that my music hasn't been co-opted or stolen.

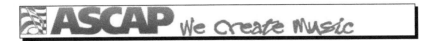

Yes, sometimes they are too draconian in their approach and go after college students who are file sharing among themselves, so there's that. I do feel good that when it comes to working with other artists, we can split the credit and monetary gain easily, by telling ASCAP what our involvement was on a project. Every time the music sells or is published, we will receive our fair cut. If you live in the States, check them out at http://www.ascap.com/.

BMI

Broadcast Music Inc. (BMI) is a whole lot like ASCAP. They exist as an alternative to ASCAP, and having them both in the States means they kind of check up on each other. When doing business overseas, I have some friends who use BMI to interface with other international agencies that might have slightly different rules than the States, but overall, BMI is pretty much the same as ASCAP in most ways.

Check them out here:

http://www.bmi.com/

In other countries, there are many different kinds of agencies for this kind of thing. For instance, in Europe there's SESAC.

SESAC

SESAC is the largest performance rights organization in Europe, and has been around for a very, very long time. They also have a U.S. branch, which is nice for crossover, and are very well established. If you live anywhere in Europe, it would be a great idea to be in touch with these people. They will help you determine your publishing, performing, and other rights.

So what about the rest of the world, huh?

Well, there are many, many, many performance rights organizations out there, and here is a link to all the ones that Wikipedia knows of:

- Mexico: SACM (México). Visit them at `http://www.sacm.org.mx/`
- Santa Lucia: Hewanorra Musical Society
- USA: ASCAP, BMI, and SESAC
- Argentina: SADAIC
- Australia: APRA
- Austria: AKM
- Belgium: SABAM
- Brazil: UBC
- Bulgaria: MUSICAUTHOR
- Canada: SOCAN
- Chile: SCD
- Colombia: SAYCO
- Croatia: HDS
- Czech Republic: OSA
- Denmark: KODA
- Estonia: EAU
- Finland: TEOSTO
- France: SACEM
- Georgia: SAS
- Germany: GEMA

- Greece: AEPI
- Hong Kong: CASH
- Hungary: ARTISJUS
- Ireland: IMRO
- Israel: ACUM
- Italy: SIAE
- Japan: JASRAC
- Korea: KOMCA
- Lithuania: LATGA-A
- Malaysia: MACP
- Netherlands: BUMA
- New Zealand: APRA
- Norway: TONO
- Panama: SPAC
- Peru: APDAYC
- Philippines: FILSCAP
- Poland: ZAIKS
- Romania: UCMR
- Russia: RAO
- Serbia: SOKOJ
- Singapore: COMPASS
- Slovakia: SOZA
- South Africa: SAMRO
- Spain: SGAE
- Sweden: STIM
- Switzerland: SUISA
- Taiwan: MUST
- Thailand: MCT
- Trinidad: COTT
- Ukraine: UACRR

- United Kingdom: PRS, PPL
- Uruguay: AGADU
- Venezuela: SACVEN

Where to sell my stuff

Selling music is easier these days than it has ever been. Let's check out the following options.

Beatport

As we are focused on dance music, I highly recommend checking out Beatport. Visit it at `https://www.beatport.com/`.

Beatport is an amazing community of dance music that just keeps growing and becoming more influential in the music industry as time moves on. It is one of the easiest ways for DJs and audiences to find their music, and the delivery service is solid.

iTunes

Well, iTunes is pretty good, I guess. It definitely is the largest online music store you can find. Though some of the rules, depending on where you live, can be a little hard to navigate.

Also, if you don't have a label, Apple won't even talk to you. So what are the options? How do you get your music into the iTunes pearly gates (I guess I should say gated community)?

CD Baby

Silly name aside, CD Baby has good relations with Apple, and if you go with them, they'll get you into that iTunes place.

They'll also print up physical CDs for you, if that's still a viable delivery platform for you. Check them out at www.cdbaby.com.

Tunecore

Tunecore is very similar to CD Baby, but they also do singles as well as albums, and have a less silly name.

Visit them at www.tunecore.com.

Music labels

Ok, here's the deal...

If you are looking to get signed, I would highly suggest reading up on the legalities of signing to record labels. Many a times, signing to a record label is akin to being given a very big credit card that you must pay back, hand over fist, for your entire life, without ever truly owning your own music.

Check out books by *Moses Avalon* or *Martin Atkins*, or the writings of *Steve Albini*.

Don't be discouraged, though! The industry is going through a whole lot of change right now! There are more ways than ever to make a name (and a living) for yourself as an artist, whether or not you choose to get involved with a label.

Community

Wherever you live in the world, there is a music community around you somewhere. Sometimes you'll need to travel to an urban center, or sometimes you only need to go to the local, live music venue. When it comes to dance music and electronic music, there are underground scenes and nightclubs. There are beachside parties and mountain gatherings. There's dance music all around you, and you should get out and listen to it!

Google your city and dance music. What comes up? When you are on Facebook, where are your friends going to have a good time? You should really get out of the house a couple of days out of the month, and see what's going on. Music should never be made solely in a vacuum. You need to go and see what's out there. What's the DJ spinning? Does it sound like your stuff? Can you talk to him/her after the gig, hand them a song, and see if they'll listen to it?

DJs are becoming producers and music makers these days. If they aren't making the music themselves, they are looking for a collaborator. If they aren't collaborating, they are looking for new, fresh material to play. You owe it to yourself to see what's happening in your community musically, and see if you have something to contribute. If you hear that an electronic music act is in town that you enjoy, go to the gig. Hang out afterward. Make conversation. Put yourself out there. If you don't, then you are a bedroom hobbyist, which is cool, but you might want to at least see if you have a place out there in the bigger world.

You'd be amazed at just how approachable these people can be. I have taught remixing classes, where I ordered the students to find music to remix from artists they liked... by asking the artist themselves! At least eight out of 10 would succeed, and the ones who didn't would find others that would be more open about sharing their music. I want to manage expectations by saying that Trent Reznor or Tiesto might be a bit hard to get a hold of, but up-and-coming artists aren't. Seek them out. Tell them you are learning and are inspired by them. Be respectful, though. Don't get full of yourself. That might tank you before you even get started.

User groups

Try the following user groups to get more involved in the LMMS community:

- Here's the Facebook user group at:
  `http://www.facebook.com/group.php?gid=34859703058`

- Here's the link to the sourceforge (SF) group:

    ```
    http://sourceforge.net/mailarchive/forum.php?forum_name=lmms-users
    ```

- On YouTube:

    I'm really digging LazerBlade... Sometimes videos can just be great ways to learn these concepts, and I like LazerBlade's approach. Visit them at:

    ```
    http://www.youtube.com/user/lzrbld
    ```

I think those two user groups and Lazerblade's YouTube channel are the best so far.

Now as far as meeting in person is concerned, I would suggest finding some friends, who use LMMS and meet maybe once a month to share ideas. It's great to have real people in the world to bounce your projects, ideas, and workflows off. It's also a great way to quickly and easily work through issues with the program and potential roadblocks to creativity.

Soundcloud

Soundcloud is a pretty interesting arena to try your music out in.

Be warned, though... everyone listening is going to make a comment and have an opinion on your music, so work on developing a thick skin. The Internet can sometimes be a ruthless place.

Summary

Now that we've gone on this journey of LMMS and making dance music, I'd like to leave you with a couple of thoughts:

- Music is 80 percent listening and 20 percent playing:

    When you are in your studio, try to listen to a couple of pieces of music before you even open LMMS. Try hard to pick out all of the elements you hear, and get into the emotional landscapes of the different pieces of music. Get outside of your comfort zone and listen to jazz, classical, pop, country, hip-hop, or any other style that you don't usually listen to. Every kind of music you take in will provide a rich soil to plant your creativity.

- Learning music theory will not affect your music in a negative way:

    This may sound silly, but I have known fairly accomplished music makers, who refuse to learn music theory because they believe it may hinder their creative development. There is a reason they call it music theory and not music law. Music theory can be absolutely beautiful when you study it. The patterns are beautiful, and the logic is inscrutable. A friend of mine compares it to a crystalline structure that he likes to turn this way and that when he looks at it. It catches different moods and emotions, but contains a structure that is complete. I highly recommend at least learning your major scales and modes, and exploring writing in different keys. It is a wonderful way to get an idea of the full breadth of possibility in music. Don't be afraid of theory; it's just more of a tool to have in your belt than a creed to follow.

- Make friends with others who make music:

    The more people you have to bounce your music off and the more ears you can trust, the better. It's a wonderful feeling to have friends that you can trust with your music. People who can give perspective and help enrich your music with their experience of it. Don't make music in a bubble.

I sincerely hope that you've enjoyed this book, and explore all I have talked about within. I enjoy teaching people as much as I love making music. Go forth and make some banging beats, dense emotional landscapes, and soaring melodies.

Pop Quiz Answers

Chapter 3: Getting Our Hands Dirty: Creating in LMMS

Question No.	Answer
1	A four on the floor kick pattern happens every quarter note of a pattern.
2	A break beat does not have a four on the floor pattern. It uses a different sub-division.
3	In Techno, the bass is off the beat.
4	The three types of hihats in dance music are open, closed, and pedal.
5	Drag up and down on a beat with the middle mouse button.
6	Right-click on the steps area, and choose **Add Steps**.

Chapter 4: Expanding the Beat: Digging Deeper into the Art of Beatmaking

1	2	3	4
b	d	a	c

5	6	7	8
b	a	a	c

Chapter 5: Making Spaces: Creating the Emotional Landscape

1	2	3	4	5	6
b	c	a	b	d	a

Chapter 6: Finding and Creating New Noises

1	2	3	4	5	6	7
c	b	a	b	c	d	a

Chapter 7: Getting it All Stacked Up

1	2	3	4
b	a	c	b

Chapter 8: Spreading Out the Arrangement

1	2	3	4	5
c	b	c	a	b

Chapter 9: Gluing the Arrangement Together

1	2	3	4	5
b	a	b	a	c

Chapter 10: Getting the Mix Together

1	2	3	4	5
a	b	c	c	a

6	7	8	9	10
a	c	b	a	b

Index

Symbols

1176 by Universal Audio 269

A

absorption
  vs. diffusion 36, 37
accent button 325
Acid house music 87, 88
additive synthesis 303
ADSR parameter 327
Advanced Linux Sound Architecture. *See* ALSA
Aglaia, electronic music artist 161
Akai MPD32, MIDI control surfaces 18
Akai MPK49, MIDI keyboard controllers 17
ALSA
  about 19
  used, for setting up MIDI 20
American Society of Composers, Authors, and Publishers. *See* ASCAP
Amount knob 151
amplifier 310
amplitude modulation 305
AM Radio Bass element 240
analog keyboards 96
answers
  pop quiz 349-351
anti-node 258
Aphex Twin, electronic music artist 160
arpeggio modes 321
arpeggio section 319-321
arranging
  about 221, 222
  pop song arrangement 222
ARTWORK directory 11
ASCAP 340
attack stage 269, 311
Audacity
  about 28
  sound sculpting in 184-189
  URL 28
audio energy 256
Audiofile processor
  about 59
  samples, editing with 58, 59
audio interfaces 24
audio samples
  creating 28
audio streams
  separating 259-263
automation
  building 131
  used, for sweeping filter 119-124
  using, on instrument effects 129
Automation Editor window 123
Automation Track element 139
Automation window 124, 128

B

BACKGROUND ARTWORK directory 11
balanced cables
  about 178, 179
  versus unbalanced cables 176

band pass EQ 279
bandwidth 278
bandwidth knob 286
bars
   about 326
   Bowed on/off option 327
   motion option 327
   pressure option 327
   speed option 327
   spread option 327
   vibrato option 327
bass
   about 93
   adding, to Beats+Bassline Editor 61, 62
   drum machines 97, 98
   electric bass 94, 95
   guidelines 118
   other notables 101
   pitch friends, making with harmony 109, 110
   placing 109
   samplers 100, 101
   synth bass 95
   upright bass 94
bass drum
   about 90
   listening, steps for 90
Bass, FreeBoy instrument 331
bass line
   pitch, changing 65
bass pattern
   opening, in piano roll edition 64, 65
beat
   building, by setting stage 55
   creating 118
   elements, adding to beat pattern 60, 61
   harmonies, adding 106-108
   pattern, creating 57, 58
   turnaround, giving 111, 112
   variation, adding to beat pattern 60, 61
Beat+Bassline Editor's pattern
   getting, in song editor 136
Beat+Bassline Editor window 105
Beat+Bassline element 138
Beatport
   about 343
   URL 343

Beats+Bassline Editor
   about 49, 55, 104
   bass, adding 61, 62
   beat pattern, creating 57, 58
   drums, adding 56, 57
   elements, adding to beat pattern 60, 61
   instruments, muting 66
   note length, editing 62, 63
   root pitch, editing 62, 63
   samples, editing with Audiofile processor 58, 59
   stage, setting to build beat 55
   variation, adding to beat pattern 60, 61
bit depth 193
bit invader instrument
   about 322
   interpolation 323
   knob 323
   normalize 323
   S button 323
bits and samples 192, 193
black notes 112
BMI
   about 340
   URL 340
Boards of Canada, electronic music artist 160
Bowed on/off option 327
Braindance music 88
breakbeat music 88
Brian Eno, electronic music artist 159
bridge
   about 222
   for nirvana song 224
   for peter gabriel song 225
   for pink floyd song 225
   for radiohead song 224
   purpose 224, 225
Broadcast Music Inc.. *See* BMI
build 92
bussing 261

C

carrier 303
carving 276
CCmixter
   about 27

URL 27, 183
CD Baby
  about 344
  URL 344
channel
  instrument, routing on FX-Mixer 69
channel buttons, FreeBoy instrument 331
Chicago style house music
  about 83
  creating, steps 83-85
CHORDS button 318, 319
Chorus button 333
choruses 222
clipping 50, 257, 258
clones
  sending, through effects 209-212
closed hi hat 91
communities
  for selling music 343
compression
  using, in LMMS 270-272
compressor 269
condenser microphone
  about 22
  diaphram 23
controller rack 51
Controls button 72, 151
control surfaces, MIDI
  Akai MPD32 18
  KORG nanoKONTROL 2 17
  Novation Zero SLmkII 18
CPU usage
  reducing, FX channels used 156
CPU usage display 53
Creative Commons licenses 182
crests 258
Crossfade parameter 327
cutoff 277
CUTOFF knob 122, 247

D

damping parameter 283, 284
Dancehall music 88
dance music
  about 75
  bass 93
  bass in, fitting 80-82
  beats, creating 76-79
  drums 89
dance music, styles
  about 83
  Acid house music 87, 88
  Braindance music 88
  breakbeat music 88
  Chicago style house music 83
  Drum and Bass music 88
  Jungle music 88
  New York house music 86, 87
DAWs
  about 42
  EditorWindow 42
  Mixer 42
dead button 325
decay knob 269
DECAY parameter 324
decay (release) 269
delay
  versus reverb 152-155
delay-based plugins 280
delay stage 311
diaphram 23
diffusion
  about 153
  vs absorption 36, 37
Digital Audio Workstations. *See* **DAWs**
digital realm 257
digital recording 175
digital synthesizers 96
dirty bass 206-209
dist, organic instrument 329
dist parameter, LB-302 325
DIST, Kicker 324
dropouts
  about 238, 239
  creating, with accompanying pitch fall 239-244
Drum and Bass music 88
drum loop
  about 168
  used, for creating pattern from samples 168-174
drum machines
  about 97, 98
  New Wave 97

Synthpop 97
drum machines, bass
   The LinnDrum 99
   The Roland TR808 98
   The Roland TR909 98
   The SP1200 100
drums
   about 89, 265
   adding, to Beats+Bassline Editor 56, 57
   bass drum 90
   elements 265
   head 89
   hi hat 90, 91
   panning 265
   snare drum 92
   tom-tom 92
dynamic microphone
   about 22
   microphone pre-amp 22
   trim knob 22
dynamics
   about 268
   range 268

E

Early Reflection mode 153
echo
   about 280
   exploring 280-282
edit menu, main menu bar 44
EditorWindow 42
effects
   clones, sending through 209-212
EFFECTS CHAIN section 158
electric bass
   about 94
   listening, steps for 95
electronic music artists 159
elements
   adding, to beat pattern 60, 61
   ambient elements, adding 212-214
   smoothing 212
END parameter 324
envelopes
   about 310
   attack 311

   decay 311
   delay 311
   hold 311
   release 311
   suatain 311
ENV/LFO tab 246
EQ
   about 119, 274
   band pass EQ 279
   high cut 277
   high pass EQ 277, 278
   low cut filter 277
   low pass EQ 277, 278
   low pass filter 277
   parameteric EQ 278, 279
   Shelf EQ 276
   types 276
   using 275, 276
Equalization. *See* **EQ**
exponential 298
Export command 184

F

Facebook user group 345
field recording 175
file management
   about 12, 13
   projects directory 13
fill 93
filter
   about 119, 274
   sweeping, automation used 119-124
filter sweep
   about 244
   creating, steps for 245-250
first reflection 153
flat 112
FL STUDIO INSTALLATION directory 12
four on the floor 77
FreeBoy instrument
   about 330, 331
   Bass 331
   channel buttons 331
   LVol 330
   RVol 330
   SRS 331

SSL 331
STime 331
SwDir 331
Treb 330
Vol 331
VSwDir 331
WPD 331
freesound website
  URL 182
Freeverb
  exploring 283
frequency 257
frequency modulation (FM button) synthesis 304, 305
Full Scale (FS) 257
Function tab
  arpeggio modes 321
  arpeggio section 319-321
  CHORDS button 318, 319
  using 317
FX
  exploring 70
FX bus
  reverb, setting up 156-158
FX channels
  about 256
  using, to reduce CPU usage 156
FX-Mixer
  about 50, 256
  instrument, routing to channel 69

G

GAIN parameter 324
Garage House music. *See* **New York house music**
Grado SR80 headphones 35

H

Haas effect 282
Haas settings 282
half step 113
handheld recorders
  about 180
  Sony PCM-M10 181
  Zoom H4n 181
hardness option 326
harmonies
  adding, to beat 106-108
head 89
help menu, main menu bar 45
Hertz (Hz) 257
high cut filter 277
high pass EQ 277, 278
hi hat
  about 90
  closed hi hat 91
  listening, steps for 91
  open hi hat 91
  pedal hi hat 91
hold stage 311

I

Imp button 335
Indaba music
  about 26
  URL 26
instrument
  about 129
  adding 203
  bars 326
  bases, creating 203-206
  bit invader instrument 322
  FreeBoy instrument 330
  kicker instrument 323, 324
  LB-302 instrument 324
  mallets instrument 325
  muting, in Beats+Bassline Editor 66
  organic instrument 328
  oscillator section 295
  parts 294
  PatMan instrument 332
  percussion 325
  reverb, putting 129, 131
  SF2 instrument 333
  tubular bells 325
  vestige instrument 334
  vibed instrument 335, 336
  ZynAddSubFx instrument 337
instrument filters
  activating 308, 309
Instrument plugins tab 76
Instrument Track element 138

interpolation function 323
In the Air Tonight 93
iTunes 343

J

Jungle music 88

K

keyboard controllers, MIDI
   Akai MPK49 17
   enabling, in song editor 67
   M-Audio Axiom Pro 16
   Novation SLmkII 16
keyboards 266
kicker instrument
   about 76, 323
   DECAY parameter 324
   DIST parameter 324
   END parameter 324
   GAIN parameter 324
   START parameter 324
knob function 323
KORG nanoKONTROL 2, MIDI control surfaces 17

L

LADSPA 12, 71
LADSPA PLUGIN PATHS directory 12
large floor tom-tom 93
LB-302 instrument
   about 324
   accent button 325
   dead button 325
   dist parameter 325
   slide button 325
   slide parameter 325
   VCF parameter 325
   Voltage Controlled Oscillator (VCO) parameter 325
leads 266
leaving headroom 264
Left loop-point 137
LFO 52
LFO Depth parameter 327
LFOs 312
LFO Speed parameter 327

limiters 269
limiting 269
Link Channels button 280
Linux
   LMMS, installing 10
   MIDI, setting up 19
Linux Audio Developer Simple Plugin API. *See* LADSPA
Linux Audio Developers Simple Plugin API. *See* LADSPA
LMMS
   ARTWORK directory 11
   BACKGROUND ARTWORK directory 11
   compression, using 270, 271, 272
   FL STUDIO INSTALLATION directory 12
   installing 9
   installing, on Linux 10
   installing, on OS X 10.6 10
   installing, on Windows 9, 10
   instruments 293
   LADSPA PLUGIN PATHS directory 12
   main menu bar 43
   MIDI, setting up 16
   modulator, assigning 312-315
   resources 11
   song template, opening 42, 43
   SOUNDFONT directory 12
   sound, outputting 21
   STK RAWWAVE directory 12
   VST PLUGIN directory 11
   WORKING directory 11, 12
LMSS samples
   about 168
   pattern, creating with droom loop 168-174
long form patterns
   setting up 104-106
loop length set
   getting 198
   loops, setting 198-202
loop mode, PatMan instrument 332
loops
   setting 198-202
low cut filter 277
Low Frequency Oscillation. *See* LFO
Low Frequency Oscillator. *See* LFOs
low frequency sound 264
low pass EQ 277, 278

low pass filter 277
LVol, FreeBoy instrument 330

M

Mac OS X
  MIDI, installing 20
Main Beat element 240
main menu bar
  about 43
  edit menu 44
  help menu 45
  project menu 44
  tools menu 45
major key 113
major scale
  about 113
  figuring out 113, 114
make-up gain 269
mallets instrument 325
mastering
  about 290
  range 268
masteroutput 68
master pitch control 53
M-Audio Axiom Pro, MIDI keyboard controller 16
microphone pre-amp 22
microphone preamp 178
microphones
  about 21
  condenser microphone 22-24
  dynamic microphone 22
  recording with 29-32
MIDI
  about 304
  control surfaces 17, 18
  installing, in Mac OS X 20
  keyboard controllers 16, 17
  setting up, for LMMS 16
  setting up, in Linux 19
  setting up in Linux, ALSA used 20
  setting up, in Windows 19
MIDI controller keyboard
  black notes 112
  white notes 112
minor scale 114

Mixer
  about 42
  using, in project 68
mixing
  about 255
  exporting 287-289
modulation . *See* modulator
modulator
  about 303
  assigning, in LMMS 312-315
  envelopes 310
  Low Frequency Oscillator (LFOs) 312
  using 310
modulator parameter 327
motion option 327
music, composing
  on fly 33, 34
  with studio monitors 35
music composing, laptop configurations
  about 33, 34
  earbuds, selecting 34, 35
music composing, with studio monitors
  about 35
  absorption vs. diffusion 36, 37
  chair 38
  computer noise 35
  hum 35
  Owens Corning 703 Insulation 36
  parallel walls 36
  room noise 35
  rug, for hardwood floors 36
  speakers choice 37, 38
Music labels 344
music selling, communities for
  Beatport 343
  CD Baby 344
  Facebook user group 345
  iTunes 343
  music labels 344
  Soundcloud 346
  sourceforge (SF) group 346
  Tunecore 344
  user groups 345
  YouTube 346
music studio
  external hard drive, requisites 9
  system requisites 8

N

New Wave 97
New York house music 86
node 258
noise 297
normalize function 323
notch filtering 279
note length
    editing, in Beats+Bassline Editor 62, 63
notes
    inputting, in Piano-Roll editor 141
    playing, in Piano-Roll editor 141-144
Novation SLmkII, MIDI keyboard controller 16
Novation Zero SLmkII, MIDI control surfaces 18
number
    adding, to note 115

O

one-eighth-inch mini stereo cable 180
open hi hat 91
organic instrument
    about 328
    dist 329
    exploring 329
    pan 329
    randomise 329
    vol 329
    wave 329
    wide 329
oscillator section, instrument
    harmonic series 296
    noise 297
    oscillators, exploring 299-301
    other waves 298
    parameters 298
    sawtooth waves 296
    sine waves 295
    square waves 296
    triangle waves 297
    Triple Oscillator instrument 295
OS X 10.6
    LMMS, installing 10
output volume 53
Owens Corning 703 Insulation 36

P

pads 139, 266
panning
    about 51-128
    and stereo separation 264
    considerations 267
    used, to spread song out 145-148
pan, organic instrument 329
parameteric EQ 278, 279
PatMan instrument
    about 332
    loop mode 332
    tune mode 332
patterns
    creating from samples, drum loop used 168-174
    moving, in song editor 136-138
pedal hi hat 91
percussion
    about 325
    hardness option 326
    options 326
    position option 326
    spread option 326
    Stick Mix option 326
    Vib Freq option 326
    Vib Gain option 326
performance rights organizations 341, 342
Phantom Power 29
phase 298
Phase modulation (PM button) synthesis 303, 304
physical modeling 336
Piano-Roll editor
    about 48, 108, 144, 206
    bass line pitch, changing 65
    enabling, in song editor 67
    notes, inputting in 141
    notes, playing 141-144
    pattern, opening 64, 65
    using, in song editor 66
pipe organ 303
pitch fall
    dropouts, creating with 239-244
plate reverbs 284, 285

plugins
  about 70
  FX, exploring 70
poles 277
pop quiz
  answers 349, 351
pop song arrangement
  bridge 222
  chorus 1 222
  chorus 2 222
  chorus 3 222
  verse 1 222
  verse 2 222
position option 326
project
  arrangement 227-234
project menu, main menu bar 44
projects directory
  about 13
  first project, saving 13, 14
  tips, for sharing 15
P, vibed instrument 336

Q

Q (quality) setting 278

R

Radiohead
  about 25
  URL 25
Ragga Jungle music 88
randomize, organic instrument 329
ratio button 269
recording
  digital recording 175
  field recording 175
  on main computer 175
release stage 311
Remix comps
  about 26
  URL 26
repetitive music 225
resonance 277
reverb
  about 153
  button 333

  mode 153
  setting up, on FX bus 156-158
  versus delay 152-155
R/Haas Delay settings 281
Right loop-point 137
Room Size knob 283
root pitch
  editing, in Beats+Bassline Editor 62, 63
R Time knob 152
RVol, FreeBoy instrument 330

S

SACM (México) 341
sample clearance 166
sample rate 193
samplers 100
Sampler Track element 138
sampling
  about 166, 174
  early sampling 166
Sasha and John Digweed, electronic music artist 160
sawtooth waves 296
S button 323
scale
  numbers, assigning to notes 115
SESAC 341, 343
SF2 instrument 333
sharp 112
Shelf EQ 276
sidebands 304
side bar
  exploring 54
  new parts, adding to song editor 139-141
sine waves 295
slapback delay 153
slide button 325
slide parameter 325
slope 277
small tom-tom 93
snare drum
  about 92
  build 92
  listening, steps for 92
song
  imagine song, analyzing 223, 224

key, using 115-117
one song, analysing 225-227
spreading out, panning used 145-148
template, opening 42, 43
song, breaking down
art 225
One song, analysing 225-227
song by John Lennon, breaking down 223, 224
song editor
about 47, 135
Automation Track element 139
Beat+Bassline Editor's pattern, getting 136
Beat+Bassline element 138
elements 138
Instrument Track element 138
MIDI keyboard controller, enabling 67
new parts, adding from side bar 139-141
pattern, moving 136-138
piano roll, enabling 67
piano roll, using 66
Sampler Track element 138
samples 215
sample track, adding 215-218
Sony PCM-M10 181
soundbible website
URL 183
sound cards 24
Soundcloud 346
SOUNDFONT directory 12
sourceforge (SF) group 346
speed option 327
spread option 326, 327
Spread parameter 327
spring reverbs 285
square waves 296
SRS, FreeBoy instrument 331
SSL, FreeBoy instrument 331
START parameter 324
Stick Mix option 326
STime, FreeBoy instrument 331
STK RAWWAVE directory 12
subtractive arranging 197
subtractive synthesis
about 308
instrument filters, activating 308, 309
sustain stage 311

S, vibed instrument 336
Swap Outputs button 281
SwDir, FreeBoy instrument 331
sync 305
syncopation 108
synth bass
about 95
The SH-101, type 96
The TB303, type 96, 97
synthesis
amplitude modulation 305
frequency modulation (FM button) synthesis 304, 305
methods, exploring 305-307
Phase modulation (PM button) synthesis 303, 304
pipe organ 303
sync 305
types 302
waves, mixing 302
Synthpop 97
synths 293

T

tape recorders
about 256
meter 256
TEMPO 52
Tempo knob 151
The LinnDrum 99
The Roland TR808 98
The Roland TR909 98
The SH-101 96
The SP1200 100
The TB303 96
tom-tom
about 92
large floor tom-tom 93
listening, steps for 93
small tom-tom 93
toolbar
about 45
bottom row buttons, on left-hand side 47-51
other features 52, 53
top row buttons, on left-hand side 45, 46
tools menu, main menu bar 45

transition
    about 237, 238
    creating 250, 252
Treb, FreeBoy instrument 330
triangle waves 297
trim knob 22
Triple Oscillator instrument 245, 295
Triple Oscillator synth 301
troughs 258
tubular bells
    about 325, 327
    ADSR parameter 327
    Crossfade parameter 327
    LFO Depth parameter 327
    LFO Speed parameter 327
    modulator parameter 327
    Spread parameter 327
Tunecore
    about 344
    URL 344
tune mode, PatMan instrument 332
two sine waves
    examples 258

U

Ubuntu
    URL, for downloading 10
unbalanced cables
    about 176-178
    versus balanced cables 176
upright bass 94

V

variation
    adding, to beat pattern 60, 61
VCF parameter 325
velocity 65
verses 222
vestige instrument 334
vibed instrument
    about 335, 336
    P 336

PU 336
S 336
V 336
Vib Freq option 326
Vib Gain option 326
vibrato option 327
Vintage Delay Effect 151
vintage reverb
    exploring 286
vocal samples 266
Vol, FreeBoy instrument 331
vol, organic instrument 329
Voltage Controlled Oscillator (VCO) parameter 325
volume
    balancing 263
volume automation 124-128
VST PLUGIN directory 11
VSwDir, FreeBoy instrument 331
V, vibed instrument 336

W

wave, organic instrument 329
W/D knob 158
Wet and Dry 158
Wet Level knob 283
white notes 112
whole step 113
wide, organic instrument 329
Windows
    LMMS, installing 9, 10
    MIDI, setting up 19
WORKING directory 11, 12
WPD, FreeBoy instrument 331

Y

YouTube 346

Z

Zoom H4n 181
ZynAddSubFx instrument 337

[363]

Thank you for buying
LMMS: A Complete Guide to Dance Music Production Beginner's Guide

About Packt Publishing

Packt, pronounced 'packed', published its first book "*Mastering phpMyAdmin for Effective MySQL Management*" in April 2004 and subsequently continued to specialize in publishing highly focused books on specific technologies and solutions.

Our books and publications share the experiences of your fellow IT professionals in adapting and customizing today's systems, applications, and frameworks. Our solution based books give you the knowledge and power to customize the software and technologies you're using to get the job done. Packt books are more specific and less general than the IT books you have seen in the past. Our unique business model allows us to bring you more focused information, giving you more of what you need to know, and less of what you don't.

Packt is a modern, yet unique publishing company, which focuses on producing quality, cutting-edge books for communities of developers, administrators, and newbies alike. For more information, please visit our website: `www.packtpub.com`.

About Packt Open Source

In 2010, Packt launched two new brands, Packt Open Source and Packt Enterprise, in order to continue its focus on specialization. This book is part of the Packt Open Source brand, home to books published on software built around Open Source licences, and offering information to anybody from advanced developers to budding web designers. The Open Source brand also runs Packt's Open Source Royalty Scheme, by which Packt gives a royalty to each Open Source project about whose software a book is sold.

Writing for Packt

We welcome all inquiries from people who are interested in authoring. Book proposals should be sent to author@packtpub.com. If your book idea is still at an early stage and you would like to discuss it first before writing a formal book proposal, contact us; one of our commissioning editors will get in touch with you.

We're not just looking for published authors; if you have strong technical skills but no writing experience, our experienced editors can help you develop a writing career, or simply get some additional reward for your expertise.

Getting started with Audacity 1.3

ISBN: 978-1-84719-764-1   Paperback: 220 pages

Create your own podcasts, edit music, and more with this open source audio editor

1. Teaches basic techniques for using Audacity to record and edit audio tracks - like podcasts and interviews

2. Combines learning to use software program with the simple theories behind digital audio and common audio terms

3. Provides advanced editing techniques and tips for using Audacity beyond a first project

Sony Vegas Pro 11 Beginner's Guide

ISBN: 978-1-84969-170-3   Paperback: 264 pages

Edit videos with style and ease using Vegas Pro

1. Edit slick, professional videos of all kinds with Sony Vegas Pro

2. Learn audio and video editing from scratch

3. Speed up your editing workflow

4. A practical beginner's guide with a fast-paced but friendly and engaging approach towards video editing

Please check **www.PacktPub.com** for information on our titles

CryENGINE 3 Game Development: Beginner's Guide

ISBN: 978-1-84969-200-7   Paperback: 348 pages

Discover how to use the CryENGINE 3 free SDK, the next-generation real-time game development tool

1. Begin developing your own games of any scale by learning to harness the power of the Award Winning CryENGINE® 3 game engine

2. Build your game worlds in real-time with CryENGINE® 3 Sandbox as we share insights into some of the tools and features useable right out of the box

3. Harness your imagination by learning how to create customized content for use within your own custom games through the detailed asset creation examples within the book

Blender Game Engine: Beginner's Guide

ISBN: 978-1-84951-702-7   Paperback: 220 pages

The non programmer's guide to creating 3D video games

1. Use Blender to create a complete 3D video game

2. Ideal entry level to game development without the need for coding

3. No programming or scripting required

Please check **www.PacktPub.com** for information on our titles

Lightning Source UK Ltd.
Milton Keynes UK
UKHW05f1852190218
318128UK00004B/180/P